Father O.S.B Ignatius

Mission Sermons and Orations

Father O.S.B Ignatius

Mission Sermons and Orations

ISBN/EAN: 9783743332324

Manufactured in Europe, USA, Canada, Australia, Japa

Cover: Foto ©ninafisch / pixelio.de

Manufactured and distributed by brebook publishing software (www.brebook.com)

Father O.S.B Ignatius

Mission Sermons and Orations

"Behold! I bring you Good Tidings of Great Joy."—S. Luke ii. 10.

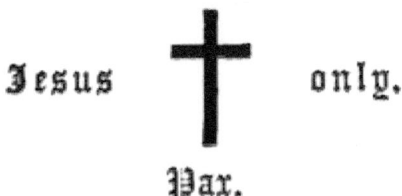

Pax.

MISSION SERMONS

AND

ORATIONS

DELIVERED BY

FATHER IGNATIUS, O.S.B.,

(REV. JOSEPH LEYCESTER LYNE),

Evangelist Monk of the Church of England,

AT WESTMINSTER TOWN HALL.

EDITED, WITH AN INTRODUCTION,

BY

J. V. SMEDLEY, M.A.,

Corpus Christi Coll., Camb.

LONDON:

WILLIAM RIDGWAY, | HAMILTON, ADAMS & CO.,
169, PICCADILLY, W. | 23, PATERNOSTER ROW, E.C.

MDCCCLXXXVI.

[*The rights of reproduction and translation are reserved.*]

TO

THE GLORY OF GOD,

AND

To the Memory

OF

LOUISA GENEVIEVE LYNE,

The Dearly Loved Mother

OF

THE REV. JOSEPH LEYCESTER LYNE

(FATHER IGNATIUS)

THIS VOLUME IS INSCRIBED.

Introduction.

INTRODUCTION.

A very strong desire having been expressed by members of the congregations who have attended the London Mission services, held by Father Ignatius (the Rev. Joseph Leycester Lyne), at the Westminster Town Hall, that some of the sermons and orations, delivered by the Rev. Father at these missions, should be published, it has become my pleasing duty and privilege to carry out this desire.

And nothing could be more natural on the part of those who have listened to this most earnest and eloquent of mission preachers, than that they should wish to possess a volume of these sermons, and to give to others, who have been less fortunate than themselves, and have not heard any of them delivered, the opportunity of reading the Gospel message so simply proclaimed by this evangelist monk.

But there is another excellent reason why this volume should be published; and that is, because of the misconception which still appears to exist, among both clergy and laity, as to the doctrines taught by Father Ignatius.

Some Catholics complain that the good monk is too protestant for them; and, on the other hand, some Protestants aver that he is too catholic—even going so far as to suggest that he is a "Jesuit in disguise"! The consequence is that many, of both schools of religious thought, deprive themselves of hearing him altogether.

The reasons, therefore, for publishing this volume are, first, that the "Primitive Catholic Christianity," preached by this evangelist monk, may be further spread; and, secondly, that religionists of all shades may know exactly what Father Ignatius *does* preach, and what views he holds upon ecclesiastical, and other, subjects.

It cannot well be gainsaid that, certainly within the last three hundred years, no human being who, by the laying-on of hands, has been admitted to the diaconate in the Church of England, has been the subject of more misrepresentation and persecution than has the Rev. Joseph Leycester Lyne.

Of course, at the period, 1860, when the young deacon received his call from God to become a monk, *e.g.*, a solitary, the state of things in the Church of England, both as regards outspoken doctrine and ritual, was very different from what it is to-day; but there can be no doubt that at the outset of his monastic life "Brother Ignatius," as he was then styled, was an out-and-out ritualist.

I have it, from his own truthful word of mouth, that, at that period, he was, unconsciously, little else. "I loved our Lord, though," he said, "all my life; but did not *know*, so did not trust *His* love to *me*."

Those were the days when even to preach in a surplice was enough to stamp a priest or deacon as a "Romanist;"*

---

* We have recently been reminded of a striking instance of the prejudice against the surplice, in the days to which I refer, by the chroniclers of the persecution of the late Rev. W. T. E. Bennett, when vicar of St. Barnabas, Pimlico.

Upon his discarding the academic M.A. black gown for the

and when the very sight of a cross in wood, marble, or brass, either inside or outside a church, would bring about the ears of the offending incumbent or curate, an avalanche of mobbism and cries of "No Popery," of which, in the present day, we have but an occasional faint echo.

But in 1866 a complete change came over the young monk. Disbelievers in, and scoffers at, sudden conversion will doubtless be incredulous of the statement; yet it is nevertheless a fact, that on a certain evening—the very moment, as well as the place, are sacred fixtures in his mind—when walking on the sea-shore in the Isle of Wight, the young deacon became *suddenly* "a converted man."

Possibly the change in the mind, heart, and spirit of the then much-talked-of, insulted, ridiculed and persecuted —even to violence—young ritualist, had been the result of years of struggle and unconscious preparation; but the fact remains that, from that moment, Joseph Leycester Lyne entered upon a new spiritual existence.

"He was born again," as he would himself express it, into the new life of a Christian. He was transformed from a hot-headed, earnest *ritualist* monk into an equally hot-headed and out-and-out in earnest *evangelist* monk, with "Jesus only" as his watchword; but *behind* this, (in its proper place,) followed the same ritualism, the same love of the beautiful to be offered to God in His divinely appointed service—the type and figure only of

---

ecclesiastical vestment, known as the surplice, that good Christian man, the late Earl of Shaftesbury (then Lord Ashley) in the heat of his feeling on the subject, made use of these memorable words: "I would rather worship with Lydia on the banks of the river than with a London surpliced-priest in the temple of St. Barnabas!"

the living reality; not the reality itself. To use his own favourite now-a-day's expression, he had, all his life previously, been putting "the cart *before* the horse!"

It might have been supposed that such a complete metamorphosis in the spiritual life of the Rev. Joseph Leycester Lyne—such "a change of front," in fact—would have given him a respite from his persecutors; but not at all. Instead of his finding himself in smoother waters, he now became confronted by two classes of " persecutors and slanderers " instead of by one!

Whilst Brother Ignatius, in conjunction with his friend, the late Rev. James Purchas, had been aiding and supporting, if not leading, the then rising Ritualistic school in the Church of England, many of that school, both clergy and laity, had given him tacit encouragement; while others, who were in the advanced guard of the movement, were among his most earnest and ardent supporters.

As an instance in point, in the year 1864, the late Rev. Edward Stuart, the then vicar of St. Mary Magdalene's, Munster Square, addressed a letter to the Bishop of London, the late Dr. Jackson, in his own pleasant, caustic style, heading it " Fair Play for Brother Ignatius;" and towards the end of this letter Mr. Stuart wrote :—

"Brother Ignatius himself may be a 'clerical error,' perhaps; 'Punch' says he is, and in such a matter 'Punch' is, of course, infallible; but I can assure your Lordship that, whatever error there may be about Brother Ignatius, there is no mistake whatever as to the warmth and heart and life, and actual success (if that is to be taken into account), of the sermons and services held in his monastery chapel."

The monastery was at that time at Norwich.

Brother Ignatius, because such a decided ritualist, had always been the special, and favourite, target of the Low

Church party; by whom, however, it was to have been hoped that the *evangelist* monk, so soon as his earnest and vigorous preaching of pure evangelical doctrines came into force, would cease to be persecuted; but instead of this, as a rule, wherever the monk preached (and he was now more often heard outside his monastery than before his conversion) the rancour and uncharitableness of the ultra-Protestant element showed itself even more and more against him.

These good folk could not see beneath the surface; and the Monastic Habit* was a cause for rabid revilings from even many excellent Protestants, whose prejudice against "the monk" blinded their spiritual eyes, and rendered them incapable of receiving the Gospel message from his lips.

On the other hand, directly the converted monk was found to be preaching Christianity, pure and simple, and not "Churchianity," as the first desideratum for sinful men and women; and to be telling the people that *until* they had accepted Jesus Christ as their own personal, atoning, all-sufficient Saviour, "their righteousnesses," forms and ceremonials, were all "as filthy rags," (no matter to what *outward* Church they might belong); the High Church and Ritualistic party also turned their backs upon him, denouncing him as a heretic, and schismatic, and actually charging the good monk with preaching against the Sacraments of the Church, and with general disloyalty to her!

History only repeats itself; for were not Wesley and Whitefield, at the period of the great revival in the Church of England, at their hands, when they preached

---

* It was from the hands of the late Rev. Dr. Pusey that Father Ignatius received his first Habit.

Jesus Christ, and "Jesus only," as the essence of the Church's life, denounced in the same manner?

Had but the Catholic Tractarians, who followed later on, instead of giving the cold shoulder to the descendants of the Evangelical revivalists, extended to them the right hand of Christian fellowship, and so have united the Catholic and **Evangelical** schools in the Mother Church of England; **the** painfully anti-Christian state of things in our **Church to-day**, would not be matter of history; **and** the *independent* sect known as "Wesleyan" would never have existed!

This opposition to, and malicious persecution of, **Brother Ignatius**, continued, in a greater or lesser degree, for some years; until, at length, the storm would seem to have so well-nigh spent itself, and his persecution to have so far died out, (with only here and there an unenviable exception) **that when the Rev. Father Ignatius, O.S.B., Evangelist Monk of Llanthony Abbey, is,** by the **grace** of God, permitted to leave his Monastery in the Black Mountains of South Wales, to preach the **Gospel** to the people, he is welcomed by **vast congregations, who** assemble from all parts to hear him **and profit by his teaching.**

As some people question the right of Father Ignatius, **the** Benedictine Monk, *because still a deacon*, to the appellation of "Father," I would here observe that while he was learning his Rule and Office, and none had taken their vows "into his hands," he was styled "Brother"; but after two years of probation, with (as in the case of St. Benedict,)* God's Providence for his novice Master;

---

* St. Benedict, Abbot and "Father," was never admitted to the **Priesthood.**

when he had learnt his Rule and Office, founded the first House, and others took their vows to him; he, as the Rule requires, assumed the title "Father." The Professed are called "fathers," the Novices "brothers."*

Neither space nor intention will permit me to give more than a very brief outline of the religious life of this unique man—unique, in that it would be difficult to point to any cotemporary in the generation in which he has lived —who, in spite of his impulsiveness and other weaknesses (of which he is himself only too conscious,) can be compared with him for single-mindedness, devotion, and faithfulness to his calling; **steadfastness** and loyalty of purpose in the midst of disappointment, loneliness, and desertion; **forgiveness** of injury, persecution, and slander; and unswerving bravery in standing *alone* to his convictions!

Nevertheless, it can in very truth be said, that Father Ignatius has been,—and by the clergy of his own Church in particular,—the most persecuted, maligned, slandered, and misunderstood cleric in all England!

To listen to some of the clergy of the Church of England, even at the present day—and I speak perhaps more particularly now of our friends holding important cures in High Church centres—criticising and finding fault with Father Ignatius, you would imagine that he had but just arrived upon the scene, and not that he had been a most prominent figure in the ecclesiastical world of the nineteenth century, for more than a quarter of it!

And the criticisms are, to say the least, ungenerous; for these clergy seem to forget, while making them, that they are maligning a man, who, some twenty-five years ago,

---

* See Rule of St. Benedict.

received torrents of persecution, (sometimes even in the form of brickbats and rotten eggs,) for leading the way to do, and for doing, that which these same reverend gentlemen are now quietly permitted to do without persecution!

The clergy of this same school are also wont to question whether these Llanthony Missions are as fruitful as other Missions held in their own churches, because no statistics are published as to the number of persons, who, through them, have been brought to Baptism, Confirmation, and Communion.

Compelled, in many dioceses, where the churches are not open to receive the monk to preach, to hold his services in hired halls; driven from font and altar to town-halls and assembly-rooms, it would not have been surprising if such statistical results were not forthcoming; but, notwithstanding these impediments, those who have been taught by him know well enough that *A Record* of the results of his mission work is not wanting!

And these criticisms have their inconsistent side also.

To require the statistics which these clergy demand from the brother-missioner whom they barely countenance, and who is ostracised by some of the bishops of the Church to which he belongs, is surely not unlike expecting a fisherman to fish without a landing-net, and to find fault with him if he happen to let a single salmon, trout,—or even minnow—drop back into the stream; or like expecting a shepherd, upon the mountain-side, to pen his sheep without a fold!

But even statistics such as are said not to exist, have come to my hand.

Soon after I had first heard Father Ignatius preach,

Introduction. xiii.

and had become aware of these criticisms, I addressed a letter to a clergyman, the vicar of a well-known town in North Wales, in whose parish, I was informed, more than one of the Llanthony Missions had been held.

The vicar being an entire stranger to me, I naturally apologised for my letter, pleading, by way of excuse, my anxiety to know the truth, or otherwise, of what I had heard.

I received reply in due course, from which the following is an extract. The letter, from the Rev. E. Rhys James, the Vicar of Llangollen, is dated January 24th, 1885.

"You wish me," he said, "to write the results of our mission here. I can only say that *God only knows* the true amount of good done to the thousands who flocked to hear Father Ignatius : but results enough have already come, and are continually coming, to my knowledge and to that of my fellow-workers in this parish, to enable us to thank God for having sent him to hold his mission here. There is a decided advance along the whole line. Whole families have been turned and notorious sinners saved. Our parochial Guild has been trebled and new life put into all our Church workers. A family from London happened to be staying here at the time, and all were converted to Christ, and went back to town rejoicing that they had ever visited our beautiful valley. Our *communicants* have not only increased, but all the old ones have found a new treasure in the Vineyard—peace, joy, security, rest in Jesus. We are better, happier, and brighter Christians than before. * * * I regard our dear Father Ignatius as an inspired medium, chosen of God above most, if not all, others to draw souls to Jesus. * * * *He seems to lead the way himself and not to point to it.*

"I can only say in conclusion, let any one who doubts his mission work, go and hear him for a week and follow him through the whole course of the octave, and then judge for himself, what he thinks of him. He will find him to be truly a right reverend father in God— and what more can anyone wish ?"

I received like testimony from the rector of a large parish in Birmingham.

It may, perhaps, be well that I should now state how it has come to pass that I find myself, to-day, editing and publishing this volume of sermons.

It was one of those circumstances we are too apt to term "accidents," which first brought to me the acquaintance of Father Ignatius; an acquaintance which soon ripened into friendship.

I have often thanked God for an illness which, in the autumn of 1884, took me into South Wales, there to recruit my strength; for whilst staying, first at Carmarthen, and then at Tenby, I had the privilege of attending the missions, which were being held, at those places, by Father Ignatius. It was at the close of the Tenby Mission that I became personally known to him.

To say that I was impressed by his preaching, would but faintly describe what I desire to say. The first sermon I heard at Carmarthen awoke me to the fact that till then I had been living in a state of spiritual lethargy; and during the mission at Tenby, by God's grace, the Gospel message, delivered in its simplicity, by this Evangelist monk, was permitted to reach me, and to do that for me which four decades of a superabundance of dogmatic teaching had failed in doing.

From that moment I determined, God helping me, to give to the Rev. Father Ignatius all the aid in my power to extend his opportunities of holding these missions.

I would fain, under other circumstances, have omitted further reference to myself, or to my work in this matter;

Introduction. xv.

but that I feel it will be of interest to many to know the steps I took to accomplish my object.

In December, 1884, I offered the services of Father Ignatius to the Bishop of Bedford, as one of the missioners in the then approaching West London Mission of February, 1885; undertaking, on his behalf, that he would, in all respects, conform to the usages of the church in which he might be called upon to officiate, and wear the surplice over the Habit of his Order. I, of course, did this with the consent and approval of the Rev. Father.

The Bishop of Bedford kindly referred me to the Rev. Canon Furse, one of the three Commissaries of the Bishop of London for the West London Mission, who took up the matter warmly.

It will be remembered that the late Bishop Jackson had, some fifteen years before, inhibited Father Ignatius from preaching in the churches of the diocese of London, on the ground, (to quote his Lordship's own words) "that the Church of England did not sanction Monastic Orders."

The good Bishop had apparently forgotten the long roll of the holy monks of the early British Church; that half England was evangelized by the monks of Lindisfarne; and that, under the auspices of the British monks, S. David, S. Gildas, and S. Cadoc, the waning faith in Ireland was revived!

Canon Furse, therefore, instead of plunging into the subject at once with Bishop Jackson, and risking an offhand refusal, kindly wrote to the Bishop, asking his Lordship to make an appointment to see him upon a matter of importance connected with the coming West London Mission.

But "man proposes and God disposes." Bishop Jackson

named, for the interview, the morning of the Feast of the Epiphany, January 6th, 1885—the day of his death!

I was then advised to address myself to the Dean and Chapter of St. Paul's, by whom, in the interval between the death of a Bishop of London and the appointment of his successor, the business of the diocese is transacted; but after the sudden and lamented death of Bishop Jackson I did not proceed further in the matter.

I was so very desirous, however, that Father Ignatius should be heard again in London, that, having already, through the kind suggestion of Canon Furse, been in treaty for the Westminster Town Hall for the Rev. Father's use should he have helped in the West London Mission, I then obtained his consent to hold an eight days' mission there, on his own account, later in the spring; and accordingly in April—May, 1885, the first mission at Westminster was held.

The necessarily heavy expenses of a mission in London had naturally weighed with Father Ignatius in his consideration of my request; but I was able to overcome this difficulty, by raising a fund, among a few friends, to discharge the expenses of printing, advertising, &c.; and a gentleman in the congregation kindly came forward and paid for the hire of the Town Hall.

Thus, the first of the present half-yearly missions, at Westminster, came to be held; and I am truly thankful for having been permitted, in ever so small a degree, to assist in their establishment. Three Missions have now been held there—the second in October, 1885, and the third in May, 1886; and if it had pleased God to have given to Father Ignatius the physical strength to enable him to conduct it, the fourth mission would (D.V.) have been held, in the same place, during the present autumn.

Indeed, the fixture, for the mission, was made for October 17th, though afterwards postponed to November 14th; but in consequence of the continued weak state of his health, the Rev. Father has been obliged to further postpone it. If strength be given him, however, he is hoping that he may still be able to hold a few services in Westminster before Christmas. I ask the prayers of all that the Rev. Father may soon be restored to health and strength.

[It will be remembered by those who attended the mission in May last, that it was with difficulty, owing to the great physical exhaustion, from which he was suffering, that Father Ignatius was able to conduct the mission—that he was in fact unable to deliver the two concluding orations.]

After the mission of October, 1885, an Oration on "The Church of England and Disestablishment" was delivered by Father Ignatius, at Westminster Town Hall; and it so much pleased those who heard it, that, at the request of many, the address was again given at St. James' Hall on November 18th, 1885, when the great hall there was crowded.

It was the eve of the elections, when "Disestablishment" was the subject uppermost in the minds of all—"the Battle of the Churches," as the Marquis of Salisbury aptly called it, was pending.

The Nonconformists, supposing that the monk, who had been so strangely persecuted by members of his own Church, could only have something to say in favour of the disestablishment of the Church of England, came in crowds to hear him denounce her; but they were not long in discovering their mistake, and finding that the ostracised monk was, in truth, the staunchest defender possible of the old Mother Church; and these same Nonconformists, in spite of themselves, were very soon in the van of the applause by which **Father Ignatius'** most eloquent, loyal, and logical address was received; cheering him to the echo, when he appealed to members of every dissenting sect, "**as** honest men, and as British citizens," to rally round the old Church of England, when attacked by the sacrilegious hands of infidel revolutionists!

As I had made part of my work to consist in having the mission sermons and orations, delivered by the Rev. Father Ignatius in London, taken down in shorthand, I **was** able to have the Oration on "The Church of England and Disestablishment"* at once published; and so great was the demand for it, that a second edition was called for in less than a week—*the Church Defence Institution* alone ordering 500 copies for distribution.

And here **I should** like to give a typical instance of the manner in which the Rev. Father is often misrepresented by the press.

The *Daily Chronicle*, doubtless quite unintentionally, in reporting the address on "Disestablishment," asserted that Father Ignatius had told his hearers that "it did not matter what *outward* church they joined if they belonged to Christ." Now, what Father Ignatius *did* say—and it is that which he always teaches,—was that *until* a

---

* "The Church of England and Disestablishment." An Oration delivered by Father Ignatius. William Ridgway, 169, Piccadilly, London, W.—Second Edition. Price 6d., by post 6½d.

man has become more than a nominal Christian, it matters, naturally, but little to what *outward* Church, or society of Christians, he may belong. A vast difference!

As a member of the divinely-appointed British branch of the "Catholic and Apostolic Church," the monk had impressed upon his hearers that evening, that *when* the Gospel message had entered into the heart of a man, it *then* became the duty of the believer to inquire if there were still, on earth, a *visible* Church "which continued in the Apostles' Doctrine, Fellowship, and Worship;" and then to join himself to that Church as the Institution of Christ Himself.

At the close of the October Mission, 1885, it was the unanimous desire of the congregation at Westminster, that a petition should be presented to Dr. Temple, the newly appointed Bishop of London, begging that his Lordship would sanction the preaching of Father Ignatius in the churches of his diocese; and forthwith the following petition was drawn up, and soon signed by many thousands of people, both clerical and lay.

To THE RIGHT REV. THE LORD BISHOP OF LONDON,

We, the undersigned, humbly petition your Lordship, as the Chief Pastor of this diocese, to sanction the preaching of the REV. JOSEPH LEYCESTER LYNE—Father Ignatius—in the churches of London.

We make this Petition in consequence of the great spiritual blessings which GOD is vouchsafing to his ministrations throughout the country; and that we feel it a matter of great regret that our National Church should not be reaping the advantages of such a Ministry.

Your Petitioners learn with satisfaction that the Rev. J. L. Lyne is himself perfectly willing to preach in the churches, and to wear either surplice or black gown—whichever may be customary—over the Habit of his Order.

LONDON, *October* 29*th*, **1885.**

This petition was not, however, presented to the Bishop; for the reason that, on good authority, we were reminded that the inhibition of a bishop lapsed with his death; and further, that as the Rev. Joseph Leycester Lyne had officiated in the diocese of Exeter, without hindrance from Dr. Temple, it was reasonable to suppose that his Lordship would place no obstacle to his doing so in the diocese of London. In other words, that there was no need for a petition.

It was at this time that Canon Trench, the vicar of All Saints', Notting Hill, placed his pulpit at the disposal of the Rev. Father Ignatius, "if he would accept it, and help him in his efforts to make his church the church of the people."

Canon Trench was then just about to try and transform "All Saints'," with its old, exclusive pew-rent system, into a "free and open church."

The offer was accepted; and on the evening of the first Tuesday in Advent, December 1st, 1885, the monk preached once again from a London pulpit after his inhibition of sixteen years!

The usual teapot-tempest element was not wanting; but I was personally grateful for it, as it was the means of eliciting, from the Bishop of London, his Lordship's mind and intention as to the preaching of Father Ignatius in the churches of his diocese.

Upon Canon Trench informing his churchwardens that he had offered his pulpit to Father Ignatius, one of them announced his intention of writing to the

Bishop to ask his Lordship's instructions and advice upon the matter; at the same time notifying Canon Trench that he should feel it his duty to prevent "Mr. Lyne" from ascending the pulpit stairs unless he could produce his licence from the Bishop!

The following is a copy of his Lordship's reply to the churchwarden :—

FULHAM PALACE, S.W.
Nov. 30th, 1885.

MY DEAR SIR,—There is no illegality in Mr. Lyne preaching in All Saints' Church at the request of the incumbent, though, of course, the Bishop could prohibit it.

Mr. Lyne has done and said a great many very silly and some very wrong things.

But it hardly seems to me to be worth while to give him the opportunity of calling himself a martyr and a victim of persecution.

People need not go and listen to him, and I do not think many of those who do, will get much harm from so foolish a man.

I should look on it in a different light if he had been announced as a preacher at one of the Sunday services.

Yours faithfully,
(Signed)   F. LONDIN.

The Bishop's letter, although very clear and satisfactory upon the question of the "no illegality" of "Mr. Lyne's" preaching in the churches of the diocese of London, in cases where the incumbents themselves should make offer of their pulpits, might, it must be confessed, have been kinder in its tone.

With the greatest respect for his Lordship, and for his holy office, I know that I do but express the opinions of many other people, as well as my own, when I say that it was much to be regretted that Bishop Temple should have allowed his evident annoyance at having been consulted at all as to the preaching of the monk at "All Saint's," to have shown itself in such unnecessarily severe, discourteous, and uncalled-for remarks.

Not only did "people go and listen" to some of the "silly things" which this "so foolish a man" preached from the pulpit of "All Saints'," on the evening in question; but, I believe I am correct in saying that never before had so large a congregation been found within the walls of that church.

The subject of the sermon was "Waiting for the Coming of our Lord Jesus Christ;" and through the kindness of Canon Trench it was printed in the "*All Saints' Parish Magazine*;"* and I subsequently had it published in cheap form for general circulation.

There was a good deal of correspondence at the time, in some of the Church and local papers, upon the Bishop's letter; and if space had allowed, I should like to have quoted several of these letters. Particularly were the writers puzzled at the distinction which Bishop Temple made between Father Ignatius being announced to preach on a week day and on a Sunday!

I think it due to Canon Trench, however, to insert a letter which he addressed to the "*Bayswater Chronicle*" on the whole subject:—

ALL SAINTS', NOTTING HILL,

Dec. 30*th*, 1885.

SIR,—As a good deal has been said about Mr. Lyne being at All Saints', I may perhaps be allowed to add a word.

It must be allowed that, in strictness, an incumbent should

---

* "Waiting for the Coming of Our Lord Jesus Christ." An Advent sermon, preached by Rev. Father Ignatius, at "All Saints'," Notting Hill, on Tuesday evening, December 1st, 1885. William Ridgway, 169, Piccadilly, London, W.—Price 2d., by post, 2½d.

always ask the Bishop, before he invites a clergyman from another diocese to occupy his pulpit.

But there are many questions bishops had rather *not* be asked, and this was just one.

And our excellent wardens were quite within their right (and duty, if they felt it so) in asking if there were any irregularity. But there was none, and so no harm was done.

But ought Mr. Lyne to be invited to preach in church?

I think so; *for I grudge him alike to the music-hall and the monastery.* No man should be judged too hardly by what he has said or written—who has not?—**wrongly** or foolishly, in a lifetime. If so, who could stand?

In the last eighteen years, I have, from time to time, heard "Father Ignatius" preach, both in and out of churches, and never without being impressed.

The other night in our church an immense congregation heard him gladly. The sermon will be published, and many will, no doubt, be glad to read it. I have never heard him preach any other doctrine; and both the doctrine and the man—in his earnestness and simplicity—in my judgment, *are wanted* in our pulpits.

But since to myself, as to most other clergy, the bishop's *wish*, if expressed, is a command, in the cause of freedom I deprecate a too free use of the right of reference to "the Ordinary." There is not a church in which commissions and omissions many, could not most easily be scheduled for reference. I certainly know one, in which, if such reference were made, we should probably lose both our altar lights and our prayer meetings, and possibly our Revised Bible.

But no one would wish it. And so of Mr. Lyne. No one *need* hear him; but if they do—and often—the better I think for them and also for him—*for I grudge him to the monastery.*

Your obedient servant,
(Signed)   W. R. TRENCH.

There can be little doubt that Father Ignatius, during his remarkable life, has said and done things which would have been better left unsaid and undone. But, as Canon Trench so truly asks in his letter: "Who has not?"

It is very easy to criticise; but, it seems to me that it would be doing Father Ignatius better justice to give prominence to the exceeding reality and sincerity of his work, life, and character, than to search out his weaknesses and defects.

But adverse, and even unkind, criticism of a public man—when made openly—is not in itself dishonourable. It is the underhand, and anonymous, attempt to injure the work of a good man (to which I regret to say Father Ignatius is even now occasionally subjected), which is alike despicable and dishonourable.

[I may mention here that having obtained the consent of Father Ignatius to hold a mission at Cambridge, I went up, early in the Lent Term, of the present year, for the purpose of making the necessary arrangements; but on finding that the Rev. W. Hay Aitken was already in the field to hold a mission, at St. Mary's, during that Term, I decided to give up the idea for the present.]

In the choice of the "Mission Sermons" and "Addresses to Christians," contained in this volume, my object has been to select those which, as a whole, will the most fairly represent the Gospel teaching of Father Ignatius.

I have especially given the Address on "The Lord's Mother," in view of the Rev. Father having been more misrepresented concerning his reverence for the Blessed Virgin Mary than on almost any other Scriptural subject.

With regard to the "Orations," published with the sermons, my aim also has been to make choice of those which treat upon the leading ecclesiastical, and other, subjects, on which Father Ignatius is known to hold very decided opinions, and about which he is so much misrepresented and misunderstood.

The Orations are here offered in the same spirit in which the Rev. Father is wont to deliver them. He invariably prefaces these addresses by telling his hearers that he does not desire them to accept his views, or his readings, on these subjects, as infallible; that he does but offer, for their consideration, the results of his own investigations for what they are worth. He may, he tells them, be wholly wrong and they wholly right; he is simply there to state the conclusions to which he has arrived; whilst they, on their part, have kindly come to hear him.

Father Ignatius' views on Monasticism and Monasteries, it must be conceded, are natural enough in one who has felt himself called to the life and vocation of a monk; and if, in his lectures on the subject, he be found to indulge in no uncertain criticisms of those who destroyed the monasteries of the Church of England, he may surely well be excused.

What he has to say on this subject will be found in the Oration: "Why were the Monasteries of the Church of England destroyed?"

Father Ignatius is also, as is well known, often taken to task by our ultra-Protestant brethren, for expressing his very decided opinions upon the "Reformation;" and in such a manner that it really would appear as if the subject were one about which discussion were not permissible.

But I should like to ask why a subject of so much interest to all English Christians should not be openly spoken of and discussed; and especially seeing that, *mirabile dictu*! there actually do exist professing members of the Church of England, who still maintain that our

Church was founded by that wicked old Tudor King Henry VIII.!

The question is one which, fortunately, is contained in an historical nut-shell. The Church of England is either of divine or human origin. Either the Church of England was founded in this land, in Apostolic times, or it was brought into existence, in the sixteenth century, by Henry Tudor!

There happen to be some members of the Church of England (and among them the Monk of Llanthony) who, because the Bible, tradition, and ecclesiastical history have told them so, believe that what is known to-day as the British Branch of the Catholic and Apostolic Church, was planted in this land, in the Apostolic era, eighteen hundred years ago!!

At the request of many, I have included, among the "Orations," the address which Father Ignatius delivered (by special request), at the close of the May Mission, 1885, upon "The Apparitions at Llanthony;" and I do so the more readily, because I consider it to be only fair that he should be read on this subject—notwithstanding that, in these unbelieving nineteenth-century days, it is the fashion to treat with levity and ridicule, anything and everything which claims to touch upon the supernatural.

Having myself visited the spot where the alleged manifestations took place; and being convinced, as far as one can be under the circumstances, that what has been stated to have been seen by eight persons, at various times, could not, from the configuration of the ground, and for other sufficient reasons, have been caused by artificial means (as has been suggested), I confess that I should be very glad if the invitation, or challenge, which Father Ignatius gives, to have the matter sifted, to the bottom, could be accepted.

It will be seen in the oration on this subject, that the Rev. Father invites the formation of a committee to investigate the evidence of the several witnesses; and that he naïvely expresses a preference that such committee, if possible, should be composed *of lawyers, who are also atheists.* The reason for this, I take it, being that such a subject, at the hands of a combination of this kind, would be more likely to be treated, if not with greater dispassion, at any rate, with a very decided prejudice and natural incredulity.

It is not to be expected that what the monk stands up before his fellow-men, and states calmly and absolutely to be a true account of what he, and seven others, saw, will be generally believed—as the ordinary run of people choose to ignore the possibility even, of miracles, in the present day! But *believing* Christians, who, of course, *must* believe in the supernatural, cannot call in question the illimitable power and will of Almighty God, to vouchsafe to man any manifestation that He pleases; albeit that such manifestation may not altogether accord with their finite preconceptions of what the Infinite should, and would, do.

At the risk of the ridicule which possibly the suggestion may provoke, it appears to me that to one who has lived the life of devotion to his God which this good man has done, and who has been persecuted, ridiculed and taunted by the world for his "madness" for so doing—it is not altogether unnatural that his life of faith and suffering should have received a special, supernatural recognition from on High.

Readers of the story may do well to think twice before they reject, as a *fabrication*, and therefore as a "blasphemous imposture," the united testimony of the several witnesses who testify to having seen these apparitions in the Monastery Church, and in the Abbot's meadow at Llanthony, in August and September 1880.

Although the consideration of the monastic side of Father Ignatius' life is altogether foreign to the object in view in the publication of these sermons, I feel that these introductory remarks of mine would be incomplete, did I not refer to his attempt to revive the Monastic Order of S. Benedict in the Church of England.

To human eyes, most certainly, the attempt made by Father Ignatius, during a period of twenty-five years, to restore monasticism in our Church, not only has not been a success, but is, apparently, a dismal failure.

But who shall gauge the effects of *the first strivings* of this single-hearted, single-handed Christian soldier in his career of following out, to the letter, that which, in spite of all opposition, he believed, and believes, to be God's will that he should do and suffer for His glory, for the good of others, and the welfare of his Mother Church!

Whether the life and work of Ignatius the Monk have, in this respect, been really a failure or not, must be left to the *future* to determine. "God's ways are not as man's ways;" and already indications are not wanting that the years of intercessory prayer, and the absolute dedication and subjection, by Joseph Leycester Lyne, of his whole being to the will and service of God, are beginning to show their fruits in unmistakable evidences, in so many directions, in England, of Christian men and women yearning, in various degrees, to live the life of the Cloister. We have had this subject only very recently brought before us in the columns of the *Church Review* and other religious papers.

With so many of our London churches comparatively empty; with the "labourers so few and the harvest so great;" with the bishops and minor clergy and laity calling for help on every side, to try and cope with the mass of sin and ignorance by which we are surrounded— I should here have felt it my duty to have humbly made the strongest appeal possible to the chief Pastors of our Church to utilize, in some regular and definite work, in the Church of England, the great spiritual and mental gifts, and the almost matchless power of Father Ignatius as a Mission preacher, did I not know that the monk's obligations to his monastery, unfortunately, (beyond his occasional mission preaching) render this impossible.

But there *is* a desire—which, in common with so very many English churchmen and churchwomen, I would fain express; and that is that the holy office of the Priesthood should no longer be withheld from the Rev. Joseph Leycester Lyne, deacon.

And I would here take the opportunity, in all respect and reverence, to humbly pray His Grace the Archbishop of Canterbury, on behalf of thousands of petitioners, to entertain this very natural and earnest prayer.

When we find not a few upon whom this holy office has been conferred, devoting so much of their time, their energies, their talents and their study to the enjoyment of race-courses, theatres, and other essentially worldly pursuits and amusements, it does seem hard and inconsistent that one, who was admitted to the diaconate twenty-five years ago, should be denied the priesthood because *he has given up the world entirely and all its pursuits*—because, in other words, he is *a monk!*

I have, in my possession, a printed copy of a letter, addressed, by Father Ignatius, to the late Bishop of London in 1873, after Bishop Jackson had refused to allow him to officiate in the churches of the diocese of London, on the plea *that he was a monk.*

The question which headed the letter was: "*May a Monk serve God in the Church of England or not?*" And what its writer had to say to his lordship is so apposite to the question of the deacon's admission to priest's orders, that I feel it right now to give the following extracts from the letter:—

"*A Letter to the Bishop of London by Ignatius, the Deacon, and Monk of the Order of S. Benedict.*

"My Lord,—

"As you have decided to give me a negative answer to the question that heads this letter, I feel it to be due to the public in general, to the Church of England, in which I was baptized, confirmed, and ordained, and to my own congregations, in particular, to address this letter to you. My object in doing so is this: to show just cause and reason, from God's Word, from Church History, and from the present necessities of the Church of England, why you should rescind the inhibition, by which I am prevented from exercising the Gospel Ministry in the churches of your diocese. . . .

"My Lord, I have a history, as well as any other clergyman in London. There is no mystery whatever connected with my career, or any part of it. I have testimonials as to my moral and religious character to produce, which will enable you to trace me from the present day, back to my early boyhood.

"If your Lordship, on perusing these letters, should declare that your inhibition casts no imputation upon my character; then, it either does so upon my orthodoxy, or upon yourself, and you lay yourself open to the charge of tyranny, and a misuse of your Episcopal power, against a helpless and innocent person.

"I must, then, in the next place, enter upon the question of orthodoxy. And here I grant, that if your Lordship simply goes by hearsay, you may condemn me as a Calvinist, because I have very often been falsely accused of holding Calvin's theory of Election. *This, however, I beg utterly to repudiate*. At the same time, I believe and teach that 'no man can come unto Christ, except the Father which hath sent Him draw him.'

"Again, I have been accused by others of being a 'Papist.' This accusation I can also easily disprove. Were I a 'Papist,' I could have my heart's desire accomplished at once, without any further persecution or labour, viz., that of being a monk in a properly ordered monastery. But I cannot accept the dogma of Papal Infallibility or Supremacy either. I firmly accept and acknowledge the Nicene Creed, as the Universal Church has received it, as the only authorized test of orthodoxy, . . . and I acknowledge the Infallibility of the Bible as the Word of God. . . . Your Lordship has plenty of Clergymen in your diocese who do *not* do this, and yet they continue unmolested in their ministry. I could name the churches in your diocese where fundamental articles of the Christian Religion are *not* held, but denied; the Clergymen of these churches, your Lordship is bound, by your Consecration Oath, to banish from our midst, as you do myself, who hold the whole truth of the Church's Faith. Why do you not do so? . . .

Thus, my Lord, I have now asserted my orthodoxy, and have cleared my character, as a Clergyman of the Church of England, from the implied imputation of heresy, which your Lordship's ban has cast at me. . . .

"To this your Lordship will probably reply,—I do not impugn your morality, or your orthodoxy; nevertheless, I feel it best, under the 'present circumstances' of the Church, not to sanction an order of preaching monks or friars. And yet, by *tacit* approval, an order of *preaching heretics*, who deny the Infallibility of the Bible, an order of drunken and adulterous Clergy are permitted, and are *at this moment* holding benefices, and preaching in the Church of England. By *implication*, my Lord, you assert that '*monks*' are worse than infidels, drunkards, and adulterers. . . . 'S. Chrysostom' is a name that appears in the end of the Morning and Evening Services of the Church of England. Who is this S. Chrysostom? A '*monk*.' This S. Chrysostom calls 'Monkery' 'The Divine Philosophy introduced by Christ;' further, he states that the life of a monk is **the** 'life of angels upon earth!' . . .

"Your Lordship has **also, no** doubt, objected that Monasticism is part and parcel of Popery. My Lord, S. Chrysostom was **not a** Papist; **the Monks** of **the early** British Church, S. Aidan, S. Columba, &c., **were** not Papists; the Monks of the Eastern Churches **were not Papists**. Again, my Lord, the first founder **of the Church** of Canterbury, the first Archbishop of the Church **of** England, was **a** canonized Monk. I refer to S. Augustine, the Benedictine Monk. It is the *very same rule*, that I follow, to which S. Augustine owned allegiance: read it, my Lord, and then say why the Holy Life which it prescribes should render it necessary for you to inhibit one who lives by its sacred precepts.

"In an interview which your Lordship was condescending enough to grant to me this **year** at London House, you gave as one of your reasons for not allowing **me to preach,** that '**the Church of** England did not sanction **Monastic orders.' You** might just as well prevent Clergy who **were Freemasons from** preaching, for **the same** reason, and rightly **too, for the Church** of England has never authorized Freemasonry. **But, if you recollect,** my Lord, I ventured to **correct** your **Lordship when, by a** *lapsus linguæ*, you stated that the English **Church** did not sanction Monastic orders. I showed you that *she does*, and had ever done so, in harmony with the teaching of S. Chrysostom and the whole Church of Christ. *That, in particular, she had formally authorized the Rule of St. Benedict for the monasteries of England.* You attempted to correct, or rather to limit, my statement, by asserting, through another *lapsus linguæ*, that if she sanctioned monasteries before the Reformation, yet at the Reformation she closed them. This strange forgetfulness of history on your Lordship's part astonished me! The Church of England, at the so-called 'Reformation,' had none to close. The Papal Legate Wolsey sacrilegiously destroyed twenty monastic houses, and the curse of God came upon him for it. Henry VIII.

destroyed the rest, *not* because the Monks were so bad, but because they were so good; and because, while *they* stood in the way, his lusts were opposed. . . .

"We have, then, ascertained thus much: That your Lordship refuses to allow a lawfully ordained Clergyman of the Church of England to exercise his office in your diocese, at the call of a large congregation, not because there is the least stain upon his character, moral or religious, but because he lives the life that is extolled as the very highest, by the chief authorities quoted by the Church of England. . . .

"The late Bishop of London's inhibition of me was caused by a misunderstanding, and has been removed by him, since he (Dr. Tait) became Archbishop of Canterbury. . . .

"Dissenters ask me why I do not throw off my allegiance to the Church, as they have done, and stand upon my individual liberty. My answer is simply this,—I can only find true liberty *within* the Church, and, suffer as I may, for my faithfulness to her, I nevertheless enjoy that which I could not find outside her pale, even the 'answer of a good conscience towards God.' . . .

"I am, my Lord Bishop of London,

"Your faithful Servant and Fellow Citizen,

(Signed) "BROTHER IGNATIUS, O.S.B., MONK."

I have, in these Introductory remarks, desired and tried to speak of Father Ignatius, his tenets and his work, with as little partiality as possible; and to give prominence even to the various (though erroneous) opinions which I am aware are held concerning him and his public teaching.

And there are two of the latter instances to which I have yet to refer; the one as to his holding and preaching Calvinistic doctrine, and the other concerning his teaching on the Blessed Sacrament.

The good Father, in his letter to the late Bishop Jackson, just quoted, has himself sufficiently repudiated the false accusation made against him, that he holds the doctrine of Calvin; hence I need say nothing further on this subject.

I may frankly mention, however, that I have heard it stated (oftener, it is true, by those whose prejudices have not even permitted them to go and hear the monk preach, than by those who have heard him) that, if his preaching be not Calvinism, it is a mixture of Calvinism and Romanism!

As mountains are sometimes more easily to be moved than prejudice, I have contented myself by replying to such accusers: " Go and hear him."

But if the accusation be a true one, then was it equally true of the great S. Augustine of Hippo, and happily is true to-day of some of our best and most revered preachers in the Church of England; who, in common with the Rev. Father Ignatius, hold, teach, and preach to the people, the pure Evangelical faith, backed by Catholic dogma!

And to accuse the Rev. Father of preaching against the Sacraments is only another false accusation against him. It is the *abuse* of the Sacraments against which he preaches; not against the Sacraments themselves. No human being living, I venture to say, knows how to—and does—honour, value, and revere the Blessed Sacrament of the Altar more than the Rev. Father himself; but against the conventionalism,—the too common practice of partaking of the Sacrament by people, whose lives are at variance with the sacredness of these Holy Mysteries — the earnest, plain-spoken Christian monk, preaches with all the power and spiritual force which have been given him.

The teaching of Father Ignatius concerning the Blessed Sacrament is plainly set forth in the sermons now published. It is briefly this: that he would have those only approach the Holy Table or Altar who have a personal faith in Christ as a personal Saviour.

In concluding these, I fear, altogether too protracted Introductory remarks, I feel impelled, from all that I know of the Rev. Father Ignatius, and from what I have heard from his lips, both publicly and privately, to express my decided conviction that, of the many good qualities and traits for which he will be remembered, in years to come—long after his acknowledged weaknesses shall have been forgotten—two very prominent characteristics of this misrepresented and misunderstood Evangelist Monk, will be, his *wholesale denunciation of the unreal in Religion*, and his *staunch loyalty to the Church of his country*—to that Church, at whose hands he received treatment little short of contumely.

The following words of loyalty and devotion to his Mother Church with which Father Ignatius closed his Oration on "*The Church of England and Disestablishment*," will fittingly conclude the Introduction to this volume of a few of his Sermons :—

"Let us have the Gospel in the Church of England simply preached and freely offered, and I am sure numbers of outsiders will flock back again to the olden Church. Jesus Christ says to each one of us : ' You shall be witnesses of Me ;' and if our Church of England be filled with living witnesses of Christ, as an Almighty Saviour, He will take care of the Church of England, and we need fear then no Disestablishment or Disendowment either.

"Our grand old National Church, which has braved the tempests of 1800 years, will brave them still. Jesus is at her helm. Our Mother Church, which has nursed, in her bosom, the Briton and the Roman; the Saxon and the Dane; and the stately Norman too—

welding these contrarian races into the one Brotherhood of the English nation; She will still continue the Great Nursing Mother for Eternity of the succeeding generations of the English.

She still exists, more full of life and energy than ever, GOD'S ESTABLISHMENT OF EIGHTEEN HUNDRED YEARS!

"An historical phenomenon, indeed, still casting her mighty roots in British hearts as well as on British soil!

"Uproot that Church, oh, lovers of Revolution and Change, if ye can and if ye dare! A mighty Vengeance of Recompense will overtake you. Truest Liberty will receive a shock to her foundations. Our Throne and Constitution must soon pass away, if the Church *which created them* should cease to be!"

If, by the publication of this volume, I may be permitted, in any degree, to remove the scales of prejudice and error from the mental eyes of any who may have done the Rev. Joseph Leycester Lyne, deacon, the injustice to impugn his loyalty to the Church of England, or to pronounce his Scripture teaching as schismatic; and if I may be further allowed to cause it to dawn upon the detractors of Ignatius, the Monk, that second to his Gospel preaching of "Jesus only," his aim and desire is to induce and develop, in the Church of England, a spirit of true Christian sympathy—a bond of Godly union—between Catholics and Evangelicals; some, at least, of the objects I have had in view will have been gained.

J. V. SMEDLEY.

Oxford and Cambridge Club,
    Pall Mall, S.W.
        October 6th, 1886.

Editor's Preface.

EDITOR'S PREFACE.

I desire, in the first place, to take the opportunity of thanking the few kind friends, who, during our Westminster Missions, contributed to the little fund which we raised for meeting the cost of the shorthand notes of these Sermons and Orations; and to whom we are, therefore, primarily indebted for their publication.

As all are aware, who have ever had the privilege of attending the Llanthony Missions, Father Ignatius preaches entirely *extempore*—without making any notes even for his sermons.

Compared with printed matter, derived from MSS. furnished by the preacher himself, the results of even *verbatim* notes of *extempore* sermons must always fail to do justice to the preacher. But I feel sure that the readers of this volume will make every allowance for such unavoidable defects, inherent to all addresses prepared from shorthand notes. I must, however, commend the stenographer for having, on the whole, I think, very satisfactorily executed his task.

I have to apologise for the volume not appearing quite so soon as it was originally promised; but for this delay I must ask forgiveness on the plea that (except perhaps by those who have had a like experience) it would be difficult to realise the amount of hard work and time that the preparation for press, and revision, of the shorthand notes, has entailed upon me; but I need not say that I assign this reason for the delay, in no spirit whatever of complaint; for "the labour of love" has, throughout, been to me one of exceeding pleasure and privilege.

I am glad and grateful to be able to state that, although still suffering from great bodily weakness, the Rev. Father has kindly given the final revision, to all the proofs, which his weak state of health would permit; and though this has delayed the publication of the volume a little longer, I am sure that all will agree with me that it was worth waiting for.

My thanks are also due to my friend Miss E. C. Phillips, author of "St. Aubyn's Laddie," "Peeps into China," etc., for her kind assistance in supplying the foot-note texts to the very many Scripture quotations made by Father Ignatius in his sermons, and for much valuable help rendered in other ways.

Although, as I have stated in my Introductory remarks, I have endeavoured to select those sermons which would most fairly represent the Gospel teaching of Father Ignatius, I have also tried to give, in this first series, as many as possible of the Sermons that were delivered at the October Mission, 1885—the first course that I had consecutively taken down.

To the possible criticisms which may be made by some, concerning a frequent repetition in these sermons, I would remark that such repetition is unavoidable, inasmuch as every sermon, preached by the Father, even when composing one of a course, is, as regards the Gospel Message, which he comes to deliver, complete in itself. It will even be seen that in his Orations, also, Father Ignatius does not fail prominently to introduce the Gospel Message.

Our book has assumed much larger proportions than was originally proposed, the number of pages being nearer five hundred than three hundred.

Feeling sure also that a portrait of Father Ignatius would lend additional interest and value to the volume, I have supplied it.

Those who have ordered copies of this work before publication, so as to kindly assist in meeting its cost, will be interested to know that—as far as can at present be seen—such orders will have met nearly one-half of the sum required.

I may say that no responsibility of any kind has been incurred by the Rev. Father Ignatius; but after the cost of the volume has been discharged, by the ready sale which, please God, I trust it may have, I look forward to the pleasure of having it in my power to hand the profits to the Rev. Father to assist in meeting the heavy expenses of holding his Missions— a thank-offering, in token of my own personal gratitude to, and loving reverence for, him.

I need scarcely remind even the most thoughtless that one of a monk's privileges is to be *absolutely unendowed*.

It is hoped that a quick sale of this book may enable me shortly to reproduce these Sermons and Orations in a cheaper form, in order that the poor, as well as the rich, may have the privilege of reading them.

Just before going to press, the characteristic lines, which will be found on the opposite page, were received by me from Father Ignatius.

J. V. S.

Editor's Preface.

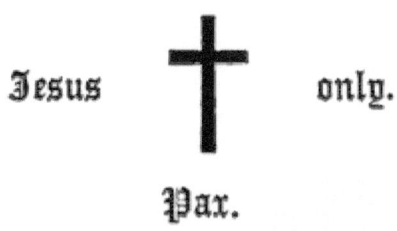

Jesus only.

Pax.

To the Reader,

The following pages, are, from a literary point of view, entirely unworthy of perusal.

The critic will find ample room for his work.

Wholly *extempore* addresses read but poorly. The tone, manner, and action of the speaker, may add some interest to his words which, apart from these, are worse than meagre and poor.

The ONLY merit of these discourses is that they are full of the Bread of Life, "*Jesus*," as an egg is full of meat; and as God blesses the weak and foolish things of this world to His Praise, He can bless even this poor book to the Salvation and joy of many a poor, tired, sinful soul.

IGNATIUS OF JESUS, O.S.B.,
Monk.

Llanthony Abbey,
   Abergavenny,
October, 1886.

ERRATA.

Page 125, line 3 from top, read "messengers" for "millions."

Page 207, line 5 from bottom, read "cœnaculum" for "canaculum."

CONTENTS.

Mission Sermons.

I.	PAGE.
Jonah's Mission to Nineveh	1
II.	
Jesus Christ and the Brazen Serpent	19
III.	
Jesus Christ, the Living Bread	37
IV.	
Jesus Christ, the Merchantman	55
V.	
Jesus Christ, the King's Son	71
VI.	
Jesus Christ, the Good Shepherd	89
VII.	
Jesus at the Grave of Lazarus	107
VIII.	
Jesus Christ, the Sabbath of God	135
IX.	
On the Results of the Mission; or, "The Great Promise Fulfilled"	155
X.	
Jesus Christ and the Ark of Noah	173
XI.	
Jesus at Bethany: Scene at the End of the Mission	190

Addresses to Christians.

XII.
THE LORD'S DAY ... 219

XIII.
THE LORD'S CROSS ... 239

XIV.
THE LORD'S MOTHER ... 253

XV.
JEHOVAH-JIREH ... 273

Orations.

XVI.
VALIDITY OF ORDERS AND SACRAMENTS IN THE CHURCH OF ENGLAND ... 297

XVII.
THE PROTESTANT CHURCH: WHAT IS IT? ... 321

XVIII.
RITUALISM: THE GOOD IT HAS DONE, AND THE HARM IT HAS DONE ... 339

XIX.
WHY WERE THE MONASTERIES OF ENGLAND DESTROYED? ... 371

XX.
THE APPARITIONS AT LLANTHONY (*by special request*) ... 391

AND

INTRODUCTORY PRAYERS.

I.

Jonah's Mission to Nineveh.

SPECIAL PRELIMINARY ADDRESS TO CHRISTIANS ON THE MISSION.

Sunday Morning, October 18th, 1885.

Jonah's Mission to Nineveh.

Prayer before Sermon.

O God, we believe in Thee. We believe that Thou art just. We believe that Thou hast revealed Thyself to us by the face of Thine own Incarnate Son Jesus Christ, and we now find that we are indeed as ignorant as little children. But we come before Thee, at this time, to be taught of Thee; for we can never know anything about Thee unless Thou Thyself wilt teach us.

Thou hast made our hearts to hunger after Thee, and Thou hast made us to realise that there is a void within us which nothing but Thou canst fill. Oh! how our hearts adore Thee because Thou hast not remained cold and silent towards us, but hast sympathized with us, and hast given us Jesus to be our Prophet and our Priest.

And Thou hast taught our hearts, by the power of the Holy Ghost, to believe, and we believe Thy Word, and that it is a living Word. We believe that it is an Almighty Word, a satisfying Word; we believe that it is a comfortable Word, a peaceful Word; we believe that it is a loving Word, and we believe also that it is the Word of an Almighty God.

Please look upon us, Father—in the all-powerful Name of Jesus Christ we plead before Thee—and consecrate us during this week with Thy Spirit's power. Thou hast promised power to those that believe in Thee—power to wipe away the cobwebs of unbelief, of materialism and rationalism from the hearts of men; and may Thy power now come down and so touch the hearts of men, and influence their lives, that they may become bright, shining lights, for Thy Glory, in the midst of "an evil and adulterous generation."*

O Father, make this a mighty "place of business" this week, and let us all be good "business men," in earnest about the tremendous work of eternity. Heavenly Father, help me to realise that I am speaking to dying men, who have only a few short moments to stop in this world, and the story of whose work will be but as a dream, that is passed, when they shall stand in the presence of their God and of infinite eternity.

Help me to help them to realise this reality, that they may "make their calling and election sure."† I know the difficulties that are in my way—the difficulties of sin, of unbelief, of the world, and of the power of evil spirits; but Thou art mightier than them all, and we believe that Thy Word is Almighty like Thyself, and therefore with good courage we will preach it.

Only do Thou anoint both preacher and people with Thy Holy Spirit, that the blessed results promised in Thy Word may come to pass in us, and that many may "go out with joy, and be led forth with peace"‡ before the mission shall end.

O God, grant that many who may hear me this week may have cause to bless the occasion when they entered into our assembly; grant that many may pass "from darkness to light, and from the power of Satan unto God, that they may receive in this place forgiveness of their sins, and inheritance among them which are sanctified by faith."§

Father, for Jesus Christ, His sake, hear our prayer. Amen.

---

* St. Matt. xii. 39.
† 2 Peter i. 10.
‡ Isaiah lv. 12.
§ Acts xxvi. 18.

"JONAH'S MISSION TO NINEVEH."

SPECIAL PRELIMINARY ADDRESS TO CHRISTIANS ON THE MISSION.

" Arise, go unto Nineveh, that great city, and preach unto it the preaching that I bid thee."—Jonah iii. 2.

It strikes me, beloved brethren, that this exhortation is very necessary to the ministers of God at the present day, when we have so much of rationalism and materialism to contend with, and when there are very many among ourselves who think it best not to preach the Gospel in its simplicity, but to try to suit it to the age in which we live; when the Gospel, in its simplicity, is considered a kind of insult to the intellect of man, which has now reached such a pitch of refinement and progress.

And what is the consequence of this? The consequence is that God's Word, preached to suit the day, falls flat and does but little of the good that it might do; and, with a vast amount of rhetoric and oratory, with a vast amount of philosophic argument and metaphysical reasoning added to it, it brings but few results to the hearts and lives of men, whose hearts are not reached and therefore whose lives are not profited: for all the philosophy of the brain and the mind cannot influence the heart and the life.

But when Christ is lifted up in the old-fashioned, simple way in which the apostles and early saints lifted Him up, then men are drawn to accept and to profit by that wonderful love of which they are told; feeling it to be, at all events, something worth having, if they can only obtain it.

So I would call attention to my text, and to the story from which it is taken, because we have there a very similar position, on the part of God's servant, to that which God's people occupy at the present day.

Poor Jonah was flesh and blood, the same as you and I are; poor Jonah was a matter-of-fact sort of person, judging from the little we learn of him; but, when the Spirit of God moved his heart and conscience to go to Nineveh, he knew that he was commanded, by the Lord, to convey a *message*.

And mark, my brethren: that message was a very unpalatable message; it was an unreasonable sort of message to be delivered to the great city—the greatest city of the civilized world at the time. Jonah was to tell the people of that mighty city that if they did not repent and turn to the God of Israel, their city should be overthrown in forty days! On the face of it, this would seem to be a most ridiculous thing to do, and was most absurd from a humanist's point of view.

Just consider for a moment what the position of Jonah was! He was a member of the despised tribe of Israelites; a people taken, as captives, into Assyria, and whose name had become a by-word among the nations; and their peculiar opinions upon religion were ridiculed by the philosophers of the world, by the schools of the West, by the pantheists, with their metaphysical subtleties, and by the Buddhists, with their philosophical and peculiar casuistries; for even if you speak to the followers of Buddha at the present day, you will find them very clever fellows indeed.

They are clever philosophers and well-read metaphysicians; and it was because the religion of the Buddhist did not ask human nature to believe any thing that it could not square, in the same way as a Cambridge wrangler would square a mathematical problem, that it flourished and numbers, at the present day, 500 million followers.

Now look at the position of Jonah, who is sent with an apparently ridiculous message from a ridiculed God! Belonging to a despised nation, he is, as far as we know, totally unprepared, from an educational point of view, to have any influence with this great city—the gigantic city of Nineveh, to walk through which it took three days.

Imagine what that immense city was like! It stood upon the Tigris, and was crowded with the merchandise, the wealth, and the power of the East; and we can well imagine the influence which Nineveh had among the nations of the world! Surely she sat as a queen upon the bosom of the royal stream, on the shores of which her palaces and quays were built: yea, like the lordly stream which washed her quays, she sat a queen among the nations.

And Jonah, a despised Israelite, is told to go to that great city and not to preach what *he* pleases: mark that! but—*to preach what God tells him.*

And the message which God told him to deliver was only calculated to give offence and to make him appear ridiculous in the eyes of the people of Nineveh; and if they had had any lunatic asylums in those days, probably the first impulse of the people would have been to take him to one. For he is to tell them that their great city of wealth, of power, philosophy, and art, whose philosophical academies comprised the learning of the world, will be overthrown in forty days if they do not turn to the despised God of the despised children of Israel.

And what is the power that will be put to work to overthrow the city of Nineveh? Will it be that some marvellous tide will sweep up the Tigris, from the sea, and submerge, in the depths of its waters, the city, its palaces, its temples, and its market-places? Or will it be that some unknown storm will sweep over the eastern plains, carrying all before it, and the gigantic city shall pass away? Or shall the earth open her mouth and swallow it up? What shall be the power and what the manner, what the catastrophe, or what the cataclysm, by which this strange wonder, the destruction of Nineveh, shall be accomplished?

Thus may Jonah have reasoned and have tried to get away from this, as I said (humanly speaking), absurd mission, and he struggled with the Spirit of God; but It proved too strong for him, *and he went to Nineveh.*

And, dear brethren, what do you think must have been Jonah's one single consolation? *He believed that God had spoken to him, he believed that God was Almighty, and that God's power would accompany him on his journey!*

He had learnt from his cradle upwards, at an Israelitish mother's knee, to believe that *God* had brought his forefathers out of the land of Egypt, in spite of the powers of Pharaoh and his hosts; that *God* had led His people triumphantly through the tide of the Red Sea, swept by the mighty gales, fresh from the sweetness of God's own hand, on either side leaving a firm dry passage in the deep; and how that, when their foes had come down from the western hills, with a mighty crash the waters had fallen back and overwhelmed the enemies and the foemen of the Lord.

He knew how that God had watched over His

people, amid all the intricacies of their wanderings in the Arabian peninsula; how, that His strong arm had supplied their wants in the desert, and had guarded each one of the thousands of pilgrims towards the land of promise; he knew how when they thirsted He had opened up waters for them from the rock, and when they hungered had caused manna to fall and quails to feed His people.

Jonah believed, too, that when Amalek had come out against the children of Israel, with all his mighty hosts, God had hearkened to His people's prayer, and down from the Heavens had swept his Mighty Powers upon the hosts of Amalek; so that ere the sun had sunk down in the west, Israel had won the victory by the power of the Lord of Hosts.

All these stories he had learnt, and he believed that it was the God who is " the same yesterday, and to-day, and for ever "* who had now given him the message to convey; and although he shrank from the Mission to Nineveh, *this knowledge was his consolation.*

And we can picture Jonah entering into Nineveh. He, no doubt, went a long way into the city before he summoned up courage to begin the delivery of his message. He must have walked miles to get into the centre of the city; for " Nineveh was an exceeding great city of three days' journey."†

* Heb. xiii. 8. † Jonah iii. 3.

Just suppose, now, that he began right away at Shepherd's Bush, and imagine him, about three o'clock in the afternoon, on the steps of the Royal Exchange! The hum and the bustle of human, commercial life is going on all around; the throbbing of the fevered pulse of business is just at its highest pitch; men are hurrying backwards and forwards and to and fro, when, all at once, the weird, strange-looking, foreign prophet springs up, amid the crowd of wondering men, and delivers his message: "YET FORTY DAYS, AND [LONDON] SHALL BE OVERTHROWN!"*

How long do you suppose he would stop there, on the steps of the Royal Exchange? He would be told to "move on," no doubt. But would he be "moved on" by the police? No, brethren, he would not! The police of Nineveh, in the past, were as strong as the police of London are at present; but all their human force stood powerless before the mandate of the Mighty Powers from another world; and ere a single hand could have reached the prophet, as the forces of this world were crying "Move on!" deep down in the hearts of the crowd the Powerful, Imperious Command of God would have cried "STAND BACK!"

And Nineveh stood back, and the despised Hebrew went forth, with his mission, and proclaimed: "YET FORTY DAYS, AND NINEVEH SHALL BE OVERTHROWN."*

* Jonah iii. 4.

He did not water down the message; he did not attempt to suit it to this or that particular school of thought, for he knew that it was the message of God, *and he trusted in the might of Him Who sent the Word.*

And what was the consequence ? As the evening shades were lengthening o'er the mighty city, as the moonlight danced upon the waters of the Tigris, as the calm of night stole over the towers and domes of that eastern town, as the places of business were closing and the quays (crowded with bales of merchandise) were becoming deserted, the vespers of Nineveh were heard, chanted with a moan of anguish from the heart of a prostrate people.

For the story which Jonah had told had passed from mouth to mouth, that the King of Nineveh had come down from his throne to fast and weep; and each inquired of each if they had heard the strange tale with which the foreign visitor was bewitching the people; and, from the greatest to the least, Nineveh heard the Word of God and put on sackcloth and ashes ! So the evil was turned away, and the message of love won the victory, *because it was the message of God.*

Just as firmly as Jonah believed the message he conveyed was Almighty, because it was the message of God, so do we Christians, who profess the name of Christ, believe in the Power of the Crucified, Divine Redeemer.

I speak not of those who are accounted wise by the world, but of those Christians I speak who, as little children, have come to Christ, Who Himself said that His Word has been "hid from the wise and prudent and revealed unto babes."* I speak of those Christians who have had the courage to come to Christ, of those Christians who believe in the Gospel message, that Jesus Christ is God Almighty; that Jesus Christ, the Carpenter of Nazareth, shed His Blood to save the world from an eternal hell.

But, you know, they say to-day that hell is not eternal. But if hell be not eternal, then Heaven is not eternal; if there be no eternal hell, there is no eternal Heaven.

I preach the simple, old-fashioned Gospel message, and the Peace of God through Jesus Christ our Lord; and all the rubbish of sectarian controversy, and all the differences of party and the wranglings of sects, are set aside; and I ask all Christians, whether they be Catholic or Protestant, to rally around me at this mission, and help me to hold up that Mighty Christ as the Bread of God, which feeds and satisfies the hearts and souls of sinful men.

And so this mission is just for one very simple object; and that is, to lift up Jesus Christ.

You see we have rather a small congregation this

* St. Matt. xi. 25.

morning, but I know that people will come, for they always do as the mission goes on; and as we lift up Christ He will draw men's hearts to Him.

Last spring, in this hall, we had Roman Catholics converted—not to Protestantism, for I should be very sorry to see a Roman Catholic turn Protestant, very sorry—*but converted to Christ.* A Roman Catholic told me, as I was going out of the hall, one day—and I shall never forget the look upon his face as he spoke—how he had learnt to trust Jesus, and how he had found the Bread of God to feed his aching, hungry soul. He was a Roman Catholic—I am not, and I never shall be.

But I have had Dissenters, too, take my hand and speak in just the same way, knowing, at the time, that I was nothing but the earthen vessel, the vile dust, which the Almighty Power of God had chosen to use, simply, perhaps, because I was despised and nothing, knowing that He could make more use of me than of those whom the world " delighteth to honour."

And so English Catholics and Protestants, Roman Catholics and Dissenters, found the Divine joy and gladness of a knowledge of Christ, even in this very hall, last spring.

And now He is going to enter this place again. And He is going to consecrate it by the visitation of His Holy Spirit. He says : " Take no thought how

or what ye shall speak : for it shall be given you "*—
and I know it will be given to me—and that, just as
Jonah's mission, in a large way, was successful, so
my mission, in its little way, will be successful, too ; and
I shall send many men and women back to their homes
and their neighbours and their struggles and their
trials, in this great modern Babylon, going forth as
" children of light and of the day ; "† and, where-
ever they move, their pathways shall be like radiant
tracks of glory from the light world of the Presence
of their God : yea, they shall be children of the light ;
and they shall not be ashamed to testify to the love
and power of Jesus, Who has filled their hearts to
overflowing.

No man, who does not himself believe, can realise
the wonderful gift that the saints of God possess.
Those who are saved can tell, generally speaking,
when a man is God's child and when he is a child of the
world. "He that is spiritual is judged of no man,"‡ and
no man can judge him ; but he can judge if others are
God's children or not. Directly a man gets up to
speak—I do not care whether it be in a Catholic
church or in a Protestant conventicle—if he be endowed
with the Holy Ghost, all believers will be able to tell
that he is sent from God; for they will hear his voice
as that of the Good Shepherd.

* St. Matt. x. 19.   † 1 Thess. v. 5.   ‡ 1 Cor. ii. 15.

Do you know Christ, and that in Jesus is eternal life? This is the question I have to ask of you. Dear Christian brethren, may you "take knowledge" of me that I "have been with Jesus;"* pray that I may say and do nothing contrary to His will, so that I may draw people to His feet; and that in this place, this week, it may be said of many: "You are the people of the living God."

And then, when the mission shall be at an end, we shall find that many a rationalistic unbeliever, and many a one, hitherto tied up and bound by the fetters of unbelief and infidelity, shall have been set free, and shall have passed "into the glorious liberty of the children of God."†

This shall be the effort of the mission; and this is the *only* effort that we ask God to bless; and on Sunday morning next, if it please God that I shall be here—and I trust that I may be—we shall see the promise fulfilled: They "shall go out with joy, and be led forth with peace."‡

And our profession is not only a profession for the future, for Christ loves you to-day; and to those who receive Him, in His fulness, as God's gift individually to them, the promise is made *to-day:* They "shall go out with joy, and be led forth with peace."‡

---

* Acts iv. 13. † Romans viii. 21. ‡ Isaiah lv. 12.

I see that among my congregation there are many Catholics—I can tell this by the way in which they make the triumphant sign of the cross;—but supposing some of these should not be *Christian* Catholics, and should never yet have entered into the peace of God, by trusting Jesus as their very own Saviour,—shall I be doing them any harm if I send them back to the midst of their religious observances, with hearts alive with the love of One Who will illuminate their ritual, and their worship, with a reality without which it is but a dead form?

Oh Protestant brother, without Jesus your Protestantism is but an outward form, which I ask you to put aside for a season, and to come and stand side by side with me, and help me to proclaim the glad Gospel tidings!

So Christian Catholic, with your ornamental display, and Christian Protestant, with your unornamental display, come and walk hand in hand together to this work; and may God grant that our work here, this week, may be totally unsectarian and to the glory of Jesus; and may the Lord bless very many, and make them willing to help in the lifting up of a common Christ!

O Catholic, what is it that you set up upon your altar? It is the Image of the Crucifix. O Protestant brother, what Name do you profess by which to win souls? It is that of Jesus Christ.

Let us both join together to show a mocking world, outside, what our Christ is. Let us show that our religion is one of love; and that, although our outward forms are totally different, we can meet together to exalt a common Christ; and let us conspire to show that Jesus lives to-day, that He lives and moves in the hearts and minds of His own beloved people, and speaks with their lips and looks through their eyes.

Hence, other men will "take knowledge" of us that we "have been with Jesus;"[*] and Jesus "is alive for evermore."

And so, as we go forward on the blessed mission of lifting up Christ, we shall be "laying up treasure" in Heaven to place at His dear Feet "in that day when He makes up His jewels."[†]

---

[*] Acts iv. 13.   [†] Mal. iii. 17.

II.

Jesus Christ and the Brazen Serpent.

Mission Sermon.

Sunday Afternoon, October 18th, 1885.

Jesus Christ and the Brazen Serpent.

Prayer before Sermon.

O God, Almighty Father, for Jesus Christ's sake, bless the people. Help them to listen to Thy Word. Bless me and help me to speak with the power of Thy Holy Spirit so that Jesus Christ may, not only be lifted up but may, be looked upon and trusted, and received, and taken into the hearts of many here present, as Thy free Gift to them this day; so that many who came in here, without Christ, may go out under the influence of His power, and trusting in His promise, "I am with you always."*

Let the power of the Holy Spirit be manifested in our midst, and grant that many may "go out" (from this place) "with joy, and be led forth with peace."† Grant this, O Heavenly Father, for Jesus Christ's sake, Thy Son our Lord. Amen.

---

* St. Matt. xxviii. 20. † Isaiah lv. 12.

"JESUS CHRIST AND THE BRAZEN SERPENT."

Mission Sermon.

" And as Moses lifted up the serpent in the wilderness, even so must the Son of Man be lifted up: that whosoever believeth in Him should not perish, but have eternal life."—St. John iii. 14 and 15.

Does it not often strike very many of us, beloved brethren, when we hear sermons preached, that many of the preachers do not believe what they are preaching? Does it not often strike us that a very large number of those who profess to be Christians do not believe the Bible any more than those who utterly and entirely deny it? We see, plainly and distinctly, that of sermons that are preached there are far more which have no effect upon men's hearts and lives than of those which do have an effect upon them. How do you account for this?

People come and tell you they are disappointed, and that Christianity and the Bible seem to have no power over them.

What is the meaning of all this seeming failure on the part of this preaching to the people at large?

What *is* the meaning of it? Do you not think, if you look very quietly and calmly, and in a matter-of-fact, practical way, into the matter, that it is this: We have now, in our midst, a Christianity that is made up of such an enormous amount of ritual and outward formality and dogmatism, that the majority of preachers to the people have lost sight of the original Message of God to a dying world?

When the Gospel was sent at first it was sent—not to organised Churches,—for there were then none in existence—but it was sent just as a simple message to a world which was lying in misery and sin. Men were groping in darkness and endeavouring to find something to satisfy the hungerings of their nature.

Human nature had tried to right itself; civilisation, art and science had done their best, and they were only failures—nay, they were worse than failures, for they made men wise; who became worse and worse, instead of better and better. In fact man developed into a mere intellectual animal.

Civilisation and enlightenment were utterly useless so far as feeding the souls of men was concerned, and utterly useless, too, to satisfy the cravings of man's inner being. Then there came a Voice, with a Message, and it was just the Message contained in the words following our text: "God so loved the world, that He gave His Only Begotten Son, that whosoever believeth in Him should not perish, but have everlasting life."*

The very instant a man is willing to accept Christ, with the hand of simple trust, by taking Him at His own Word and thus coming to Him, that instant he is accepted, for he has come to the Saviour who has said: "Him that cometh to Me I will in no wise cast out."†

It is so very simple. "God so loved the world" that He gave His only begotten Son to die for it; and anyone who accepts Christ accepts God's rest and enters into His peace.

But instead of this being preached, it is directly or indirectly put on one side, or covered up with such an enormous amount of externals—I do not care whether they be Protestant or Catholic—there is such an amount of *system* introduced into the preaching of the Gospel, that *the* Message is not heard at all.

The strife of tongues and the wranglings of sects drown the sound of God's Message of Peace and Love; and, instead of the quietude of His great calm, there is war and strife, there is noise and distraction and unrest.

In our text our blessed Lord tells His messengers what they are to lift up. It is Jesus. And He tells

* St. John iii. 16. † St. John vi. 37.

them how He is to be lifted up—"as Moses lifted up the serpent in the wilderness."*

Moses lifted up the brazen serpent at God's command, that whosoever had been bitten by the fiery serpents, and then gazed upon it, might live. No matter how deep the poison might have been in his veins, the promise was, that if he looked at that serpent, he should live. It must have seemed a most absurd piece of intelligence for intelligent men (such as the Israelites and the Egyptians were at that time) to receive. Egypt was the nursery of human science and human philosophy, and the learning of the Egyptians was nothing at which to sneer; and to tell them this seemingly absurd story, regarding the lifting up of the brazen serpent, was only calculated to provoke their laughter.

But God said to Moses: "Take the serpent of brass, where the people can see it, and put the serpent of brass on a pole, and anyone who gazes on that serpent, if he be bitten, shall live." God set Moses to lift up this piece of brass in the sight of all the injured ones; and we know that everyone who looked at it lived.

God says now that there is to be no noise, no argument about His Message, no concessions to the demands of human wisdom, no softening down of the Message;

* St. John iii. 14.

but His preachers are to tell the people : " Here is a Crucified Jew Who is the Creator of the universe, Who is Almighty God, Who has taken our nature upon Him, in order to know our needs and to pay our debts, that we may have eternal life and pardon from sin ; and His preachers are to proclaim that *whosoever* will look up to the Cross of Christ, with a simple, trustful love and accept His eternal love, righteousness, pardon, joy, peace, and holiness are, *directly they look*, inheritors of His Everlasting Life ; and He declares that "they shall never perish, and no man shall pluck them out of His hand."*

This is what we are to tell to the people. We know that it is a thoroughly unphilosophical mode of teaching them. It is the old, primitive Gospel Message, which we are to preach at the present day. But the nineteenth-century Christian takes all kinds of exceptions to this Gospel, by which the supernatural in the Gospel becomes "smaller by degrees," and " beautifully less," in the lives, and hearts, and minds of the congregations of the present day.

And yet I have never known anyone look up to Christ who has not gone away satisfied; and whose life has not been totally changed, because he knew that his sins were blotted out and his debt was paid, and he

* St. John x. 28.

had "the witness of the Holy Spirit bearing witness with his spirit, that he is the child of God."*

What is it that produces this wonderful change in the hearts of men wherever Christ is lifted up? It is the power of God—it can be no other. You can explain that change on no other hypothesis.

And this is the simple promise that God has attached to the preaching of His Holy Word: "It shall not return unto Me void."†

Now, just for a moment, I will refer to the picture which God depicts in the text. Doubtless it was a usual custom of the Israelites, after their day's march, in the desert waste, to gradually form their streets of tents on the burning, sandy plain. As far as the eye could reach there was nothing but a vast expanse of burning sand, and as the sun sank in the west, and the moon rose over the distant mountains, of the Arabian peninsula, what a strange scene would be presented to the eye!

All at once a vast city, as far as the eye can reach, springs up: it is a city of tents. The women, in the tents, are preparing for the evening meal, the men and children, in the streets of canvas, are talking over the news of the camp, the difficulties of the way, which difficulties must have been countless and gigantic in the extreme; for many a time, in their desert journey,

* Rom. viii. 16.   † Isaiah lv. 11.

the people must have hungered, and many a time they must have thirsted and craved for water. There was plenty about which to talk in those canvas streets.

And no doubt, when the people had done talking of the difficulties and the wanderings of the way, they would begin to recount tales of the luxuries of the Nile banks, whence they came, and to tell of the shadows that the vines and pomegranates in Egypt threw upon the pathways, by the side of the delicious streams of water—the tributaries of the Nile.

In the desert waste the Israelites were a lonely nation in the world; and many of them may have longed to get back to the security of the land that they had left; and then, no doubt, they thought that they were foolish to go on such a reckless journey; and they complained against God and against Moses, His servant.

In the height of their rebellion the Lord sent a strange plague into their midst; whatever the animals were we know not; but they are described as being "fiery serpents!" I shall not argue what they were, for I take it that they were exactly what God said they were.

Just as if anyone asked me whether I believed that a fish swallowed Jonah, I should answer "of course I do." I believe that God prepared a great fish to swallow him; and I believe further that the God who prepared a fish to swallow Jonah could have prepared also a man to swallow the fish had he chosen to do so. It is perfectly easy to believe it all when once you admit that God is Almighty.

Well, whatever those animals were they were described, by the people who saw them, as "fiery serpents."

I can just picture the first venomous reptile gliding unseen and fixing itself upon the soft arm of some little darling, playing outside a tent door. I can hear the first wail of anguish that succeeded the first poisonous bite, and I fancy that I see the mother rushing out to ascertain what is the matter with her darling. It is now changing colour, and she carries it into the tent, while it begins to rave in its agony; and that cry is followed by a great moaning, and a yet mightier moan, that sweeps over the people, going up to the justly offended Father God.

And then the people, in their terror, flee to Moses.

What made them go to Moses? Oh! why did they not cry to God themselves? Because they felt, in their hearts, a sense of sin and the need of someone to plead their cause.

And just as the Children of Israel felt towards Moses, so we feel towards Jesus Christ! We want intercession with God.

And when God told Moses to lift up the serpent He

sent down a power upon the people to enable them to accept the invitation to look and live. There is in God's Word a power which accompanies It and enables men to take in the message and to believe it; and, in spite of unbelief and the arguments and philosophies, the materialism and the rationalism of the day, the Gospel of Jesus is winning souls just as it has done through all ages; and men are coming to believe the truths of the Gospel, and to enter into the rest of the saints, just the same to-day as their forefathers did when they believed.

The Gospel has just the same power now that it ever had, and it presents just the same phenomenon as ever: a phenomenon produced by the same cause, and one which challenges the investigation and the analysis of a doubting world outside; for the world cannot produce what the Gospel produces—a changed heart and a changed life—by any amount of philosophy.

As St. Paul wrote to the Corinthians of old: "If any man be in Christ, he is a new creature: old things are passed away; behold, all things are become new."*

And, brothers and sisters, when once you accept the Gift, you work with its mighty power, and you long to give others what you have received yourself and to

* 2 Cor. v. 17.

help others to know that their sins are forgiven; you long to help them to know who God is—that He is the Father of all those who put their trust in Him.

My brothers and sisters, when once you possess Christ then all the power of the powers of the world, all the powers of sin cannot destroy and cannot overcome you. The world has tried to destroy the Gospel power for eighteen hundred years; but, in spite of all the opposition of the past, and the opposition of the present day, the Gospel is doing its work *in drawing out* a people for God.

The Gospel never professes to save the world. It professes only to draw out a hungry crowd of filthy, wretched, dying men; to draw out a people for God. And this is what it is doing at the present day.

O! what a number of letters we received last May, all showing the results—the blessed results—of our mission, held in this hall, in that month; and all proving too that God's Word is doing its work just the same now as it ever did.

Let us determine to lift up Jesus "as Moses lifted up the serpent in the wilderness,"* and then we shall see the fulfilment attached to it; and they who gaze on Christ, and accept Him, as God's gift individually to them, shall not perish.

Not one who looks with the eye of faith into the

* St. John iii. 14.

mighty Saviour's face and trusts Him, not one who takes Christ as life eternal to his soul, not one who, by the hand of faith, lays hold of the precious Blood of Christ, as the atoning sacrifice of his soul, shall perish, for Jesus says: "They shall be mine, in that day when I make up my jewels."* And He also says: "This is the Father's will which hath sent Me, that of all which He hath given Me I should lose nothing, but should raise it up again at the last day;"† and again He says: "All that the Father giveth Me shall come to Me: and him that cometh to Me I will in no wise cast out."‡

We have only to proclaim Christ as the great High Priest of the Church, of the redeemed, for sinners, from all parts of the human family, to flock to gaze upon Jesus, to be healed, and to go away rejoicing and singing:—

> "I came to Jesus, and I drank,
> Of that life-giving stream:
> My thirst was quenched, my soul revived,
> And now I live in Him."

My brethren, this is no beautiful dream of fancy; it is no poetic imagination; it is a tremendous, practical reality to the soul; it is God's Gift, eternal life in Jesus Christ. And may God help and bless the work upon which I have entered to-day. *This week* we

---

* Malachi iii. 17.   † St. John vi. 39.   ‡ St. John vi. 37.

are going to carry on a purely unsectarian labour, and to keep all Churches and sects out of sight.

Our one aim will be to lift up Christ. We have too many in the Church who do not know Christ; and unbelief and infidelity are undermining the Church.

So many of our Clergy, alas, do not hold up Christ to unconverted worldlings as are so many of those who crowd our churches at the present day.

If we do not want to see the Church of England disestablished let us lift up Christ, for if the Church does not lift up Christ of what use is she? Let us remember what Our Lord said: "As Moses lifted up the serpent in the wilderness, even so must the Son of Man be lifted up: that *whosoever* believeth in Him should not perish, but have eternal life."*

There are plenty of Church people who will tell you that, although you have come to Jesus, you still might perish; they say Christ has done His part and left you to do your part. But it is not so. Christ is the "Author and the Finisher,"† "the Alpha and the Omega" "of our faith,"† and He says: Whosoever believeth in Him shall not perish but have eternal life. And "this is life eternal, that they might know Him."‡

There is a kind of similarity between our case and that of the Children of Israel. Man is forced to con-

* St. John iii. 14, 15.   † Heb. xii. 2.   ‡ St. John xvii. 3.

fess that this world cannot satisfy him—that this world is, to some extent, a kind of wilderness. And the older we get, and the further we journey along life's road, the more like a wilderness the world seems; and one we love and then another, falls away until, as life prolongs its chapters, they all seem to close in notes of minor; so unlike the major strains that we knew in the past, so sparkling and so bright. And gradually, like the wind, they die away into a whisper and fade into a murmur; and then we hear them no more as the hush of death steals over us.

No invention can satisfy, and no food can satisfy, the cravings, stern and imperious, of the soul within us: but Jesus Christ—He satisfies those who accept Him in His fulness.

Therefore, our desire, our *one* desire this week, will be to lift up Jesus and to exalt Christ.

And, brethren, have not any of you been bitten by some serpent, the serpent of uncleanness or of dishonesty? Have you not some secret habit or fault, of which you would gladly get rid? The poison is flowing in your veins; but Christ says to those who trust Him: "I have blotted out, as a thick cloud, thy transgressions, and, as a cloud, thy sins."* "Their iniquities will I remember no more."†

And the angel spirits take up the sound of that

---

* Isaiah xliv. 22. † Heb. viii. 12.

"No more!" and the strains steal into the presence of the King Himself. "I will remember no more;" and we go out in peace, for the gate of death has become the gate of life; and "death is swallowed up in victory."*

So I know what I am about, and what I am going to do, during our mission week; all that I seek is just to speak of Jesus.

I am a poor, earthen vessel, I am frail and fickle and vile; but may Jesus take me up and, through me, pour out the light and the power and the riches of Christ over the congregations gathered here! Thanks be to God for the opportunity of presenting Christ to many hearts, He who is God's anodyne for the wounded, and God's panacea for the sorrowing heart.

---

* 1 Cor. xv. 54.

III.

Jesus Christ, the Living Bread.

Mission Sermon.

Sunday Evening, October 18th, 1885.

Jesus Christ, the Living Bread.

Prayer before Sermon.

O Lord, Shepherd of the sheep, Who hast laid down Thy life for Thy sheep, we bless Thee because Thou art keeping Thy promise, at this time; and Thou art in the midst of us as Thou hast said: "Where two or three are gathered together in My Name, there am I in the midst of them."*

And we believe that Thou art here as a Power to comfort, and to save, to feed, and to clothe, the soul. O Lord Jesus, when we know Thee and Thy Word, we are possessed of "joy unspeakable and full of glory."†

O God, may many this week partake of the Living Bread, sent down from Heaven to feed a hungry, sinful, dying world; and grant that Thy Holy Spirit may anoint my understanding and my heart, that Thou mayest be able to use them for Thy glory and for Thy people's good.

O God, anoint Thy people also that they may hear Thy Word and, after hearing, may lay hold of the Bread of Life, and may they become satisfied with Thy goodness. Dear Lord Jesus, send many empty ones away, from this place, filled with Thy Goodness, possessed of Thee; and may they be able to say: "I am satisfied with Jesus." So shall their lives be renewed with the gladness of Heaven; so shall their hearts rest in the peace of God; and so with them shall "old things have passed away; and all things have become new."‡ Amen.

---

* St. Matt. xviii. 20.   † 1 Pet. i. 8.   ‡ 2 Cor. v. 17.

"JESUS CHRIST, THE LIVING BREAD."
Mission Sermon.

"And Jesus said unto them, 'I am the Bread of Life: he that cometh to Me shall never hunger; and he that believeth on Me shall never thirst.'"—John vi. 35.

Now, you know, brethren, this is either true or not true. Then let us take it for granted that it is true, I wonder how many persons, in this place, have proved the truth of it. Listen! Jesus Christ says: "I am the Bread of Life—he that cometh to Me shall never hunger; and he that believeth on Me shall never thirst."*

This is the test of whether a man be a Christian or not. A man who is satisfied with Christ is a Christian; he that is not so satisfied is not a Christian. "He that cometh to Me shall never hunger; he that believeth on Me shall never thirst,"* says our Lord and Saviour.

Are you so satisfied that you do not hunger after righteousness because Christ *is* your Righteousness?

Are you so satisfied that Christ is the pardon of sin

* St. John vi. 35.

to you, that you do not hunger after pardon of sin, because you have it?

Are you so satisfied that you do not *want* eternal life because you have it? Jesus Christ *is* your life, and you are satisfied with Him and live.

Are you so satisfied that you do not *want* peace because you have it? He *is* your peace.

How many are there, in this congregation, who have accepted Christ in His fulness, His love, His salvation, His purity, His peace and His joy? Very few. There are very, very few, among the crowds of professing Christian people, who are satisfied with Jesus. They do not know what it is to come to Jesus and lay hold of the tremendous realities, the practical realities, of His love. In that love there is something not only intensely real; but glorious and all-satisfying is the power of " the unsearchable riches of Christ," outpoured over starving multitudes.

Our ideas of this life are formed from our every-day experiences of it; and I am now speaking to some who have formed their ideas of life from a very long experience. Some are sixty and seventy years of age, and have had perhaps a fair share of the good things of this world.

They have tried the world, they have tried what the world can give, they have tasted its pleasures, its loves, its ambitions, its hopes, its aims; and now their lives are nearly over. They have come to the shady side of life's hill; they have long since climbed to the top, and are descending the other side, towards the strange and mystic stream, which separates them from the great beyond, whatever it may be.

And now, elder brethren, what is your experience of life? Tell me, have the cravings of your heart and intellect and spirit—have they been fed and satisfied with the world?

The world is full of charms of art, philosophy, science, rhetoric, oratory and politics. All have their pleasures and delights; and then there is the intoxicating cup of popular applause—some seek to drink of this—perhaps some of you have drunk of it, and have been popular men in your day.

I remember being at the bedside of a popular member of Parliament when he was dying. He never thought of popularity then as I, with the Bible in my hand, was by his side. Oh! if I had related to him certain memories of his past life, when some glad ovation from his friends had greeted him, he would have shaken his head with a sickening expression. What did he want with the world's glories as life was ebbing fast away? I held his hand in mine; faithful servants, wife and children were gathered round his bed. My lips were close to his ear, and I kept whispering to him—not of politics or popular applause, not of the things of this world—it was of the vast future that he was about to face, and the tremendous realities of Eternity that I whispered in his ear.

He was about to enter upon the great examination which shall succeed the college term of life; he was about to enter into the Presence of the great Examiner, who is to decide between those who are in His peace and righteousness, and those who are not; and you should have seen that man's face when I spoke words like these in his ear: "My sheep shall never perish, neither shall any man pluck them out of My hand."*

I listened to the gasping breathings of the dying man; and he was calm as I said: "And they shall come with singing unto Zion; and everlasting joy shall be upon their head."† His spirit passed away in peace.

Oh! brethren, I need not dwell upon this illustration to prove that Jesus Christ is the Bread that satisfies, that satisfies in life, in death and in eternity.

There is no real life without Christ. Life without Christ is indeed made up of inexplicable contradictions, is most illogical; life without Christ is an enigma that is past solution.

Yes, brethren, I say a man without Christ is not satisfied, for he has not laid hold of that Bread which alone can satisfy all his desires.

* St. John x. 28. † Isaiah li. 11.

Brothers, when Jesus says He is the Bread that satisfieth there is a sublime reality in the declaration.

Human life is a magnificent thing; and there is something wonderful about its compound character. The compound of the animal man is something very mysterious, puzzling and beautiful to contemplate. Oh! the powers which exist within us, and kindle anew in us, the powers that are brought into play in our compound nature!

I have felt powers within me that have startled me at times—powers only like babes in their cradles, that seemed to tell me we are only here to be prepared for the great and everlasting Home of our Father. Life, human life, is a magnificent and absorbing series of paradoxical contradictions.

If I want to look at human life in one of its dark phases, I have only to go to Ratcliffe Highway, its slums and its courts, between eleven and twelve at night, as I used to do when one of the good Father Lowder's Mission curates, at St. George's-in-the-East. I have only then to go to the low dancing saloons, or other haunts of misery and sin, and gaze upon the poor, painted girl in the street, or watch her as she dances in one of these halls of depravity and vice.

More than once have I taken such a child by the hand, and have looked up in her face and said, "You are not happy." And I have seen the tears moisten in the girl's eye when I have spoken to her of Jesus Christ. When the world has cast her off, like the coward that it is, and civilized society has given her the cold shoulder, then the Good Shepherd has come and said to her: "Come unto Me, all ye that labour and are heavy laden, and I will give you rest!"* The poor child has then sobbed her way to Jesus' Feet, and has lain down and trusted in Him; and has been raised up to a new and forgiven life.

I could give the experience of scores who have realised the truth that Jesus lives and works to-day, and is the Bread of Life, in the hearts and minds and souls of men.

He is the Bread that satisfies.

Oh! brethren, many of you know that I speak not of a poetic dream; but of a magnificent, daily, practical reality, when I speak of the power of The Resurrection in your souls.

"I am that Bread of Life!"† Brethren, when Jesus Christ enters into a man's life, He explains all difficulties, He solves all enigmas. Where storm was, when He enters, calm comes, and where darkness was, there He brings light; although you may truly say: "I must be in the dark, in part, now, because this life is the night of time, and the shades are mantling in the valley. But when I reach the journey's end, where the morn is bright upon the

* St. Matt. xi. 28. † St. John vi. 48.

mountains, I shall see the wonderful love of God and the wonderful wisdom of Jehovah, and I shall know that Jesus Christ, in truth, is the Bread of Life that has sustained me and fed me, through my earthly pilgrimage of sorrow and pain."

There is a wonderful life in the intellect; but, brethren, what is science and what is philosophy doing for man's intellect? Is it giving man's intellect rest and satisfaction and joy and peace?

A great man, of the present day, has declared that the more he knows the more he finds out how little he does know. Therefore, there is not much rest in scientific research.

Plenty of persons have entered with such avidity into scientific studies that their brains have become overbalanced; for the intellect cannot do without the food which the Creator has supplied for it.

When once we have taken Christ at His word, and have received Him—that instant we become illuminated with a light that we had not before; as we realise the height and the depth of the love of Christ.

Intellectually speaking Jesus Christ has been the Bread of Life to numbers of philosophers—the bread of repose, the bread of rest, the bread of peace, the bread of hope, and the bread of joy.

Men cease to be proud when once they have laid

hold of Christ, Who said: "Thou hast hid these things from the wise and prudent, and hast revealed them unto babes."*

"Oh!" the wise man says, "I am not a babe. I consider myself a giant in intellect and philosophy."

But, brethren, I see men and women, who have come to Christ, and have believed in Him, possessing, in their daily lives, a peace and a joy that you do not possess, and that you cannot apart from God. Therefore, as they receive all this from trusting Him, and this is exactly that for which you yearn, O weary, wandering soul, will you not come to Jesus too?

But you must come as we came. "Except ye be converted, and become as little children, ye shall not enter into the kingdom of Heaven."† Yes, you must put off the wisdom of this world, and bow at the foot of the throne of eternal wisdom and truth.

Is it too great a condescension to bow, for a moment, in prostrate obeisance—do you think it is derogatory to your dignity that you should bow before that God, Who has said: "He that shall humble himself shall be exalted?"‡

It is as though a beggar, battling in the mire with poverty, and only just beginning to learn the A B C of civilization, were asked by the Queen to go and take a present from her, and when told that he will

* St. Matt. xi. 25. † St. Matt. xviii. 3. ‡ St. Matt. xxiii. 12.

have to kneel to receive it, said, "Oh! I am not going to kneel to take it!" Then he will not be forced to receive the present.

But it would surely not be a great act of condescension to kneel, for a minute, before the throne of a loving monarch who wished to supply his needs.

Jesus said: "I am the Bread of Life: he that cometh to Me shall never hunger."* Now I know a great many would come to Christ only they are not asked to do so. They are asked to go to Church and to the Sacraments instead; they are asked to be baptized, to go to Confirmation or to Confession—all sorts of things they are asked to do. But Sacraments are utterly useless *until*—mark that word *until*—they have come to Christ; for the Holy Communion, and other ordinances, cannot operate upon a man until he has received Christ as his life.

Oh! brethren, sometimes I cannot help thinking that if, for a little while, all the churches in England would give up everything but offering Christ to the multitudes of starving souls in this woe-begone, sin-darkened country, what a vast amount of saving good might be done!

If men be not first brought to Christ what a mockery the Sacraments and other ordinances are; but how blessed and all-sustaining is that precious

* St. John vi. 35.

Sacramental "Bread" to those who do believe, and have accepted Jesus as their own individual Saviour.

Is it not however a fact that we constantly see troops of young men and women brought, in shoals, to be confirmed by the bishop, whose hearts have not been born again to holiness, who have not received Christ, and who immediately after publicly confessing Christ, and even receiving the Blessed Sacrament, go out to the theatre and the ball-room, returning deliberately to their old life of dissipation?

Then let us lift up Christ—that Saviour, for whom the teeming thousands of London are yearning—as the Bread of Life, and He will bring to them peace.

I never met a man or woman, a boy or a girl, who had received Christ, as God's Gift, who had not also received peace through Christ Jesus our Lord.

And, so you see, this is not a matter of sect or party. Catholics or Protestants, all who come to Christ—*all*, there is no distinction—shall find Him to be the Bread that satisfieth hungering souls.

What a glorious hope then, Christian people, in this congregation, you and I have of the results of this mission! How we know Jesus Christ will feed His flock in this place; and that very many will be led by the side of the green pastures of joy and pleasure, and be made to lie down by the cool waters of rest and gladness; and join with us at the end of the mission in singing the Psalm: "The Lord is my Shepherd; I shall not want."* "Yea, though I walk through the valley of the shadow of death, I will fear no evil: for Thou art with me; Thy rod and Thy staff they comfort me."†

Yes, Christ says: "I will never leave thee, nor forsake thee!"‡ and we believe it; and we believe that He is with us, shining upon us in life—illuminating our pathway, lightening our burdens, alleviating our troubles, our sorrows, and our cares; supplying us with strength to overcome sin, until, at last, we shall be more than conquerors when we come to Zion with a shout of joy; and we shall be able to say, in truth: "This is the victory that overcometh the world, even our faith."§

"I am the Bread of Life."‖ Perhaps some among my poorer brethren find life a very dismal, dark reality; perhaps some among my poorer brethren have to go home to a dingy garret, in some dark and dreary street, where they have to toil night and day—from early morning until late at night—to earn a few pence to keep bodily life within them.

Oh! what a dreary home you have, my sister; how sad and aimless seems your life. You have to work to make a shirt that may be sold for three shillings

* Psalms xxiii. 1.   ‡ Heb. xiii. 5.
† Psalms xxiii. 4.   § 1 John v. 4.
‖ St. John vi. 35.

E

and sixpence, and *you* make it ; but you only get sixpence for it—whereas the man, who does *not* make it, gets three shillings and sixpence ! And your fingers, my dear sister, are sore. Your young eyes often have no sight, because you strain your eyesight by the farthing rushlight which you can scarcely afford to buy; and, as you sit shivering, trembling, on your chair by the fireless grate, but ill clad and fed, with the dry hard crust of poverty, the thoughts of your old home when you were a girl, in the country, come to you.

Thoughts of the golden days of your girlhood steal into your brave heart, weak with much fasting, and mantle like a halo of glory around your imagination—thoughts of the time when your mother was alive and you had a loving mother's kiss at night ; and again you pass, as in a dream, through the familiar scenes of your childhood, and you hear the sound of the village bells, and the ringing, joyous cadence of the village children's voices, as you heard them when you were a village girl at home ; and then all passes away, and again you are amid your poverty and your toil.

But always there is just one star up there that throws its bright light through the casement upon you—upon you who have not a friend in the whole, wide world ; and the stars seem to talk to you and to say : " The heavens declare the glory of God; and the firmament sheweth His handiwork."*

* Psalm xix. 1.

The children of poverty talk to the stars. If they are not astronomers they study the stars; and I have been told by them what comfort they receive from those bright gems of the night-time.

But my sister, there is One beyond the stars Who loves you; Who has told you that if you will follow Him you shall be one of the jewels for His eternal Crown. He, my child, was once as poor as you are, and "had not where to lay His head."* "He was rich, yet for your sakes He became poor,"† and, last of all, He died for you, and, with His nail-pierced hands, He beckons you to Him, and He says: "Come unto Me, all ye that labour and are heavy laden, and I will give you rest."‡

I could tell you such tales of how Jesus Christ has cheered the lonely heart, and made joyful the lonely, sorrowing one; how the poor, pinched faces of the children of Poverty have been illuminated, as they have passed to the Land where "there shall be no more crying, neither shall there be any more pain."§

A little while ago some one was telling me how he had visited an old man in the workhouse, who, in the heyday of his life, had had a happy home, a loving wife and children. But gradually, one by one, they all faded away from his side; then his life grew sadder

---

* St. Matt. viii. 20.   ‡ St. Matt. xi. 28.
† 2 Cor. viii. 9.   § Rev. xxi. iv.

and more sad, as one light after another went out; and the poor man, finding himself alone and stricken down with weakness and poverty, came and knocked at the workhouse door.

He was an educated man; he had had the comforts of the world, but all had fled, when he went and knocked at that workhouse door! It was not very long before he there became so weak that he could not leave his bed, and when my friend went to see him and said to him: "O my poor man," he exclaimed, as he looked up, with a bright face, "Poor! I am not poor. I possess 'the unsearchable riches of Christ,'* that none can take from me. I am going to a king's palace, where I shall find all those who have gone before, treasured up and waiting for me."

Christ was the Bread of Life, Who fed him, and the sorrows of his life were illuminated with the light of the "Sun of Righteousness."†

Would you not be that man rather than the dying, wealthy worldling, who goes out into eternity, robed in the rags of his filthy sins; and whose poor, lank, lean, starved soul has never had one particle of living food from the fountain of Goodness?

Worldly men, you know what I am saying is true; the world cannot satisfy the cravings of the hungry soul; the world cannot satisfy the imperious claims of

* Ephes. iii. 8. † Mal. iv. 2.

the powers within; the world cannot fill the aching yearnings in the heart; but Christ Jesus can and Christ Jesus does.

"Blessed are they which do hunger and thirst after righteousness: for they *shall* be filled."*

They who already have fed upon the Bread of Life know that I have not exaggerated the beauty and the satisfaction and "the rest that remaineth to the people of God."†

Oh! then, in conclusion, I beseech all, who have not yet come to Jesus, to come to that Saviour, Who is waiting to receive you, and Who says: "Whosoever will,"‡ let him come.

And coming is not a movement of the body; it is just simply a movement of the soul, looking up to Christ, Who is present in our midst, and trusting in His promise "I will not fail thee, nor forsake thee."§

And when you come to Him, you shall find in Him all you can ever need—righteousness, strength, salvation and power, for He says: "He that cometh to Me shall never hunger; and he that believeth on Me shall never thirst." ‖

---

* St. Matt. v. 6.   § Joshua i. 5.
† Heb. iv. 9.   ‖ St. John vi. 35.
‡ Rev. xxii. 17.

IV.

Jesus Christ, the Merchantman.

Mission Sermon.

Monday Evening, October 19th, 1885.

Jesus Christ, the Merchantman.

Prayer before Sermon.

O God, our Father, Who art all-loving and all-wise and all-powerful, we believe Thy message of Love to a poor, loveless, lowly, weeping, hungering, dying world; and we, who are Thy people, long to make that message of Love and Power more truly known. And while we pray that Thy message of Love may become a message of Power, we ask Thee, Who hast promised that Thy message shall not return to Thee void, to remember Thy promise to-night, and to let Thy love and power go together into some heart that longeth for Thee, and pineth for Thy rest and peace.

O Word of wisdom—and Thou art the God of wisdom—it is from Thee alone that we draw the little sparks of wisdom which we possess. O Thou fountain of light, Thou Father of wisdom and truth, we pray Thee grant that, in our midst to-night, Thy wisdom may be revealed, and that many souls here present, clouded by the darkness of unbelief and sin, may by the power of Thy love, be brought quietly and gently and tenderly to the feet of the Good Shepherd, and may look up into His face, and trust themselves to His tender, Almighty care; and go out of this place rejoicing in their freedom.

They will find in Him "a Friend that sticketh closer than a brother,"* a Friend Who will never leave them in adversity, a Friend Almighty in compassion and wisdom and love, Who has said "Him that cometh to Me I will in no wise cast out."†

O Merchantman of wondrous toil, Who dost seek the precious pearl until Thou findest it, and then dost pay for it with the great price of Thy most Precious Blood, find some of the pearls for Thy Crown, in this place, at this time, to-night, for Thine Infinite Love and Mercy's sake. Amen.

* Prov. xviii. 24.   † St. John. vi. 37.

"JESUS CHRIST THE MERCHANTMAN."

Mission Sermon.

"The kingdom of heaven is like unto a merchantman, seeking goodly pearls: Who, when He had found one pearl of great price, went and sold all that He had, and bought it."—St. Matthew xiii. 45 and 46.

I think I am right in saying that the very best pearls are generally found in oyster-shells.

Oyster-shells certainly are very uncomely and unprofitable things to look at, and one would not think that hidden under such a rough exterior would be found gems that are at once so costly and so beautiful.

Now, dear brethren, this thought seems to be brought out wonderfully in the parable before us. It is a short parable, but it is very terse and very trite; and what it does say is very encouraging to the preacher of the Gospel.

When I am preaching, I often think that perhaps amongst my hearers are some of the most desperate characters in the place, and I am always glad when it is so, for these are the most likely to become the saints of Jesus Christ! At all events we know that no one can be a Christian unless he be a sinner; we know that no one can be a disciple of Jesus Christ unless he be a poor, lost soul; for Jesus Christ said: "I came not to call the righteous, but sinners to repentance."*

"The Son of Man is come to seek and to save that which was lost."†

Therefore, I believe, that before a man can be saved it must be proved that he is a sinner—a lost sinner.

I was very much struck, some few weeks ago, when we were holding a mission at Cardiff—which is a very bad town indeed, and where there are very low classes of people who congregate around the docks and in the slums—I was very much struck by the policeman telling a brother at the door of the hall, in which the services were being held, that some of the vilest characters in the place had been seen sitting quietly at the mission; and they pointed out one "fellow," as they called him, in particular, who had attended all the services, and who now professed to be a Christian.

Large numbers, who had never been seen in any place of worship before, thronged the hall. So testified the police. And that "fellow," who had been unspeakably bad, had been transubstantiated in a most extraordinary way and, in an unaccountable manner, (on any other hypothesis but the Gospel hypothesis)

* St. Mark ii. 17.   † St. Luke xix. 10.

he had been transubstantiated from a great sinner to one rejoicing in the knowledge of Jesus Christ; and was telling his knowledge of Christ to those outside, who had been his companions in sin before.

Yes, brethren, it does seem such a wonderful thought for Jesus Christ to liken Himself to a merchantman seeking goodly pearls. You must not form your idea of the Merchantman from the merchants of London, for this is an Eastern figure of speech. The merchants of London do not go themselves to distant countries to seek for what they require in their trades; but the Eastern merchants did. The Eastern merchantman travelled himself through desert wastes and wildernesses; he went through countless troubles, trials, dangers, necessities, and wants; he travelled, very often, in the face of most alarming dangers, just like the merchants of whom we read, to whom the children of Israel sold their younger brother Joseph, who travelled through vast tracts of desert.

We must picture to ourselves, then, a Persian or an Arabian going up into Egypt; we must fancy the toils and the pains of the way, and then we shall arrive at the thought which our Lord Jesus Christ wishes to convey when He speaks of Himself as a merchantman going forth, upon a lengthened journey, to some distant country, seeking for goodly pearls.

Sometimes, in His search for these jewels, He will have to go down into the depths of the lowest cesspools of human vice and human misery to find them. Take just a few specimens.

How far would He have to go, in His wonderful compassion, to reach the harlot of Magdala? How far would He have to persevere in His search for His pearl in her case? The sinful woman in the streets of Magdala, surrounded by the wealth and the vanity of sin, was one of the pearls of great price belonging to Him, Who is infinite purity, infinite holiness, infinite love; yes, though the woman was indwelt by seven devils, she was one of the pearls that the " Father gave to Jesus ;"* she was one of His sheep, whom He must redeem, seek, and find, and save. O! let us respect the fallen; for, under the poor, external roughness of their sin, there may be a pearl of great price which has been given, by God the Father, to the Creator Incarnate of the Universe.

Yes, Mary Magdalene now is one of the flashing gems in the crown of the King of Kings; and now, in dazzling brightness, she gleams and glows in the regalia of Heaven; for the sinner is saved; and the one " dead in trespasses and sins "† is alive; she that " was lost, is found ! "‡

Come again with me in fancy right away to Gadara,

* St. John x. 29.   † Eph. ii. 1.   ‡ St. Luke xv. 24.

cross the Galilean lake, in the fisherman's skiff, alight on its easternmost side, climb the steep path up the cliffs, and go in among the limestone tombs, just as the moon is shedding her silvery beams upon their whiteness, and see there, crouching, a maniac! a lunatic! one who has been brought to his desperate state by the sin of uncleanness.

There he is; no chains can bind him, no fetters can retain, or keep back, his hands from sin. He is beset with a legion of unclean devils and is the terror of the neighbourhood. Children and women flee from him in alarm! He lives among the tombs, and no man can bind him. Yet, *he* is one of the pearls of the King! He is a pearl that the Father gave to Jesus from all eternity! He is one of the jewels that, in purity and holiness, shall flash and flame, glitter and gleam, and glow in resplendent brightness, in the Crown of the King of Kings.

Who would have thought that Jesus, the Merchantman, would go out to that dismal Necropolis and, from the shelter of its tombs, drag out into the bright moonlight the "pearl of great price?"* But that man is the gift of God the Father to Jesus Christ His Son, and Jesus Christ is the Merchantman "seeking (for) goodly pearls."†

He does not go into the streets of Decapolis; He does not go to the priests or the Levites, or to the

* St. Matt. xiii. 46.   † St. Matt. xiii. 45.

schools of religion or morality to seek His pearls; but He goes to the vilest of the vile, He goes to the least likely of them all. The Man of infinite purity comes face to face with infinite impurity, and the Man of infinite love comes face to face with the demoniac of the mountains, the man who is possessed of a legion of devils.

And ere evening be past, and the drear shadows of night have taken the place of "the gloaming," a strange scene is witnessed. The multitude come to Jesus and see Him seated with the demoniac at His feet, now "clothed, and in his right mind."* Yes, there is Jesus, with the harlot of Magdala, on one side, and the man possessed by devils on the other side, and Mary kisses his feet, and washes them with her tears; and then, with the golden tresses of her lightsome hair, she dries them, and Jesus is not ashamed of her kiss because she is one of the pearls for His Crown.

Or again—come in fancy to the streets of Jerusalem early in the morning of the first Good Friday. They are swarming with teeming crowds from every nation and every clime, for the rumour has gone forth that the Nazarene prophet is condemned to die.

He is led forth to His doom before the gazing, mocking crowds, with two others who are to be crucified

* St. Luke viii. 35.

with Him. And these two companions are common thieves and murderers in a rebellion!

Oh! look at the expression on those men's faces, as they drag their crosses through the throngs in the streets. We can picture the hang-dog look about the criminals, a look which seems to say that they have been hardened by a course of sin; and now they are going out to meet their rightful, and just, doom. Yet one of those two men is one of the "pearls of great price;" one of those two men the Father gave to the Son and, in a few hours, he will hear the cry "To-day shalt thou be with Me in Paradise."*

And *these* are pictures, from the Gospel Story, which we all believe to be the very Word of the living God.

Thus Jesus Christ sought His jewels amongst harlots, and devil-possessed, and murderers, and thieves; and He is the same Jesus to-night; and if there be any here who are sinners of the deepest dye, remember, that under the rough, external hideousness of sin there may be hidden one of the pearls of the Merchantman, the Heavenly Traveller; and Jesus Christ has sent me here to-night to seek for His pearls and, in His Name, He bids me say to all present—all who have not yet come to Christ, all who have not yet, with the simplicity of hungry men, come to partake of the Bread, all who have not, with

* St. Luke xxiii. 43.

the simplicity of thirsty men come to drink of the Fountain—"whosoever will,"* let him come, "Him that cometh to Me I will in no wise cast out."†

Oh! the Heavenly Merchantman! When He entered upon His journey He was not sent forth, from His Father's Home, an unwilling sacrifice; but He came, a willing Victim, He came as a Heavenly Merchantman, to make the long journey here, to this little planet, where a rebel race were dwelling, who had turned their backs upon the light, the love and the wisdom of their God, and who were lying "in darkness and in the shadow of death."‡ He descended from the heavens, and the angels joined in the glad song: "Glory to God in the highest, and on earth peace, to the men of good-will."§

He comes! He comes to seek, He comes to save, that which is lost. Like a merchantman He sought for goodly pearls during the thirty-three long years of His earthly life of sorrow. He became "a Man of Sorrows,"‖ because we are children of sorrow; He became "acquainted with grief,"‖ because we are all "born unto trouble, as the sparks fly upward;"¶ and He must bear like us, suffer like us, feel temptation as we do, be human, in all points, the same as we are

---

* Rev. xxii. 17.
† St. John vi. 37.
‡ Psalms cvii. 10.
§ St. Luke ii. 14.
‖ Isaiah liii. 3.
¶ Job v. 7.

human; but without sin. He took upon Himself our nature in order that He might be a tender, sympathizing friend to fallen humanity. **He comes! He comes to seek! He comes to save!**

And He comes to that which is *lost*—for He comes to *seek*. How long does He come; how long does He seek for that which is lost? He tells us in another parable how long—"*until He find it!*"* He will find the pearls that are purchased with His own Blood —He would not pay that great price, He would not purchase them with that tremendous ransom which He paid on the Cross, and lose one. He says, "All that the Father giveth Me shall come to Me."†

So the heavenly Merchantman goes to seek His pearls. And He never goes in vain. May I believe —nay, I must believe—that there are some of His lost pearls here to-night, for He has sent me to seek them for Him, and to preach the Message of love and peace and joy to sinners. The publicans and sinners of old "were very attentive to hear him;"‡ and so it is now.

He who feels the need of Jesus never hears the invitation without a thrill of joy and a throb of gladness, saying: "Will He receive *me*? He is just what I want. If I can lay claim to Jesus as God's Gift to me, if He be really what the Gospel says He is, He will satisfy my soul. If I can plunge into the stream of His

* St. Luke xv. 4.   † St. John vi. 37.   ‡ St. Luke xix. 48.

Blood I shall be washed 'whiter than snow,'* and stand accepted before God in Jesus. ' Blessed is the the man to whom the Lord will not impute sin.'†

"If I can only lay claim to Him, and realise the gift of God to *me*, then shall I be able to stretch out the hand of an aching, hungry soul, and grasp, with a clutch of earnest desire, His blessed truth. And then, when I have laid hold of Jesus, I shall sink down into His dear arms, and listen to His Own Word, which is: 'Him that cometh to Me I will in no wise cast out;'‡ 'None shall pluck him out of My hand.'§

"Let me take the heavenly Merchant at His word; let me lie like a pearl in His hand; for, inasmuch as He shed His Blood for me, He paid the debt of my sins to the ' uttermost farthing.' "

My brother, art thou a great sinner? Jesus is a great Saviour. Hast thou turned thy back upon Him? His great love is now entreating thee; the exceeding might of His compassion is touching thy heart; and the Holy Ghost has anointed me to speak and to tell thee, who hearest, that He waiteth, He calleth for thee.

Do I see a tear in some one's eye? To that one I would say: " He careth for you." You may reply, " I never knew anybody cared for me. No one has cared for me since my mother died."

Or, is it that the companion of your manhood is now

* Ps. li. 7.   † Rom. iv. 8.   ‡ St. John vi. 37.   § St. John x. 28.

a heap of dust in the lonely grave; and the world, which was so full of life and sunshine for you, is changed, and sunshine plays around your earthly path no more; you walk along the dull, dark road of life; and the thought that nobody cares for you makes your life a bitter mockery and a sad and fleeting dream.

"Nobody cares for me! did I hear you say? O yes, Somebody does; and sweetly the companionship of Christ reveals itself to the lonely soul. The Lord Jesus Christ is indeed the greatest of all friends, for He cares for *all* who "come unto Him."

"Can a woman forget her sucking child....? Yea, they may forget, yet will I not forget thee."*

And so the love of Jesus gently wooes the sinner and wins the sinner, who lets himself fall, almost unconsciously at first, into the tender Merchant's mighty arms, until he realises, in deed and in truth, the meaning of the cry, "Into Thine hand I commend my spirit; Thou hast redeemed me."† And he lies, like a pearl, in the heavenly Merchant's palm, and says, "My Beloved is mine, and I am His."‡

The pearl of great price is found! Oh! realise the great price that was paid for it. As the Apostle St. Peter says: "Ye were not redeemed with corruptible things; but with the precious Blood of Christ."§ Or St.

---

* Isaiah xlix. 15.   ‡ Song of Solomon ii. 16.
† Ps. xxxi. 5.   § 1 Pet. i. 18—19.

Paul to the Corinthians: "Ye are bought with a price: therefore glorify God in your body, and in your spirit."*

And brethren, when the soul realises this, the result is always the same. When once the soul realises that Jesus Christ is enough to satisfy all its cravings, life becomes utterly new to such a man; and with the apostle he can say: "Old things are passed away; behold, all things are become new."†

I remember a poor girl who had led the "life of the lost" for some time, attending our mission at Birmingham; and she sent a letter to be read to the congregation, in which she told how she had come to see how Christ loved her; and how the love of Christ had overcome and satisfied her, and had led her to the determination to live for Christ, and to trust His promise; and that this, now, was the one great ambition of her life.

And only a few months ago a letter came from another girl, of the same class, in Manchester, who two years before had been brought to Christ; and she told in this letter how He had kept His promise to her for the last two years, which time had been a new life to her; and how good a Saviour she had found Jesus Christ to be!

He was, He is, the power that held her, that holds us, up, that keeps us safe, that gladdens our hearts, and satisfies hungry and thirsty souls.

* 1 Cor. vi. 20. † 2 Cor. v. 17.

I know my words are very poor, and feeble and faint, but there is a power, in the Message, for it is the Word of God, and that promise must be true: "My Word shall not return unto Me void."*

And I know that hearts now are opening to God, as the heavenly Merchantman in the still, white moonlight goes seeking for His pearls, who are lying in the field of the world, and oh! He shall soon come to some weary heart in this congregation and say: I have found my "pearl of great price!"†

Dear brother or sister, will you surrender to the heavenly Merchantman to-night? Will you let Him take you up and carry you in His arms, and look up in His face, and trust Him just as you are, while we sing:

> "Just as I am, without one plea
> But that Thy blood was shed for me,
> And that Thou bidd'st me come to Thee;
> O! Lamb of God, I come."

Brethren, I have no doubt, before this week is over, that I shall know who are some of the pearls that have fallen into the heavenly Merchantman's hand, because letters are coming to me already; and how happy I shall be to hear who are the pearls that have been found to-night!

Oh brother! oh sister! hesitate no longer; but at once drop into the Merchantman's clasp, for then you

---

* Isaiah lv. 11. † St. Matth. xiii. 46.

can say: "I know that I am safe," for He promises to those who come unto Him that He will "never leave them," but will be with them always, and will make their lives a totally different thing, in deed and truth, from what they were before. You shall go on your way rejoicing, knowing that He Whom you have trusted is "Jesus Christ the same yesterday, and to-day, and for ever;"* "Who is able to keep that which you have committed unto Him"† to-night.

No one shall be missing *There*, who has come through the rough and stormy way, through the sorrows and persecutions, the harass of sin, the unbelief, the tears of this short, dying life, with Christ at his side. No one, who, amid the daily round of troubles, trials and scandals, has had the sheltering arms of Christ around him, sustaining, holding him up and bearing his burden, shall be missing in the Homeland of Heaven, "in the day when He makes up His jewels."

Then, when you look back upon your earthly pilgrimage, and your once sin-stained existence, *then* you shall understand the necessity for *all* the trials, by the way; for "then shall we know even as also we are known,"‡ as we stand in the full light of the eternal day of the Presence of our God. Amen.

---

* Heb. xiii. 8.   † 2 Tim. i. 12.   ‡ 1 Cor. xiii. 12.

V.

Jesus Christ, the King's Son.

Mission Sermon.

Wednesday Evening, October 21st, 1885.

Jesus Christ, the King's Son.

Prayer before Sermon.

O Almighty Father, Who hast sent a message to this world, of sin and sorrow, by the lips of Thine Only Begotten Son, in our flesh; and Who hast not only given Him to bring the message of peace and reconciliation, but hast given to all such as believe in Him the free, full and perfect gift of eternal Life, be in our midst to-night. We bless Thy Name for the countless multitudes who have received Him and are satisfied with Him; we praise Thee for the joy and peace that have inflowed their lives, and the cleansing power which Thou hast poured upon their hearts.

But while we praise Thee for those that have received Thy Word, we again entreat Thee on behalf of the vast masses of our fellow-men who have not received Thy message of Love. And grant also that many men, without Christ now, may, before this service shall be over, receive Him as Thy gift individually to them, and that they may go out rejoicing in "the unsearchable riches of Christ."*

O God, look upon the sorrowful ones, look upon those who are tired of the world and weary of its changes, its wrongs, its cruelties, and its pains; look upon those who have already had their fill of the world's cup of pleasure, and have already tasted the bitterness of the dregs, and would fain turn to another cup, even the cup of joy and the "cup of salvation," that is filled by Thee. Grant that many such an one may come to the marriage Feast that Thou makest for

* Eph. iii. 8.

Thy Son. O Heavenly Father, make the Gospel marriage Feast, that Thou makest for Thy Son, a reality for some here present to-night; make them not only to hear the invitation but to accept it, and to-night to sit down at the grand banquet which the Gospel provides for poor, tired, hungry, sinful men; and may they go out cleansed from sin by faith in the Precious Blood.

May they feel that joy received from directly trusting in Jesus, and may they be able to say: " I know Whom I have believed."[*] O Heavenly Father, give to me words—give to me grace to utter the words—endow me with Thy Holy Spirit that I may proclaim Thy sweet invitation to captive, sin-bound souls, in such a way that they may take in with a hungry, grateful longing, Thy blessed Word. By the power of Thy Holy Spirit sanctify their hearts with a solemn sense of the presence of Jesus, and the calm of the Holy Ghost, that they may be able to listen with the hush of Heaven upon their souls. Hear and answer our petitions, for the glory of the Name of Jesus; and pour a blessing upon our souls for the same Jesus' sake. Amen.

---

[*] 2 Tim. i. 12.

"JESUS CHRIST, THE KING'S SON."

Mission Sermon.

"The kingdom of Heaven is like unto a certain king, which made a marriage for his son."—St. Matth. xxii. 2.

What a wonderful picture our Lord gives us in this parable of the marriage of the king's son.

I kept you waiting just now trying to find whether it is in Hosea,* Amos, or Micah that we have a most remarkable resemblance to this parable. The resemblance there is more than a mere similarity, for there is a practical matter-of-fact illustration of the teaching—the prophet is told by God to go and marry a harlot. God tells the prophet he is a type of Himself, and that the poor woman is a type of Israel, which is a type of Christ's Church.

Oh! the bride of the King's Son is a poor, lost, depraved, filthy wretch—that is the bride!

The Scriptures tell us that Christ's Church is made up of lost sinners; the Scripture describes the people who make up Christ's Church as a mass of "wounds, and bruises, and putrefying sores."† Jesus Christ, Himself, tells us that it is "the publicans and harlots

---

* Hosea iii. 1, 2, 3. † Isaiah i. 6.

that go into the kingdom of God,"* and that He is "not come to call the righteous, but sinners to repentance;"† that it is the lost whom Jesus Christ came to seek and to save, *the lost.*

You know, beloved brethren, what it is to see the sneer of the worldlings over our "lost sisters," as they call them. *But they are the type of the Church.* Take one of our most degraded, woe-begone, sin-stained sisters—she is a type of Christ's Church. The lowest, most abandoned outcast is Christ's bride—she is the bride that the King hath chosen for His Son.

The King says: "The kingdom of Heaven is like unto a certain king, which made a marriage for his son."‡

The great King of Heaven, in His Almighty Sovereignty, willed to create a race of mortals and endow them with free will, so that, if they chose, they could turn their backs upon Him and rebel against the Master of the magnificent household of the universe; they could go to the greatest depths of sin if they chose, and they did choose; and our hospitals, our lunatic asylums, our battle-fields, our reformatories, and our Magdalene hospitals, all show to what human nature can sink.

Go to the back slums of the vilest parts of our gigantic cesspools of humanity, called cities, and there

* St. Matt. xxi. 31.   † St. Matt. ix. 13.   ‡ St. Matt. xxii. 2.

see human nature in the vilest garb in which it is possible to behold it! When I had the privilege of living among the very lowest in St. George's-in-the-East, I saw there to what human nature could sink.

Talk about man progressing from the monkey! I think, when human nature is left to itself, it will progress downwards to a degradation that is unspeakable and unimaginable.

It is all very well to set up an apotheosis of humanity; it is all very well to talk of civilisation, enlightenment, education, science, art and philosophy; but what can all these do to raise the masses of the human family? What have they done? I say, without fear of contradiction, that the pictures of degraded humanity, in this city, which exist at our side to-day, exceed in horror any that have existed in the teeming pages of human memory, which we call history.

It is all very well for people to sit after their dinners, over their wine, and talk of politics, and the difficulties of our social problems; but they do not know of what they are talking, unless they have taken their stand in the midst of the rotting multitudes, that are seething in this cauldron of agony and tears and dying and woe, untouched by the power that would regenerate them; perhaps because others have been too selfish to carry the magnificent panacea of God to them.

We have fed on Jesus ourselves; shall we not

therefore care also for the misery and woe of the masses from amongst whom Jesus Christ is to pick out His bride?

Brethren, let me ask you to consider the tremendously exaggerated picture that Jesus Christ gives to us here. The King makes a marriage for His Son—but there cannot be a marriage without a bride; and the Word of God tells us who the bride is—the bride is the Church, and the Church is a magnificent international, cosmopolitan fraternity, drawn out from every "kindred, and tongue, and people, and nation,"* by the utterance of the Message of Love and Power of our God, Who says: "Go and preach the Gospel to every creature."†

Then the power that accompanies the Word draws people to Christ, and they find in Christ a fountain of perfection, a fountain of refreshment, a healing balm for the wounds of their souls and intellects—yea, a balm for the sores and pains of this sorrowful life. Yes, they will find Jesus Christ, and His Cross, turn the bitter waters of Marah into sweetness; for, of God is righteousness, of God is wisdom and of God is the power that can loose the chains of sin and enable the captive to bound " into the glorious liberty of the children of God."‡ They will learn to enjoy a new atmosphere, and to appreciate the truth of St. Paul's magnificent declaration: "If any man be in Christ, he is a new

* Rev. v. 9. † St. Mark xvi. 15. ‡ Rom. viii. 21.

creature: old things are passed away; behold, all things are become new."*

Brethren, the marriage of the King's Son is a beautiful picture of mystery; but it is also a beautiful picture of fact.

It occurs to me that a great many religious teachers make a great mistake, when proclaiming the Message of God—and this great mistake, made by so many preachers, is that when they preach the Gospel, they begin by dilating upon the hideousness of sin. It is quite wrong—utterly wrong—we are not told to do that. Supposing a physician comes to visit a patient, who is in great agony, and begins by abusing the patient for his suffering. That would be a pretty beginning, but that is how many religious teachers set to work.

Brethren, I say we have no authority for that.

Then some religious teachers tell sinners what they must give up. We are not told to do that. People who come to our mission say: "You do not insist, as you should, upon the giving up of sin, and the necessity of sorrow for sin." I am not told to do that—it is quite a mistake to suppose that I am. I am not told to go to the sinner and say: "You wicked wretch, you must be sorry for your sins or Christ will not save you." I am to tell him to come just as he is; I am told to say " Jesus loves you; and yearns for you, and

* 2 Cor. v. 17.

thirsts to save you, and if you will only let Him He will keep you 'as the apple of His eye, and will hide you under the shadow of His wings.'"*

The marriage feast is a joyful feast; and it is exactly that to which the Gospel invitation is asking you to come. I am not told to ask the sinner to give up his sin; though when the sinner has accepted Christ, there will not be any room in his heart for the love of the world; for when Jesus comes into the heart the love of the world is driven out. And that power comes in which helps the sinner to overcome the world by Him Who says: "My grace is sufficient."†

Therefore, you see, the invitation of the Gospel is an invitation to a feast; not to give up anything, but an invitation to come and *accept* something.

God invites all, and says: "Whosoever will, let him take the water of life freely."‡ "Ho, every one that thirsteth, come ye to the waters."§ "Come unto Me, all ye that labour and are heavy laden, and I will give you rest."||

The message of the Gospel is: "I give you this—take it." And it is not only a feast to which you are bidden, but a marriage feast, and the bride is the Church. You remember the words St. Paul used to his converts, which he had gathered out of heathen

---

* Deut. xxxii. 10; Ps. xvii. 8.   † 2 Cor. xii. 9.
‡ Rev. xxii. 17.   § Isaiah lv. 1. || St. Matth. xi. 28.

Rome—and you know St. Paul went among heathen nations that were civilised and were marvellously polished and marvellously enlightened, whose arts and whose sciences had reached the highest pitch of perfection; therefore when I say "heathen" I do not wish to convey a false impression, for St. Paul was preaching to educated intellects. Out of the midst of the learned nations of the past he was gathering out a people for Christ—and what does he tell them when they have come to Christ? He says: "For I am jealous over you with godly jealousy: for I have espoused you to one husband, that I may present you as a chaste virgin to Christ."* What an extraordinary statement! We just heard that the bride of Christ was utterly lost, that she was poor, lost and fallen.

Ah! my brethren, when the lost and the fallen one is brought to Christ, His blood washes her "whiter than snow."† Christ is the "Garment of Salvation,"‡ His Holy Spirit consoles and sanctifies; and then the redeemed is joined to the Redeemer, as St. Paul says: "He that is joined unto the Lord is one Spirit."§

We are told that the Church is made up of lost sinners; but we are told also that Christ is an individual, personal, ever-present Saviour.

My brethren, this is the Church of Christ; "the Bride, the Lamb's wife;"* the Church which the Father

* 2 Cor. xi. 2.   † Ps. li. 7.   ‡ Isaiah lxi. 10.   § 1 Cor. vi. 17.

gave to Jesus is the Church which is called out by the preaching of the Gospel. Some of you know, and have realised most intensely, the reality of what I am saying—do not you know what it is to be married to Jesus and joined to Him by the joints and bands of the Holy Ghost? You know what it is to be in a loving Saviour's arms and to hear His voice, saying: "No man shall pluck you out of His hand."†

Did not His promise make us partakers of His Divine Nature? Does not He say: "As many as received Him, to them gave He power to become the sons (and daughters) of God?"‡

Oh! yes, many of us here know the reality of a heart joined to the Lord, and "what God hath joined together, let not man put asunder."§ He will "keep us as the apple of the eye; He will hide us under the shadow of His wings."‖ And He says to His bride, and to every individual soul that makes up the Church: "He that toucheth you toucheth the apple of His eye."¶ He gave Himself for you, for we are told: "He loved the Church, and He gave Himself for it;"** and "He is the Head of the Church."††

Yes, my brethren, it is His Church. He did not mean the Protestant, or the Catholic Church; but a body

---
* Rev. xxi. 9. † St. John x. 28. ‡ St. John i. 12.
§ St. Matt. xix. 6. ‖ Ps. xvii. 8. ¶ Zec. ii. 8.
** Eph. v. 25. †† Eph. v. 23.

made up of all those who have accepted Christ, as God's gift to them.

The Church is made up of that company of saved sheep of whom Jesus says: "I know My sheep, and am known of Mine."* I would ask you, my brethren, individually, each one of you, are you joined to the Lord, by the power of the Holy Ghost? Have you ever come to the Gospel Feast to which all are invited? "Go," says the Lord to His disciples—"Go and preach the good news to every creature."† You have heard the invitation. Have you accepted it? You have had the Gift of God offered to you. Have you received it? Is it yours? Can you say: I know that "God has given to me eternal life, and this life is in His Son."‡ St. John said: "He that hath the Son hath life; he that hath not the Son of God hath not life."§

"O, come unto Me!" He cries to the weary pilgrim to-night, for "He is the same yesterday, and to-day, and for ever:"|| "Come unto Me, all ye that labour and are heavy laden, and I will give you rest."¶

Brethren, this is a weary world, and many are tired and faint as life's journey goes on towards the goal, and age begins to enfeeble our nerves and to still our pulses; and quiet, mystic death is stealthily

---

* St. John x. 14.   † St. Mark xvi. 15.   ‡ 1 John v. 11.
§ 1 John v. 12. || Heb. xiii. 8.   ¶ St. Matt. xi. 28.

drawing nearer and more nigh, and then comes the question: "Does not the world get weary and more weary, to me who am so weary and heavy laden? Am not I heavy laden with the burden of aches and pains—moral, physical and intellectual? My body is heir to countless diseases; my poor distressed intellect longs to know all things; but the more it gets to know, the more it knows how little it does know; also my heart, how it hungers for a something that shall satisfy and give it rest!

Then Jesus says: "Come unto Me, all ye that *are weary* and heavy laden, and I will give you rest."*

And we, who have come to Him, have found rest, and know that we are of God. We know Jesus Christ has saved us and is in us. He lives in us, and we, in Him, are reconciled, and brought back to God; and Jesus lights up our hearts with the rays of the Sun of Righteousness; and from the gate of death we pass to the gate of life and come to the marriage Feast of Heaven.

"We have washed (ourselves clean) in the Blood of the Lamb,"† and are robed in the best robe from the wardrobe of Heaven, the Righteousness of Christ.

So we have come to the Feast, and when we come to the Feast the King says to each one of us: "You may be the bride of My Son if you will." The love

* St. Matth. xi. 28.   † Rev. vii. 14.

of Christ first wins our hearts and then the love of Christ sustains us. So Christ, in His divinely human sympathy, wins the souls of weary, hungry, restless, sinful, dying men; and the sheep, when they hear the Gospel Call, come flocking into the fold.

Still is the Gospel quietly doing its work, amid storms of rationalism, materialism, and unbelief. For what is the Gospel's work? It is to draw out a people for the Lord of glory—out, from the masses of sadness and sorrow, a people of gladness and joy shall come who shall be the sons and daughters of morning, the salt of the earth and lights in the darkness of earth's shades.

There is no one who is unsaved, at this moment, who need remain so a moment longer, for the loving message is: "Whosoever will,* let him come." Do you feel your need? Do you feel your lost estate? Do you feel that you are restless, and that sin is staining you from head to foot, and in heart and mind and soul? Do you feel destitute of any righteousness which is worthy of God? All your needs are not forgotten by Christ, Who says: "Come; for all things are now ready."† The Robe of Righteousness and the Peace of God are ready for you. Only just look up to Jesus, Who is present, in our midst, speaking *in* you, speaking *to* you.

* Rev. xxii. 17. † St. Luke xiv. 17.

"In Him dwelleth all the fulness of the Godhead,"* and of His fulness you may receive if you will only lay hold on Jesus, Who *now* is proffered as God's Gift to you; and, in the words of the Holy Virgin Mary, the Mother of Jesus, you may then sing: "My soul doth magnify the Lord, and my spirit hath rejoiced in God *my* Saviour."†

The marriage of the King's Son has taken place in this hall to-night, for Christ has promised that "His word shall not return to Him void, but it shall prosper in the thing whereto he sent it."‡ And this is *whereto* He sends it, to draw out poor, naked sinners, and to clothe them with His Righteousness; to draw out sin-stained souls, and to wash them in that Blood which makes them "whiter than snow."§ Then the poor, lost soul, that only a moment before was a mass of sin and corruption, is cleansed; Christ takes away the filthy garments from him and gives him a change of raiment; and the soul is filled with the peace of Jesus Christ; and he may go out with a shout of joy and he shall sing: "I will greatly rejoice in the Lord, my soul shall be joyful in my God; for He hath clothed me with the garments of Salvation, He hath covered me with the Robe of Righteousness."‖

So, beloved, to-night the King's Son is present in

---

* Col. ii. 9. † St. Luke i. 46, 47. ‡ Isaiah lv. 11.
§ Ps. li. 7. ‖ Isaiah lxi. 10.

this hall, and has found His bride in some poor, lost sister, who may have travelled here from some of the slums of London and now is trembling in our midst.

The world has cast her off and the world's sneer is beaming its ironical gaze upon her; and oh! the bitterness of the world's irony — the world destroyed her first and then the world casts her off. But she is the bride of Jesus, Who says to her: "thy sins are forgiven"* thee, "go, and sin no more."† "I will never leave thee, nor forsake thee."‡ "When thou passest through the waters, I will be with thee; —they shall not overflow thee."§

My brethren, this is, then, what it is to preach the Gospel—to proclaim the marriage of the King's Son; and God blesses the Word, and gives it power and goes with it, and it prospers. I may see before me now a young orphan girl who has to go all the way back to Whitechapel after this service. There she lives alone; nobody cares for her, and she is hard at work from morning until night; but she can go back to-night, to her little room, and say: "Somebody cares for me. Somebody loves me—even me."

And to-night there will be a light in that lonely room, shining so brightly, above the poor rush-light that flickers in the socket. Yes, brethren, it is

* St. Luke vii. 48.   ‡ Heb. xiii. 5.
† St. John viii. 11.   § Isaiah xliii. 2.

a light that will never go out; it is a light that nothing will extinguish; it is the light of liberty and love that will shine upon her from the light-world of the presence of God.

There is a Home eternal in the Heavens—her Beloved is keeping it for her and her for it. A place has been prepared for her—" I go to prepare a place for you "*—and she is now to be prepared for the place until the King shall call her into the brightness and the glory and the peace of the Homeland of Heaven, when she " shall see Him as He is."†

---

* St. John xiv. 2.   † 1 John iii. 2

VI.

Jesus Christ, the Good Shepherd.

Mission Sermon.

Thursday Evening, October 22nd, 1885.

Jesus Christ, the Good Shepherd.

Prayer before Sermon.

O Lord Jesus Christ, Shepherd of the Flock of God, Who hast sent a Message of Love and Peace and Salvation into the world, and hast given such power to the Message that It must "prosper in the thing whereto Thou sendest It"*—even to gather out the people whom the Father has given to Thee: we pray Thee grant such power to the preaching of Thy Word to-night, that many of the " lost sheep of the House of Israel"† may be gathered in! Grant such a shower of blessing to this congregation that the power of Thy Holy Spirit may, in very deed and truth, be felt upon us; and, as Thou hast, by Thine Apostle St. Paul, declared to us that Thou choosest "the weak things of the world to confound the strong,"‡ behold one here who is weak and foolish; and O Lord, do Thou take me and use me, for Thy Glory, for the gathering together of Thy people, and for the consolation of some here present.

We do not speak to Thee as to a far-away God, but as One Who is in our midst, even "the Son of Man," Who is "come to seek and to save, to-night, that which is lost."§ And we know that Thou art just "the same yesterday, and to-day, and for ever."‖

Dear Lord Jesus, the Bishop and Shepherd of our souls, be to-night amongst the lost ones here, as Thou wast amongst the lost ones by the side of the Galilean sea, when

---

* Isaiah lv. 11. † St. Matth. x. 6. xv. 24. ‡ 1 Cor. i. 27.
§ St. Luke xix. 10. ‖ Heb. xiii. 8.

the publicans and sinners crowded to hear Thee. Speak with Thy Voice of love and pardon. Let the sheep hear the Shepherd's voice and follow Him.

And now, Blessed Jesus, do Thou anoint my understanding, anoint my lips and my heart, that I may be **Thy** instrument **and Thy witness** amongst those here assembled.

To-night may Thy Name be lifted up; to-night "be **Thou exalted, Lord, in Thine Own Strength:** so will we sing and praise Thy Power."* Blessed Jesus, hear Thy people's prayer, to the glory of Thy Name, for Thine Infinite Love and Mercy's Sake. Amen.

* Ps. xxi. 13.

"JESUS CHRIST, THE GOOD SHEPHERD."

Mission Sermon.

"I am the Good Shepherd, and know My sheep, and am known of Mine. As the Father knoweth Me, even so know I the Father: and I lay down My Life for the sheep."—St. John x. 14, 15.

Brethren, although this is such a very common subject and thought, yet it is a subject that is not in the least comprehended by the majority of professing Christians. They do not seem to think that our Lord is a "Good Shepherd;" in fact they make Him out to be a bad Shepherd, a very helpless Shepherd, who loses ever so many of His sheep. They make Him out to be a Shepherd who lets ever so many of His sheep go to everlasting damnation. Therefore they make Him out to be a bad Shepherd.

But *I* am not here to talk of Him as a *bad* Shepherd, but to talk as one who *knows* that He is "the *Good* Shepherd."

Some of our congregations come from hundreds of miles away; they are gathered, when we have a mission, from all parts of England and there are those here now who have come hundreds of miles to this service—and I would ask why have they come?—why they have come such a long distance to attend these services? It is because they know that I tell them of a "GOOD Shepherd" whom I know and believe myself to be a "*Good* Shepherd" and that not one of His sheep shall ever perish. He says it Himself; and anyone who says that one of "the sheep of Jesus" can perish, makes "God a liar."

I believe what He says; and if I had to stand alone in the Church of England, I should, and shall, always testify to the fact that Jesus is a *Good* Shepherd; and that when He says "My sheep shall never perish,"* He means it, and will take care that not one of them does perish. "Of them which Thou gavest Me have I lost none."†

During the early part of the history of the Christian Church the Christian religion was sometimes called "the Religion of the Good Shepherd." That was one of the names by which it went.

And if you go and look into the Catacombs at Rome, you will find that one of the favourite sculptures in those dens and caves of the earth, in the days of persecution, was a figure of Jesus with a lamb in His Arms as "The Good Shepherd."

"The Religion of the Good Shepherd!"

The Colosseum would ring with the shouts of scores

* St. John x. 28. † St. John xviii. 9.

of thousands of men, women and children who stood by gloatingly watching the sheep of the Good Shepherd torn to pieces by wild beasts; and little boys and girls—children of Jesus—were given to the lion and the tiger, and were killed amid the crash of the triumphant shouts of delight from the heathen crowds, that filled the seats of the Colosseum. A little Saint Cyril, or Saint Pancras, held up before an astonished world the dignity of the Christian's life, and joyfully and triumphantly went to the fire, the torture, the flame or the wild beast, knowing that He in Whom he trusted, was a Good Shepherd, and that not one of His sheep could perish.

The short process of dying was nothing, because the eyes of the dying saw Him Who was invisible to the persecutors of the martyrs, who remembered the Promise of that God who was not ashamed to be called their God; because "He had prepared for them a City"* on High, far beyond this world of war and strife, this world of grief and wrong; far beyond this world of hate and bitterness; up there in the Homeland of everlasting Peace and eternal Rest in the New Jerusalem.

That is the Home of His sheep—the sheep of the Good Shepherd—an abiding place within the Folds upon the Mountains of Israel.

* Heb. xi. 16.

Brethren, the Church of Jesus, and each individual member of that Church, has always known that Jesus Christ is a Good Shepherd.

And now let us examine, for a short time, the origin of Christ's title to the name of "Good Shepherd."

I do not think any professing Christians would deny the fact that Jesus Christ has a people. I do not suppose that any persons, who profess at all to know Christ, and to believe the Christian revelation, would, even intellectually, deny that Christ has a people in the world, and that He always has had.

Well, how did this people become God's people? "My sheep," he calls them in the parable before us. What right has He to call them "My sheep"?* He did not call the Scribes and Pharisees His sheep. He said to them: "Ye believe not, because ye are not of My sheep."† So, you see, He claims some as His sheep, and to others He says: "Ye are not of My sheep." But what right has He to call His people His "sheep"? He tells us, "*My Father gave them Me.*"‡

It is as plain as A B C to the Christian, taught of God. There is no difficulty at all in understanding it. There were two seeds from the first—the seed of the

---
* St. John x. 14, 27.
† St. John x. 26.   ‡ St. John x. 29.

Kingdom and the seed of the Evil One. "My sheep," Christ calls His people, and He says "The Father gave them to Me."

I do not know if the children of God here like being called sheep. I do not think that a sillier animal could have been selected by our Blessed Lord; and sheep are also very destructive. They are very, very injurious to our crops of winter greens at Llanthony; and we are obliged to employ a man to mind our crops just because the sheep are the very pests of our lives. Therefore, when our Lord says we are His sheep, I repeat that I do not think it is a very complimentary expression, because it shows that His people are very silly, very helpless, and mischievous, always getting into pickles and difficulties, muddles and messes. We often find sheep on the mountains smashed to pieces through falling over dangerous precipices.

But, dear brothers and sisters, that is just what God says we are like! He says His people are perfectly helpless, very foolish, very mischievous, and get into a great deal of trouble. I feel myself that I was all that. I was foolish and ignorant until He, by His Holy Spirit, taught me. I know that I was utterly helpless, too; and that often, before I knew the Good Shepherd, I felt sure I must be damned.

But after I came to the Good Shepherd, I knew that I could *never* be lost, because my Shepherd, Who is

Almighty, had told me so, and that I am "kept by His Power."*

And then I was mischievous—and even now I often want my own will and my own way in the midst of some horrible trial or persecution which I am called upon to bear. Many of you know the dreadful character I have from a dear relation: and some people even say that I am not fit to preach on account of it. You, dear souls, whom my heart is yearning to save, do not know the weight of the affliction which God calls me to bear; and how year after year I have lived groaning in anguish both of mind and body.

But I believe that I have needed this trial and training. And you need your trials too.

My brethren, we all are very mischievous. We give the Good Shepherd such pains.

And, worse than all, it was necessary that the Good Shepherd should die for us. He had to lay down His life for us. He had to go forth amid the perils of the strife, alone and poor; and then He died for us on Good Friday morning, eighteen hundred years ago. The Shepherd was slain, but the Flock liveth for evermore. "I lay down My life for the sheep"† said Christ.

And then He rose again with a Resurrection Life, and that Resurrection Life of Jesus is the life which

* 1 Peter i. 5. † St. John x. 15.

He gives to His sheep; and every believer can say "I live; yet not I, but Christ liveth in me."*

Brethren, the work and duty of every true Evangelist is to go out and gather in the sheep of Christ. We want to go out amid the multitudes of men and women who are steeped in unbelief and sin; who are under the influence of sin and of the powers of darkness and of sorrow; and to raise our voices and say: "Whosoever will,"† let him come unto Me. "Him that cometh to Me, I will in no wise cast out."‡ As His ministers, we should be witnesses for Christ; and not those who are ordained ministers only, but every believer in Jesus.

The Gospel of Jesus is still calling a people out from the world to feed on Him. Oh weary brother, worn and tossed with the battle of this life, God's Spirit is breathing upon you; and NOW—if you will —you may feel the hallowed influence of that Spirit; and when once you have felt it you seem to say: "If I could only kneel at that Shepherd's feet and trust Him, as *my* Shepherd; if I could only do this, I should rejoice."

Are there any here now who have never come to Christ? If there be, they can come *now*. What is it that is making them wish to come? It is the beautiful influence of the Holy Spirit that makes Jesus' people

---
* Gal. ii. 20. † Rev. xxii. 17. ‡ St. John vi. 37.

yearn to know and to taste of His Love and Power. *This* is "the day of (our) Salvation; *now* is the accepted time."*

It is the day of His Power when His Word is calling out a "people" from a world "dead in trespasses and sins."† Come, therefore, "all ye who labour and are heavy laden,"‡ and "seek ye the Lord while He may be found, call ye upon Him while He is near."§ "The Spirit and the Bride say, come!"‖

Perhaps some of you may say: "But how shall I come?" He tells you how—"He that believeth on Me."¶

It is just trusting Him; it is just taking Him at His word; it is just accepting Him as the Father's gift to the soul. This is what it is to come.

Oh, how simple is that act of coming! How simple is that act by which the soul raises itself and takes hold of Jesus! And then, when once we have accepted Him—when once we have accepted Jesus as God's gift to us—then He holds us and keeps us and declares that nothing "shall pluck us out of His hand."** Then the sheep lies down upon the Bosom of the Shepherd, "strong and tender;" then the sheep is at rest, for it hears the voice of the Shepherd saying, "He that toucheth you toucheth the apple of

* 2 Cor. vi. 2. † Ephes. ii. 1. ‡ St. Matth. xi. 28.
§ Isaiah lv. 6. ‖ Rev. xxii. 17. ¶ St. John vi. 47.
** St. John x. 28.

His eye.* Jesus loves the Church for which He died; and the Church is made up of all those who come to Him, and whom the Father draws to His feet, by the grace and inspiration of the Holy Ghost.

My brethren, God grant that everyone in this congregation may to-night be at peace with God and safe in the arms of the "Good Shepherd!" He knows who are thus safe in His arms; though I cannot tell.

But I know that the Spirit of the Lord is here—in this Westminster Town Hall to-night—and I also know that the work of the Lord *must* prosper when the Word goeth out with power.

Whether it be the atheist, the materialist, or the rationalist, all may come under the influence of that Word; and whether it be the most bigoted rationalist, the vilest of all the company, who struggles and rebels and would resist with his finite wisdom the infinite wisdom of God, the moment he comes under the power of the Holy Ghost he falls at the feet of Jesus and says, "Here I am! Lord, I believe; help Thou mine unbelief."†

My brethren, I could tell you such stories to show that nothing is too hard for the Lord. But look at the pictures furnished in the Gospel stories themselves. Look at that lost sheep, that man possessed

* Zec. ii. 8. † St. Mark ix. 24.

of a legion of unclean devils living among the tombs! He was drawn to the feet of Jesus, and was seen there by the multitude, "clothed, and in his right mind."*

Look at Mary Magdalene sitting at the feet of Jesus, bathing them with her tears, and drying them with the hair of her head; and Jesus was not ashamed of her! Look at the lost sheep on the cross —the dying thief. What a glorious promise was extended to him! "*To-day* shalt thou be with Me in Paradise."†

How speedy is the work of love!

And see what a good hope we have when we preach the Gospel—"the secret things (that) belong to God"‡ are revealed to us. He has revealed His Gospel to us so that we may have the power of utterance of the Word of Life; that it may succeed and "prosper in the thing whereto He sends it."§ My brethren, God grant to each one of us this willing mind, that not one of us shall ever be among the number of those who have rejected Christ—those of whom He says: "Ye would not come to me."‖ "Ye are not of my sheep."¶

And now, in conclusion, think of the security of the soul, that to-night, in this congregation, has come to

* St. Mark v. 15. † St. Luke xxiii. 43. ‡ Deut. xxix. 29.
§ Isaiah. lv. 11. ‖ St. John v. 40. ¶ St. John x. 26.

Jesus. It is saved for ever. Saved for ever with an everlasting redemption; with an everlasting salvation. Saved! "By grace"—I am told to say to the saved—"by grace ye are saved."* Yes, dear souls, lie down now in the Good Shepherd's Arms in faith, and say to thyself "He loved me; He gave Himself for me;"† The "Good Shepherd gave His Life for the sheep."‡

Will you let Him take you? He, Who says: "I will never leave you nor forsake you"?§ You may say, I would, but my nature is so weak and fickle and changeable; and the powers of the world may pluck me from His hand. But Christ says: "None shall pluck thee out of My hand."‖ You may say again: My nature is so vile and the world, the flesh and the devil may perchance win the victory. Christ says: "My grace is sufficient for thee."¶ As thy need is—"As thy days, so shall thy strength be."** Is it peace? Is it peace? Listen, "Thou wilt keep him in perfect peace, whose mind is stayed on Thee: *because* he trusteth in Thee."†† Trust Him and believe, and thou shalt be saved.

Jesus Christ is the "*Good* Shepherd," "He laid down His life for the Sheep."‡‡ "He calleth His Own

---

* Ephes. ii. 5. † Gal. ii. 20. ‡ St. John x. 11.
§ Heb. xiii. 5. ‖ St. John x. 28. ¶ 2 Cor. xii. 9.
** Deut. xxxiii. 25. †† Isaiah xxvi. 3. ‡‡ John x. 15.

sheep by name,"* and He will forget none "in that day when He makes up His jewels."†

Do you want anything more? If you do, God has no more to give. Jesus is all that God can give you, and if you have accepted Him, God has supplied all your need, and "will supply all your need in Christ Jesus."‡

And, beloved, some of you may be rebelling because of the quiet and calm teaching of this evening, and saying that it is all new to you. I am sorry to say, and I am ashamed to say, it is no doubt new to many. And yet you may go to a bookstall and buy a copy of the Bible for fourpence! What is the Bible? Shall I tell you? It is the "Lamb's Book of Life"§ on earth, and it is available to all at the present day.

But there are numbers who come to me and say: "I have never understood the Bible before—I have read it as a task, as a duty; but I never before saw it in the light in which I see it now!" Ah! directly the soul is married to Jesus the soul bears her Husband's name; for this is the "new name whereby she shall be called."∥ When she hears the Bridegroom's voice His words are sweeter than honey to the taste.

And now I should like to ask the congregation—

* John x. 3. † Mal. iii. 17. ‡ Phil. iv. 19.
§ Rev. xxi. 27. ∥ Isaiah lxii. 2.

and to ask it very quietly—if I have spoken any skilful words to-night, or whether I have attempted any human arguments, or the use of any logic or philosophy? No, we preach not " with enticing words of man's wisdom, that your faith should not stand in the wisdom of men, but in the power of God."* The wisdom of the world is foolishness, but the simple Gospel of Jesus is sufficient for us; and, in spite of all the sectarianism, of all the rationalism, of all the phases of nineteenth-century unbelief, it is the same almighty Gospel and the same " Power of God unto Salvation, to everyone that believeth."†

Some of you, no doubt, are Roman Catholics, and some Anglo-Catholics, like myself; some of you are Methodists, some of you are Plymouth Brethren, and some are Salvation Army people. But, whatever and whoever you are, you know that what I have now been saying has only to do with the flock of Jesus.

I never attempt at my Mission services to take away a member of the Roman Catholic Church or the Salvation Army to another form of *outward* belief. What I do is just to try and bring weary, hungering souls to the feet of the " Good Shepherd "; to enable each one to look up in His face and say " The Lord is my Shepherd, I shall not want;"‡ and to send

---

* 1 Cor. ii. 4, 5.   † Rom. i. 16.   ‡ Psalm xxiii. 1.

them back to their worship full of Jesus and of His wondrous Love.

What I preach is that *without* Jesus no Church or work is of the least avail, for it is in Him you shall "have Peace"*—in "Jesus Only."

And the love of our brethren is the great mark of the children of God—the great mark of those souls that are saved.

Lord Jesus, Thou hast blessed Thine own Word, and we praise Thee.

---

* St. John xvi. 33.

VII.

Jesus at the Grave of Lazarus.

Mission Sermon.

Friday Evening, May 21st, 1886.

Jesus at the Grave of Lazarus.

Prayer before Sermon.

O God, enthroned on the highest heights of the universe, Who rulest, by the supreme power of Thy will, all the forces of nature which Thou hast created and dost command; Who speakest to the vast systems of the planets of space and they obey Thee, in the law that Thou hast given them; we bow down before Thee as creatures of a day, shortly to turn to dust and mingle with the soil of this our little, tiny planet that floats in space; and as we realise our nothingness we marvel at the exceeding greatness of Thy loving kindness in caring for us. Oh! Thou hast made us with a free will, and our free will is turned towards selfishness and sin, and this world of ours is peopled with a multitude of rebels against Thee and Thy laws. Care and sorrow strew our oceans with wrecks, and our vast continents with tears; and dying is the end of us all.

Father, look, we pray Thee, with the eyes of Thy tender compassion upon us here present, who have gathered out from the crowd, that is restless and weary and hungry, to seek after good things that may satisfy the wants and hungering of the soul and intellect and mind that exist and work within us.

O Father, hast Thou spoken to this world, or hast Thou maintained a solemn silence from the first? Has man really never heard the voice of His Father God? Hast Thou never sent a word of love, or healing, or instruction, or rest, or comfort, or liberty to men? Blessed be Thy Name! We know that Thou hast spoken, and that Thou hast uttered Thy voice and revealed to us the thoughts Thou thinkest towards **us, that they are thoughts of peace.** O Father, we who have heard Thy message of love and pardon, of new life, of rest, of peace, of satisfaction—our hearts are fed and are full; our souls are alive in the gladness of the eternal liberty of the sons of God.

But there are many here who have not heard Thy **message, in whose** hearts Thy Word hath never yet found an echoing response. Wilt Thou grant that Thy Word **may be so** spoken to-night that souls may enter into "the peace **of God,** which passeth all understanding,"* and that Thy promise which Thou didst make to the preaching of Thy Word, by Thy prophet of old, may be fulfilled—that many may go out "with joy, and be led forth with peace."†

And now, Heavenly Father, **in the** "Name which is above every name,"‡ in the Name **of Thy** Holy Child Jesus, we beseech Thee hear our supplications, **and** grant a bountiful answer to our prayer; and He shall **have** all the glory while the blessing falls upon us—even **to Him** shall be the praise, who with Thee, in the unity of the Holy Spirit, liveth and reigneth, God for ever and ever. Amen.

* Phil. iv. 7.   † Isaiah liv. 12.   ‡ Phil. ii. 9.

JESUS AT THE GRAVE OF LAZARUS.

Mission Sermon.

Jesus cried with a loud voice, " Lazarus, come forth."
S. John xi. 43.

How many scenes from the Gospel history have been passing before our mind's eye during the past week ; and while the scenes of the Gospel have been passing before us, how God's Holy Spirit has anointed the scenes with power, and lit them up with a strange and instructive fragrance to some of our hearts !

How the stories have been coming to me every day, from some of the congregation, of the strange influence that has been at work in people's minds and hearts—certainly not from anything I can have said, for my words are nothing but the poor weak, tiny tones of a dying man ; but with the tones a power has gone forth which has been promised to the preaching of God's Word !

Now, before I come to deal with my subject may I ask my kind, patient hearers a very simple question ? What would be your opinion upon the point that I am going to propose to you? If we take it for granted that there is a God, and that God has sent a message to the world, what kind of a message do you think it would be? A simple message which every one could take in—young and old, small and great, intellectual and those of humble intellect—or a message which would require a vast amount of human philosophy and human exposition to accompany it? Which do you think the message of God, if He sent a message to this world, would be? Do you think, beloved brethren, that I am expressing a very wild and a very unreasonable thought when I say that I believe God has sent a message to man *just as he is*—sinful, weak, sorrowful, tearful, restless, peaceless, hungry, dying?

Therefore, I believe that as God *has* sent a message to man as he is, it is a message which will fill up all the voids, which will feed all the hungerings, yearnings, energisings of his wondrous compound nature; and I also believe that this message is not a philosophical message, but it is a message so simple that a little child is capable of taking it in, as well as the greatest philosopher, and the loftiest thinker that any age, or race, can produce. It is a message of God, and it is a message that is perfect. It is a message that can remedy all the ills to which man is subject; but this message is also filled with a power that is quite unique. The message itself is unique because it is divine, but its divinity is proved by the power that accompanies it; and God has promised that the Word He has sent to man "shall not return unto Him void; it shall prosper in the thing whereto He sent it, and it shall accomplish that which He pleases."* But there is only one thing that the message will not do. *It will not force a man's free will.*

If you ask me how it is that God came to make an animal with a free will such as man is, I cannot tell you. I do not know the object of all God's purposes. I only know what He has chosen to reveal. I know that God is sovereign in love, and sovereign in power; and I know that, in spite of His sovereignty in love and power, He has yet determined to create a free-willed agent in man.

Our free will and God's sovereignty seem to be opposed, the one to the other. Our free will and God's love seem at times to clash. Why did He make me with a free will when He foresaw that my free will would lead me wrong? Oh! why did He not make me like some of the magnificent automata that spangle the sky at night, like some of those beauteous worlds which follow in exquisite harmony of obedience the law wherewith God, in nature, has governed them? Why did He make me a sentient, intellectual,

* Isaiah lv. 11.

reasoning animal, with a free will to choose and to do as I please?

My brethren, is it God's will that the drunkards should be at their cups in the countless public-houses of this great metropolis? Is it God's will that men should go home in a state of intoxication, and knock down their wives, and starve their little ones? But yet it is permitted. We are surrounded on all sides by mysteries and seeming contradictions; but in spite of all these seeming contradictions there meets us face to face this magnificent fact, that wherever the word of God is accepted and believed, that word sets a man right. It makes a man peaceful, it makes him restful, it makes him happy; it makes him powerful to overcome sin, and makes him powerful to endure the sorrows of earth; so that the Apostle Paul does not in the least exaggerate when he says: "If any man be in Christ, he is a new creature;"* and the Apostle does not exaggerate either when he writes to the Ephesians, and tells them that man by nature is "dead in trespasses and sins"† before God!

He is utterly dead. He is dead as far as spiritual and eternal things are concerned just like a body is dead with regard to the senses. A dead body can neither see, nor hear, nor speak, nor eat, nor drink, nor breathe. This is exactly the condition of a man's

* 2 Cor. v. 17.   † Ephes. ii. 1.

soul, of a sinner's soul with regard to eternal things; and if the unconverted man attempt to bring his human reason to bear upon the revelation of God; and to argue out with God the mysteries that He has chosen to reveal to us, we say at once it is an impossibility. You are arguing from a finite platform about things infinite.

The Apostle said of the preaching of the Cross, I am going to "speak the wisdom of God in a mystery."* He says: "This cannot be understood except spiritually." He says: "The natural man" (that is, the unconverted man) "receiveth not the things of the Spirit of God: for they are foolishness unto him: neither can he know them, because they are to be spiritually discerned;"† and you may not argue concerning spiritual things by human analysis. You must compare spiritual things with spiritual, and that is the only way of dealing thoroughly and logically with the things of God. But he says that this word of God, which is "foolishness to the natural man," is accompanied by a power that opens the hearts and enables our minds to receive it.

Will you excuse me, for a moment, for asking you again, as thinking men, to consider the extraordinary success of St. Paul's mission to Corinth?

* 1 Cor. ii. 7. † 1 Cor. ii. 14.

We have often drawn a picture of the magnificent philosophies of Greece, and of the religions of Greece, assisted by all the magnificence of human art and science. We have drawn pictures of Grecian civilisation, which had reached the very acme of beauty; and yet a despised Jew was going forth, among the Isles of Greece, with an absurd tale that a Jewish Carpenter had been crucified as a malefactor; but that that Jewish Carpenter was really and truly the mighty Creator of the universe, and that He had really and truly shed His blood to redeem all who would believe in Him; and that there was *no* redemption *except* through the blood of this crucified Jewish Carpenter. And not only that, but St. Paul had the courage to say: "I am determined not to know anything among you but Jesus Christ and Him crucified."* You must worship, as your Creator, your God and your Redeemer, a crucified Jewish peasant, condemned to death by His own countrymen.

I ask you, as a matter of common sense, if this be an historical fact, what the power was that induced the Greeks to form churches of believers in this crucified Carpenter? Is the power a power that you can explain by any human hypothesis? Was the success of the Apostles of Christ (and wherever they went, and uttered this Gospel, they formed churches of

* 1 Cor. ii. 2.

believers), was it a power like any other power? Is there any power like it? Upon any but the Christian hypothesis, how can you explain the success of such a childish, absurd, improbable and ridiculous statement as, from a human standpoint, the story of the Gospel is?

Why, God does everything as if He were determined to turn everything here upside down. He acts exactly opposite to all man's preconceived ideas as to what God *ought* to do; and yet the Apostle Paul is quite content to preach to the philosophic Greeks and the martial Romans, "Jesus Christ and Him crucified,"* and *nothing* else. And I say we have proof sufficient of the power of this message, to a dying world, when we see that it has called out, from all generations, and in every place, wherever it be faithfully preached, a people of every temperament, every characteristic, every peculiarity, every idiosyncrasy and of every phase of unbelief; and that it can enable them to take in, as the gift of God, this mighty Christ in all His fulness to the soul.

And those men began to rejoice. They began to be very glad to find their hearts resting on a mighty Rock, their souls fed with a Food that satisfied them, and set them free from all the bondage of sin. They found themselves filled with a strange illumination of the

* 1 Cor. ii. 2.

intellect and understanding, so that they were able to comprehend, and take in, things that before had seemed utterly foolish to them.

Such is the power that accompanies the preaching of the Word of God!

And now, having made these very long preliminary remarks, I must be very brief in dealing with the subject of "Jesus at the grave of Lazarus."

I daresay some of you have read Ernest Renan's account of the raising of Lazarus; and I think, of all the possible muddles into which an author can get, poor Ernest Renan gets into one over that. You see what an extraordinary contradiction there is in the way he deals with the subject. This beautiful character, which he confesses our Lord to be; this exquisite, loving, gentle, pure, holy, noble Being, he says, must, somehow or another, have lent Himself to a fraud on the occasion. What an absolute contradiction of all he has before said of our beloved Lord! How utterly contradictory to the character which Renan himself draws of Christ! But I grant you his work is only a novel, not an historical tale at all; for Ernest Renan's Christ is not the Christ of the Bible, though he tries to make out that it is.

He begins his tale with "Christ was born at Nazareth," and he draws out a magnificent picture of the character of Jesus of Nazareth; after which he asks us to believe that he acquiesced in the most infamous fraud to make people think He was what He was not. But I only just mention this in passing to show you how horribly silly and unhistorical, though beautiful, from a literary point of view, Renan's book is.

I want to call you around the grave of Lazarus to-night, and then I want to apply our subject to my hearers; and that same power which has been promised, and that same power which always comes amongst us, by the preaching of God's Word, shall rest upon the assembly now, even though my words shall be poor and incomplete. And that holy power shall just pave the way for the entrance of the truth, into many a heart that is longing to receive it, if only it could.

The Lord Jesus, then, has returned from a distant part of the country about Jordan. He has climbed the heights that lead from Jericho—I dare say some of you know the neighbourhood very well—He has reached the eastern slope of the Mount of Olives. He has just come within sight of the dearly loved village of Bethany. The Lord Jesus had had some very social, happy times in the house of Lazarus. He loved Mary Magdalene so much, and Martha her sister; and Mary Magdalene loved Jesus too, for He had met her far away in the midst of a life of sin, and His words of love and power had drawn her out of her misery, and had wooed her back to her dear old village home of Bethany. She was named after Magdala, in Galilee, because her foul life had been spent there; but now she is Mary of Bethany again. She is restored to her home, and Martha and Lazarus have gladly received the sister, who was decoyed away by the infamy of cruel, heartless deceit.

This little home of Bethany, therefore, is a home that appeals to the hearts of Christians very much, because Jesus has rested there, has had bodily refreshment there; His tired, aching head has been refreshed by the soft breezes that blew through the little cottage casement in the village, on the eastern slope of the beautiful Olivet hill.

Bethany! There is a charm about Bethany to a Christian ear and a Christian heart, because it seems as if Bethany were a kind of oasis in the life of the Man of Sorrows; for Jesus was not content only to take our nature; He loved His people with such a love that He "hath borne our griefs, and carried our sorrows." * "He was despised and rejected of men; a Man of Sorrows and acquainted with grief."†

Therefore, in the midst of the surrounding shadows that fell upon Jesus, in His short pilgrimage, Bethany was a little tender oasis in His desert journey. Martha was attending on Jesus, for Martha loved Him and tenderly waited on Him; Mary loved Him with a great

* Isaiah liii. 4. † Isaiah liii. 3.

love and sat at His feet, and drank in the wondrous power of His divine teaching; and Lazarus loved Him too. But now, He has come to Bethany when a great cloud hovers over the home.

Perhaps some of us, at this moment, in the midst of the glitter and the glare of the London season, know homes upon which a great cloud of sorrow is resting. Supposing we could get upon some high building in London and we could, with a kind of spiritual vision, see every home over which, at this moment, a cloud of bitter grief is resting; would there not be hundreds and thousands of weeping eyes, multitudes of aching, sorrowful hearts? Oh! brethren, while I am speaking to you I can just picture the great cry of human sorrow that is going up from multitudes in this great metropolis, which is indeed a cesspool of festering humanity.

My dear brethren, when I think of Jesus at the home of Bethany, when a great cloud of sorrow rested over it, and I see the consequences of the visit of Jesus to the sorrowful home, it reminds me of so many sorrowful homes that I have seen Jesus visit, and leave, Oh! such a bright sunshine of gladness, such a happiness, such a peace, such a calm, such a joy, behind Him! Jesus satisfies, Jesus heals—I was going to say a thousand-fold more now than He used to do; but it is a sort of selfish gratitude that makes me speak like that.

We now watch the Lord Jesus about to visit the home He loved so much, when it is under a cloud of sorrow. Mary is sitting in the house weeping, and Martha has gone out to the garden to meet Jesus, because she has "heard that Jesus was coming."* And Jesus lingers outside in the distance. He does not come up to them at once. He lingers, and then Martha meets him; and Jesus, with his heart so full of intense compassion, begins to talk to Martha; and she says: "Lord, if Thou hadst been here my brother had not died."†

But the Lord Jesus had kept away on purpose to let Lazarus die, so that God's greatness, and power, and love might be more manifest. Martha speaks to her much-loved Lord. He speaks to her in return. He does not let her into the secret of what He intends to do all at once. He tests her *faith*. He appeals to her knowledge of God's revealed truth, and she says she "knows that he shall rise again in the Resurrection at the last day."‡ Then Jesus calls for Mary, and Martha goes to the house, and says: "The Master is come, and calleth for Thee,"§ and Mary goes quickly to Him.

Many Jews from Jerusalem were there to mourn with Martha and Mary; and we can just picture to

* St. John xi. 20. † St. John xi. 21. ‡ St. John xi. 24.
§ St. John xi. 28.

ourselves the gradual fall of the eastern eventide as our Lord reaches Bethany.

There, in the distance, the moon is just beginning to light up the Dead Sea. Right away, down in front of you, you see the plains of Jericho; then away to the left would be Jericho itself. It is a wonderful panorama that one catches standing on that eastern slope of the Hill of Olives; and on this slope was the graveyard place, the sepulchre, of the dead. I dare say you know of what kind these sepulchres were; they were generally holes cut out in the side of the rock, with a large stone covering the mouth; so that we may imagine to ourselves that the tomb of Lazarus was a great cave in the side of the hill.

And when Jesus has seen the sisters and has spoken to them for some time, He says: "Where have ye laid him?"*

And then the scene begins to deepen in interest, and Jesus Christ is led by the sisters, followed by crowds of Jews that have come to mourn. They all go back to the grave, and as they have been speaking the shadows of the evening have been lengthening; and it is dusk by the time our Lord reaches the grave.

A stone lay on the mouth of the tomb. Jesus said: "Take ye away the stone."† Then Martha answered: "Lord, by this time he stinketh: for

* St. John xi. 34. † St. John xi. 39.

he hath been dead four days."* Jesus saith unto her, "'Said I not unto thee, that, if thou wouldest believe, thou shouldest see the glory of God?' Then they took away the stone."†

Have you ever noticed that the three stories that have been handed down to us of our Lord raising people from the dead are all of degrees? One is Jairus' daughter. She had only just died. The other was the widow's son, being carried out to burial; and the last was Lazarus, who had been four days dead and stank.

So now we have the scene very plainly before us. Here is the tomb of Lazarus, which has the stone moved away from it; and it stands out in the evening light, for the western sun is now hidden over the hill, leaving Bethany in shadow. Our Lord stands at the great black mouth of the cave. I can picture the figure of our Lord standing there, and the others in the background, at that great, black, open cave.

There stands that strange Being who is in very deed, in one sense, the centre of all human history, for somehow or another, before Christ came, all religions of all races pointed to Him. Even the heathen poets sang of One Who should come down from Heaven, and renew life, and take away the poison of the old serpent, and make even the poisonous plants to lose

* St. John xi. 39. † St. John xi. 40, 41.

their bane. All the great civilisations of the East pointed westward to a coming Reformer; and we know the mistake that was made by the millions from China many centuries ago. They were told that the further they went west the nearer they would get to the light; but these millions from China stopped in Hindostan, and thence they took back with them the philosophy of Buddha. They stopped in Hindostan instead of going to the utmost point of the west, Palestine, which was the boundary washed by the western seas. Palestine was the central point between the Western and Eastern civilisations.

Well, then, I say, standing at the open tomb, of Lazarus we see this Figure, the Figure of Him Who seems to be the central point of human history; for since Christ came, has there been a religion that has not plagiarised His Gospel and adopted a great deal of it?

Mahomet could not have flourished with his Koran and his sword, if he had not mixed up a vast amount of the Word of the living God with his teaching.

I want you to gaze on this wondrous Figure. He is only a Jewish peasant to look at; but there is a strange, mystic electricity, may I call it? that goes out from Him. It attracts to Him all the sorrowful, all the diseased, all the most sinful; and the most pure and simple little children cling around Him. The publicans and the harlots crowd to listen to Him, and He says: "The publicans and harlots" that believe in Him "shall go into the Kingdom of Heaven before"* the self-righteous Pharisees that reject Him.

There is a charm about Jesus that follows Him wherever He goes. Even the leper cries out: "Lord, if Thou wilt, Thou canst make me clean."†

Who, besides Jesus, has ever dared to claim the love of humanity to such an extent that he could say: "He that loveth father or mother more than Me is not worthy of Me"?‡ Did Mahomet ever claim the love of humanity in such a way as this? Never.

But there is our Lord standing at the mouth of the tomb! I wonder what the Jews thought He was going to do; whether anybody knew what He was going to do! Here is the Prince of Life standing at the Gate of Death. Here, too, is the Gate of Life eternal, for Jesus says: "I am the way, the truth, and the life;"§ and He is standing at the grave where His friend is rotting and stinking in the embrace of death.

The spirit of Lazarus had some four days since migrated into some strange, distant realm. But we cannot talk about distance in eternity. Why, millions upon millions of miles, in our little, tiny ideas, are worth a

* St. Matt. xxi. 31.   † St. Matt. viii. 2.
‡ St. Matt. x. 37.   § St. John xiv. 6.

mere nothing in space, in eternity! But where had the spirit of Lazarus gone? It had entered into eternity and into infinity. But where—how far off from our little world? What voice could make itself heard to the distant spirit—to the far-away one?

There is a Voice that can make the whole universe to give heed; and so now we will watch and listen. And brethren, you must remember, the works of Jesus Christ were often done before vast crowds. Who saw Crishna work his works? Give me a certified date, in early history, with well-certified proof, of the incarnation of Vishnu. Where are the data, and the early proofs, of the sayings and doings of Ramah and Crishna? My brethren, they have no dates and no history. But I say that one of the most precious facts respecting *our* religion is that our religion began when history was at its greatest height of perfection. Between Herodotus and Tacitus our religion began.

Jesus Christ is no unhistorical character. Jesus Christ stood out in the bright blaze of the most intense publicity. And so here, at the working of this miracle, there were numbers around watching Him.

Even Renan does not deny the fact that these works were performed publicly; and he has the very greatest difficulty in shuffling out of them.

Well, then, we see the Lord standing at the open grave. Everyone's attention is turned towards

Him. We are told that the Jews crowded round from Jerusalem in multitudes. "Take off the grave-clothes." Does He say that? No. The body is allowed to remain in the tomb "bound hand and foot with grave-clothes;"* and while these grave-clothes bind him, and the dead body lies stinking in the winding-sheet, all at once the Lord Jesus raises His eyes to the evening sky. He raises His eyes towards the new Jerusalem. He raises His eyes, amidst the intense, aching hearts of the multitude, and He says: "I knew, Father, that Thou hearest Me always;"† and then He lifts up His voice, and He sends it like an echo far, far, far away—how far I cannot tell; and He cries in the hearing of the assembled multitude: "'LAZARUS, COME FORTH!' And he that was dead came forth, bound hand and foot with grave-clothes."‡

And I see the rotten figure standing in the white garments of the grave, in the great, black mouth of the tomb, and Jesus face to face with his resuscitated friend. But brethren, whence has the spirit been recalled? Oh! from the distant fields of illimitable space this spirit has returned, and has given to that body new life! The flush of health has taken the place of decay. The sweetness of fresh life has taken the place of the stinking of the tomb. Now then, you

* St. John xi. 44.   † St. John xi. 42.   ‡ St. John xi. 43, 44.

may take away the grave-clothes. "Loose him, and let him go."*

Oh! *that* night in Bethany! The awful hush of the miracle rests on the hills. It travels with the Jews right over Jerusalem, the city over the western hill. Lazarus has been raised from the dead! A spirit has come back from the realms of infinity, from the marvellous everywhere—and there is a man raised from the dead at Bethany!

My brethren, which do you consider is the greatest miracle—this temporary resurrection of the body of Lazarus, the revivifying of a few atoms of animal matter, for a few more years; or the resurrection of a dead soul from the darkness of unbelief, and from the bondage and tyranny of sin? Which is the greater phenomenon, the resurrection of a dead body to mortal life, or of a dead soul to life eternal, pardoned, cleansed, restored, satisfied, filled with peace, and enlightened with a "*sure and certain*" knowledge of an *everlasting* and *eternal* liberty, till the whole man has become renewed; his heart, will, and intellect completely changed, enabling him to believe all those things which he once ridiculed and maligned.

Some years ago in London, at one of my mission services, an atheist, who had been lecturing that very afternoon (as I was told afterwards) in one of the out-

* St. John xi. 44.

skirts of London, all at once confessed that what had been said at our service about Jesus Christ was true; and he went to a dissenting Minister in his own neighbourhood and asked to be prepared at once for baptism, and admission into that Christian sect which he desired to join; and the dissenting Minister wrote a letter to me to tell me that this man had been instantly converted while I was speaking.

I was speaking of Jesus as the gift of God to a suffering, dying, hungering world. I was giving illustrations of how Jesus Christ was what we said He was; and then all at once this man's heart opened and took the great Truth in. This man's intellect received an objective light which became subjective to him; and he believed what Jesus was; and he said, to the person sitting next to him: " What that man has said I am sure is true."

This is only one instance; but all through the ages of the Gospel, whenever Christ, in His fulness, is offered to the hungry sinner, there are sinners who come out and accept the gift. Shall you tell them, " Jesus Christ won't save you as you are; you must go and get a little better?" O no! Did our Lord Jesus Christ tell them to wash Lazarus as he was in such a state in the tomb, and make Lazarus a little more presentable? No, it was *just as he was* that he came forth; and have we not countless proofs that it is just the same with the sinner? It is just as you are that He wants you. "Whosoever will"* may come. My brethren, do you wish to have this new life? Do you wish to have this enlightening of your understanding, this rest and peace? Do you wish to know that you have eternal life and that you can never perish; that your sins are all put away for ever? *You can only know it by accepting Christ, in his fulness, as God's gift to you now.*

But how? What do you mean by accepting Christ? You tell me to come to Jesus. What am I to do? Oh! what a blessing it is that Jesus tells us how to come. Just mark that 47th verse of the 6th chapter of St. John, where our Lord, in very short, simple words, tells us what it means. "Verily, verily, I say unto you, he that believeth on Me hath—*hath* everlasting life.

Just close your eyes *now*, forget all else about you, only that Jesus Christ, the gift of God, is at your side. He wants to be to you now pardon, salvation, eternal life, peace. But He cannot do it until you give one look up in His face that simply trusts Him. *Directly* you give that look of simple trust, and take Him at His word, then He is all yours, for He says again: "He that believeth on the Son hath everlasting life."† And is there not a soul here now

* Rev. xxii. 17.   † St. John iii. 36.

dead, to whom the voice of Jesus, in His own Word, is going out, "Lazarus, come forth"? Oh! the Lazaruses that have written to me from this hall, telling me how once they were living lives of filth and sin and misery, and woe and restlessness and toil; and you should hear what they say of the new life!

Some write and say of this Book (the Bible) that, when once they have trusted Jesus, it seems to be an open Book to them, and all the promises in this Book come to them like a direct voice from the great, big heart of their loving Father God, to whom Jesus has brought them back as His reconciled children. Is there, perhaps, a sinner here to-night as hardened as he can be, living in the embrace of sin and death— or one, perhaps, who cannot believe the Word of the Gospel, yet who wishes to do so, but his intellect will not let him?

A gentleman, now among "the cloud of witnesses,"* said to me one evening after listening to my mission sermon: "Oh, Father Ignatius, Jesus Christ has won my heart to-day, but not my intellect! I cannot understand, or believe, the things in the Bible." Oh! what a joy it was to say to him: "Jesus Christ does not say, Give Me your brains; He says, 'Give Me thine heart.'† Your heart has been able to take Him in in His fulness, and your heart is at rest.

* Heb. xii. 1. † Prov. xxiii. 26.

Never mind your intellect. Give Jesus your heart, and He will take care of your intellect for you. It is 'with the heart that man believeth unto righteousness.'"* I could then see tears streaming down his eyes.

"The devil has the intellectual faith and trembles."† It is with the heart that I have to come and throw myself upon His promise; and then, as the Apostle says: "The eyes of your understanding shall be enlightened."‡

Jesus Christ changes men's hearts. He gives them peace and rest. He does what all the theologies and philosophies of earth have never been able to do. He makes a man a new creature. He makes him a contented creature, a happy, glad creature: for "if any man be in Christ" Jesus "old things are passed away; behold, all things are become new."§

Lazarus has come forth in this hall. I know that *here* Lazarus has come forth! I know that while I have been speaking there is someone who has come out of the miserable life of sin and worldliness, and has taken in this beautiful Jesus as the gift of God to him. Perhaps he will write to me before the week is over and tell me: "I was the one that 'came forth' that night."

* Rom. x. 10.
† St. James ii. 19.
‡ Ephes. i. 18.
§ 2 Cor. v. 17.

Oh! my dear brother, it is such joy to be told by those, upon whom the Word has fallen, "It was I 'that came forth;' and I am now possessed of "the unsearchable riches of Christ.'"*

I see a lady in the congregation this evening, who could tell you of a change in the whole of her family, husband, sons, and daughters, who have passed into a new life—all save one of a very large family. I know she will forgive me for mentioning it in her presence; for she is so full of the joy of that precious Saviour, Whom she has learnt to believe.

---

* Ephes. iii. 8

VIII.

Jesus Christ, the Sabbath of God.

Mission Sermon.

Saturday Evening, October 24th, 1885.

Jesus Christ, the Sabbath of God.

Prayer before Sermon.

O! Holy Spirit, help us to draw very near unto Jesus in prayer at this time. Draw us close to Him, we, Thy people, beseech Thee, O God. Lord Jesus, we are on our knees at Thy dear feet, to ask a blessing from Thee and to close another week of our shortly passing life.

The week's work is done, and now our hearts are turned towards the Lord's Day of rest. Thou art the Rest that abideth, and we would come to Thee this Saturday night to rest in Thy Presence; and we would lie down to-night to sleep resting in Thee, the Sabbath of our souls.

Oh! hold out Thy loving hands to each one of us, and draw us close to Thee, so that, when we lift up our hearts to Thee, with perfect confidence and faith, we can say of Thee, Lord Jesus, "Thou art ours and we are Thine."

And now speak to us, dearest Lord and Saviour; tell our hearts how much Thou lovest us; tell our hearts how Thou hast finished the work of our salvation, and make us to lie down in Thy love. Let us rest in peace; yea, "keep us in perfect peace, for our minds are stayed on Thee: because we trust in Thee."*

And, Lord Jesus, it is very safe to trust Thee, and it is very comfortable to trust Thee. Oh! the comfort and the rest of trusting Thee!

We bless Thee, O! precious Jesus, on behalf of everyone

* Isaiah xxvi. 3.

here present, who is able to rest in Thee as the Finisher and Accomplisher of their salvation; to rest in Thee as One Who *has* finished the work, and paid the debt, and covered them with Thine Own Righteousness. We do praise Thee because Thou hast revealed Thyself to us by Thy Holy Spirit!

And let us, this Saturday night, speak of the calm of death when the six days' work of life shall be ended, and we shall put aside earth's garments for the grave; let us, this Saturday night, speak of the calm and the rest of Paradise, and that time when the work of life, and its strife and toil, shall be for ever over; and when these bodies of sin and pain, sweet Saviour, shall be laid aside, and, in the beautiful rest of those peaceful plains, with Thy Saints, we shall be abiding; and waiting for the coming of the morning, when our bodies shall be raised with power, and we shall all be gathered together in Thy Presence, in the Land of the Free.

O! Lord, bless the words spoken at this time, and, if there be any here present who are not Thy people, bring Thy rest to those dear souls. And if now they have no calm, peaceful Saturday night and happy Sunday, like Thy people have—but go on through the wearying torture of this cruel world, and its restless, peaceless, unsatisfying strife, without Thee, and without hope of participating in the joy of Thy Sabbath—let me speak words to draw some of those dear, tired ones into the beautiful rest we enjoy. Let the Word be spoken with such a power that tears may stream down many a tired cheek for very gladness that they have found their Saviour to-night—their rest, their peace and their joy.

We know, dear Lord, we have not made these supplications in vain, because Thou art "more willing to hear" than we to receive. Lord, give us Thy Blessing; give Thy Blessing to the fallen and bring them into Thy Fold with joy, that there may be but one Fold and one Shepherd, even Thou Thyself, sweet, satisfying Jesus, our Saviour and our God. Amen.

"JESUS CHRIST, THE SABBATH OF GOD."

Mission Sermon.

"Come unto Me, all ye that labour and are heavy laden, and I will give you rest."—St. Matt. xi. 28.

And so we have come to the end of our week's Mission for Jesus, and we have come to the quiet of our Saturday-night service. Most of us are gathered here to-night to get some very real enjoyment out of Jesus—out of His Love, out of His Peace, out of His Mercy, out of His Salvation, out of His Holiness, out of His Rest.

He said Himself: "Come unto Me, all ye that labour and are heavy laden, and I will give you rest."*

Supposing we could collect together all the people in London to-night who are weary—supposing we could—Oh! what a sight it would be! What a crowd of weary, tired, pained faces we should see, with deep lines of sorrow on their brows; and there would be some desperate, half-starved-looking ones too.

And then supposing we could talk to them! I

* St. Matt. xi. 28.

am sure that out of the four millions of this city there are quite one million who are tired and weary; there are quite one million who know nothing whatever of hope, or rest, or peace.

Now, just picture to yourselves—we can hardly picture it to ourselves because we are so full of hope, so full of joy and gladness; we have such peace and rest, in Jesus, that we cannot imagine what it is to be without this blessedness (for some of us have, perhaps for twenty years, enjoyed moral and spiritual rest, and we can hardly realise what it is to be without it, but let us try just to picture to ourselves)—a poor, tired man, who perhaps has attended, once during the week, at some atheistic club, and has heard an address delivered by some very clever rationalist or materialist, who explains away all revealed religion and leaves a man standing, as it were, in a dark midnight road without any idea of God.

Such an one may be here. The world is restless about him, the world is unsatisfying, the world is cruel to him; he feels as if he would like to go out and murder and steal and slash and cut down everyone who is better off than himself, because he hates the world and everything in it. To him there is no God and no beyond, and he says: " I will get all I can here. There is no harm if I pick a man's pocket if I am not discovered. I am morally starving and I feel desperate. I should like to blow the brains out of the first rich man I meet!"

So these horrid and terrific ideas revolve in his restless, weary brain—his manly form is bowed, and his once strong muscles are now prematurely relaxing in the fearful struggle for bread. Disappointed hopes and domestic sorrows; the hideous fear of being struck down with illness and of being unable to feed his children any more—all the contingencies (the hundreds and thousands of contingencies) of this contradictory and paradoxical existence throng, and throng, around him; and his brain whirls as he faces the darkness that is before him. Oh! he is a weary one indeed!

To see such an one give a moral yawn on Saturday night! The hideous expression that comes over his face! It makes the Heart of Jesus Christ beat with sorrow, for He loves that man with a tender love; and what would we not do, if we could, to get him to taste of that joy and gladness, and that peace which the poorest Christian possesses in the knowledge and certainty of Christ.

Oh! the weary ones of London! And yet some of them will be in the low dancing houses now, laughing professionally. Do you know, the professional mirth-provokers come to me sometimes, and under the paint of their cheeks, under the forced, ghastly laugh, there is such a substratum of agony and anguish that is dreadful to contemplate. Weary, weary ones!

How many of our poor, poor fallen sisters and brothers there are who would give worlds to come to Christ, and obtain what we have obtained; and who *would* come, too, if they had only someone to show them the way and to lead them to Him! But supposing they steal into a church to-morrow morning, and hide behind a pillar and listen; what will they hear? Perhaps some metaphysical thesis or some casuistic philosophy—the holding up of Jesus Christ as a moral philosopher—and they go away unsatisfied.

Oh! the abominable iniquity of preachers who speak of Christ as a mere moral Example—who *could* give the Bread that God sends to His people, but who, instead, send hungry ones away with a stone!

The preacher does not know Christ, and does not want to know Him, and deliberately sets to work to undermine the value of the Sacraments. I could name clergymen in the Church of England who take away from the people what Christ would give to them—and they are licensed by our bishops!

My brothers, my brothers, when I think of the weary ones, waiting for the calm of holiness, and the Rev. Mr. This or That, with his black or his white gown upon his back, watering down the Word of God—in order to suit his congregation, in order to suit the poor, dark unbelief of the age in which we live!

He suits the nineteenth-century school of thought; but he does not think of the poor, tired, weary ones who, on Saturday night, want to get something out of God, and want to find Him Who says: "Come unto Me, and I will give you rest."* I say, when I hear a man offering to the people the stone of philosophy, instead of the Bread of Life, it makes me sad indeed.

Dear brethren, are we not thankful to God for the Salvation Army? I hope all of us are. I really do not know what thousands, in this great city, would do if it were not for the Salvation Army doing the work that the Church of England has left undone. It is all very well to laugh and scoff at their peculiarities. The Holy Ghost blesses their peculiarities, and by the instrumentality of those peculiarities brings "the Peace of God, which passeth all understanding,"† into the hearts and lives of the weary and heavy laden, and makes those peculiarities the media for emptying brothels and public-houses—for washing many faces with the water of charity and many hearts with the Blood of Christ.

Oh, brethren, if the Roman Catholic Church in London, and the Church of England in London, would become one great *Salvation* Army what a mighty work

* St. Matt. xi. 28.   † Phil. iv. 7.

might be done among the weary and heavy laden! Oh! what a glorious Saturday night many of the tired ones of London might then enjoy!

If the churches and places of worship would only give up something of mere outward formalism—if the Protestant would forget his protestantism, and the Catholic his catholicism, and agree to exalt that common Christ, whom Catholic and Protestant alike profess, what a harvest of redeemed souls there would be! Would to God there were such a happy Saturday night in London for poor weary and heavy laden ones! Would to God all professing Christians would seek to help forward the promotion of a universal Saturday night revival and refreshment for the poor that are weary and heavy laden, and whom Christ invites to come to Him.

And now, here is another thought, "How shall they preach except they be sent?"* By the Bishop? Yes. The Bishop of Souls, through the Holy Ghost.

No one but the Holy Ghost can send a Messenger of the Gospel to preach to a dying people—all other ordinations, in the world, cannot *make* a preacher. This can only be the work of the Holy Ghost. They are "taught of God."† "Ye have an unction from the Holy One, and ye know all things"‡ about Jesus, and can enjoy your Saturday night, and look

* Romans x. 15.   † St. John vi. 45.   ‡ 1 St. John ii. 20.

forward to the sweet rest of the Lord's Day. You are the ordained ones—you know what the love of Jesus is.

Brethren, this Saturday night meeting seems to speak to me of such wonderful, wonderful visions, and wonderful foretastes of the Saturday night to which you and I are looking forward, when we shall put off our work-a-day clothes for ever, and put on the garments of the everlasting Lord's Day.

Christian people, one of the marks of the reality of our profession, as Christians, is the love we shall have for sinners, because Christ loved them, and came to seek them, and sent us to seek them. We are not to expect them to seek us—we are to seek them, and brethren, when we seek them, what a wonderful assurance we have, in our hearts, that we shall find them.

And we do find them whenever we go out in the Master's Name!

If any of you have an hour to spare, if any of you are free on Saturday night, go and seek for one sinner whom you may bring in to the calm of our Saturday night, that at the end of his six days' work he may live trusting in Christ's mighty grace to enable him to begin a new life—the life of the rest day of salvation.

And you know it is not as if I were talking to you the rubbish that materialists and philosophers talk.

What does that rubbish give to the poor aching, hungering heart of man? Nothing at all. Brethren, I am talking of the only reality of which it is worth talking—the reality that has filled the hearts and lives of men—bringing pleasure, freedom, and peace, and joy, and gladness to countless multitudes wherever the Gospel has been proclaimed.

Oh, my brethren, Saturday night, Saturday night, to us is a time of rest and quietness. We are very tired with our week's work—one of you, perhaps, has been sitting all the week upon a high clerk's stool, scribbling away, and when Saturday night comes you are thankful enough to lay down your pen and rest.

There may be some poor clerk here who is working his very life out to support a widowed mother—perhaps he does not get as much as thirty shillings a week, and yet he tries to send half to his mother; and he shares a garret with a friend in poor circumstances, and they burn a rushlight between them that they may save something out of their poverty.

And oh! when Saturday night comes the thoughts of their church, of the delights of the House of God, the delightful refreshment of the Lord's Table, of the sweet words of Life they will hear from the clergyman's lips, who is taught of God, brings joy to them. They look forward to the very text, and after Sunday they will go back to the counting-house refreshed, and thankful for the consolations of Sunday.

Some there are who say it is right to have a game of cricket on a Sunday; but I cannot spare five minutes of the Lord's Day for all that the devil can offer me. I am a poor, tired man; I want to enjoy the rest and delight and peace of God, and to lay hold of the love of Jesus. Catch me blaspheming the day of Jesus, a day fifty times more holy than the Jewish Sabbath, for the Jews kept the Sabbath because they were under the law; I keep it because I am under grace, and I will not rob one hour of it from Jesus.

Saturday night has great and holy charms because the whole of the twelve hours of the Lord's Day are before me. There are those who talk about the enjoyment of Sunday afternoon, and hold it right to go to the opera in the evening. Let the world do what it likes with what it calls the Lord's Day; but we Christians cannot part with a single hour of it, for we want the whole of our Sundays for Jesus and ourselves.

Sunday is not to us a day of bondage or formalism; but it is the day when we draw most of life's refreshment from the well of salvation. Oh! sweet Saturday night! Oh! still sweeter Day of Jesus, our precious Sunday Fountain of strength and refreshment after the six days' toil of earth.

My dear brethren, these thoughts are intensely real; but they are not to be kept wrapped up in words. If I have a large piece of bread and I see a hungry man coming along, shall not I spare him some of it? And won't you spare something of Jesus to the hungry souls around you? When we light our altar lights, at some great Feast, all the wicks of the tapers are lit from one light; but the light with which we lit them does not go out.

You are to be God's altar taper in a world of darkness; you are to be the altar taper of the Holy Ghost, to go and kindle beautiful lights in the hearts of men, who are sitting in darkness and the shadow of death. I do not care a scrap for ceremony and ritualism, unless it spring from the heart; but if you can appreciate it Scripturally, and it is the mere outcome of an inward reality; then don't I love ritualism!

Brethren, let us all be as tapers of the altar for Jesus—we are his " witnesses,"[*] in a dark world —we who are " the salt of the earth,"[†] the " children of light and the children of the day."[‡] Oh! then, let us tell out, amid the calm of Saturday night, the joy of Sunday, to them who have never tasted the sweetness and the rest of those who know God in Jesus.

---

[*] Isaiah xliii. 10; xliv. 8; Acts i. 8; v. 32.   [†] St. Matt. v. 13.
[‡] 1 Thes. v. 5.

Two more thoughts and I have done. What is this rest that Jesus gives to all "that come unto God by Him?"* He says, "Come unto Me all ye that labour, and are heavy laden, and I will give you rest."† What is this rest? From what does it proceed? It proceeds just from this. When anyone comes to Jesus, and trusts Him, and takes Him at His word, all the clouds of doubt and misery pass away from before the sun, which then begins to shine.

When we trust in Him all the toil of seeking for salvation comes to an end. *Directly* we trust in Jesus we know indeed the rest of a *finished* salvation; we realise that *He* has finished the work, and *we* have only to enter into the rest.

See how many tired, weary people there are in the world who are continually trying to save their own souls! There is no Saturday night in their religion, because they are always at work—all the seven days they are at work—working to save their own souls, and then not knowing if they are saved or not—in fact, feeling sure that they are not.

Oh, the rest of knowing "It is finished!"‡ The quiet rest of Saturday night; knowing, in calm confidence, that "He has finished the work which the

---

* Heb. vii. 25.   † St. Matt. xi. 28.   ‡ St. John xix. 30.

Father gave Him to do,"* which was to "save His people from their sins."†

So that directly the soul trusts in Jesus it enters into rest; the rest, from working for salvation, is its own. Oh! then, with what joy and peace we can look up in His face and say: "Thou art *my* Saviour."

And it is not an imperfect work; it is a work altogether perfect, for Christ is "the end of the law to everyone that believeth."‡ He has paid my debt to the "uttermost farthing. But it is rest *in* Jesus."

Oh! sweet, sweet hour, when first the soul sinks into "the rest that remaineth to the people of God,"§ of which St. Paul speaks when he says: "We which have believed do enter into rest."‖

But, again remember that it is not a selfish, inert rest. It is a rest of perpetual work. When we have entered into the rest of His finished work we enter upon the Lord's Day of real work. It is a work of love, a restful work of joy, in serving Him Whom we love, and Whom we serve. So, brethren, you see that the rest that comes from trusting in Jesus is not a lazy rest, no slothful quiescence; but it is a mighty going forward to win pearls for His Crown—of bringing crowds of weary ones to know Him, Who has given to us joy and peace and hope and gladness.

---

* St. John xvii. 4. † St. Matt. i. 21. ‡ Rom. x. 4.
§ Heb. iv. 9. ‖ Heb. iv. 3.

And so comes Sunday. Is Sunday a lazy day? Certainly not. Why, it is the most joyously active of all the days of the week, for on Sunday we are to work, not for ourselves, but for Him " who loved us and gave Himself for us."*

This is the thought of rest that I wish to give you; and this is the rest in Jesus; the rest that strengthens us; the rest in the knowledge that He has finished our salvation, has won for us a robe of perfect righteousness, has shed His Blood, Which "cleanseth us from all sin,"† and has given to us the grace of the Holy Spirit, which shall " supply our *every* need,"‡ no matter what it shall be. " Be careful for nothing"§ —" He careth for you,"∥ and " of His fulness have all we received;"¶ and you have all your needs supplied in Christ Jesus.

And " this is the rest, and this is the refreshing !"** To-day I had a letter from a dear, young " lost " sister, and it was such a happy, sweet letter. She has entered into the rest and the refreshing of sin forgiven. And I could tell you so many stories of girls like this now numbered amongst the saints who have entered into the rest of sin forgiven; because Jesus says when He has saved us from sin He gives

* Gal. ii. 20.
† 1 John i. 7.
‡ Phil. iv. 19.
§ Phil. iv. 6.
∥ 1 Pet. v. 7.
¶ St. John i. 16.
** Isaiah xxviii. 12.

us power to overcome it—yea, "to be more than conquerors."*

So now, come, enter into the rest; you are certain to find it. You need not trouble about the result; "you shall be more than conquerors."* We know in Whom we trust, and to Whom we cry, and Who "giveth us the victory, through our Lord Jesus Christ."†

And just as we put off our work-a-day clothes, so shall we very soon have to lay aside these bodies of ours, and they shall be put into their coffins. And then our "works will follow"‡ us; and those "which sow sparingly shall reap also sparingly; and those which sow bountifully shall reap also bountifully."§ Each sacrifice of ours will be remembered, not one will be lost, not even "the cup of cold water"‖ taken from the fountain, and carried to the weary one, shall be unrecorded; and they will stand you in good stead "in that day." Oh! soon we have to put off our week-day clothes; but when "the earthly house of this tabernacle shall be dissolved, we have an house not made with hands, eternal in the Heavens."¶

Are you, dear brethren, ready for this Saturday night; are you ready to put off the earthly house of this tabernacle? Can you look up into the face of Jesus and say? "Yea, though I walk through the

* Rom. viii. 37. † 1 Cor. xv. 57. ‡ Rev. xiv. 13
§ 2 Cor. ix. 6. ‖ St. Mark ix. 41. ¶ 2 Cor. v. 1.

valley of the shadow of death, I will fear no evil: for Thou, (O Lord), art with me."*

Shall we all be glad when that Saturday night comes, when life's week of work is over, when Saturday night is coming gently upon us; and our hearts, which have never ceased to beat since the day of our birth, shall beat no more; when our throbbing brains shall be at rest and we shall (on that Saturday night) put off our earthly bodies?

Oh! then, when all the things of earth are passing away, and everything around us seems but mist and shadow, and dream; and the eyes of our spirit are opening to those eternal realities, which are not seen but are eternal; and when those who are around our beds are watching our laboured breath, as we climb the last hill, at eleven o'clock on Saturday night, and the solemnity of the hush of the death-bed is ours, and Saturday night has come, then, oh! then brethren, what shall you and what shall I do? There will be no time then for making our peace with God. It will be no time then to seek for salvation. It will not be the day of salvation then; it will be the day of judgment and of death. "*Now is the accepted time, now is the day of salvation!*"†

If Jesus be a Stranger to you now, He will be a Stranger to you then. If He be a Friend to you now,

* Ps. xxiii. 4. † 2 Cor. vi. 2

He will be a Friend to you then—a Friend Who will carry you right through the Jordan water, and land you safe on the shore of the Promised Land, where you may enter into the beautiful gardens of the eternal Sunday—the sweet Lord's Day of a joyful Sabbath.

Brothers and sisters, God is making me an instrument for giving you a happy Saturday night when that day comes. Will you have a happy Saturday night? Oh! yes, if you will look into the face of Christ and trust Him as your Saviour, Who died for you; and Who, by His Blood, has put away your sin and paid your debt to the " uttermost farthing;" and Who says to those who trust Him : " I will never leave thee nor forsake thee."*

And then we shall all meet on Sunday morning at the grand High Mass of Heaven; when the angels swing the censers of gold, and the Light is beaming in brilliancy from the Throne of God. There—where there is " no need of a candle "† and where the choirs of the Redeemed, as they sweep through the temple, sing their changeless antiphon: " Unto Him that loved us, and washed us from our sins in His Own Blood, to Him be glory and dominion for ever and ever. Amen."‡

---

* Heb. xiii. 5. † Rev. xxii. 5. ‡ Rev. i. 5, 6.

IX.

On the Results of the Mission,
or
"The Great Promise Fulfilled."

Mission Sermon.

Sunday Morning, October 25th, 1885.

On the Results of the Mission,
or
"The Great Promise Fulfilled."

Prayer before Sermon.

O Lord, Jesus Christ, we have been gathering in this place for many days, in Thy Name, and Thy Word has been spoken in this place day after day. There are souls here who, before this mission began, knew Thee not and were restless without Thee, but now have been washed in Thy Precious Blood. We do know and believe that such is the case—we know it of some and we believe it of others; and we bless Thee because Thou art faithful.

And although Thou dost promise things that, to the world, are impossible, Thou dost accomplish them; and Thou sendest forth enlightened souls as Thy witnesses of the results of Thy Power, unto a restless, sinful world. And, O Lord, their hearts are blessing Thee, and we glorify Thy Holy Name with gladness and thanksgiving.

We now beseech Thee, bless us this morning; and if there be any here who have not been attending our services, and who come this morning amongst us as strangers, not knowing what has been going on this week, and therefore not understanding a great deal of what is said, grant that some gift may be in store for them.

O loving, loving Shepherd, if there be any of Thy lost sheep here, bring them to Thee that there may be one Fold and One Shepherd; make them to feel the need and the value of Thee and Thy great Salvation, and everlasting Life. Blessed Lord Jesus, glorify Thy Name through the preaching of Thy Word, for Thine Infinite Love and Mercy's sake. Amen.

THE RESULTS OF THE MISSION, OR "THE GREAT PROMISE FULFILLED."

Mission Sermon.

"For ye shall go out with joy, and be led forth with peace."—Isaiah lv. 12.

Now, as people are so accustomed to hear texts of Scripture read without attempting to take notice of their meaning, I will read the text again. "For ye shall go out with joy, and be led forth with peace."

Here is a distinct Promise, which is alleged to have been made by God in His Own Word. Here is a distinct promise that, if His Word be preached, this shall be the result—the hearers shall go out with joy, and be led forth with peace.

Now, then, brethren, if God's Word has been preached this week, this must be the result, or else the gospel story is a lie. If this Word be not fulfilled there must be one of three reasons for its non-fulfilment. If, of those who have been attending the mission, none are now filled "with joy,"* if among them, none "have been led forth with peace,"* it is

* Isaiah lv. 12.

either because I have not preached God's Word or, if I have, that God has not kept His Promise, or that there is no God to keep the Promise, and the whole thing is a myth.

Brethren, we Christians not only believe, but we *know*, that the Promise has been fulfilled. And not only do we believe in our hearts, and know it must be so, because we have the witness that it has taken place in our own cases, but God always gives proofs of the fulfilment of His Promise; and if you were to see the pile of letters that I have received, in consequence of what has been going on in this hall during the week, some of you would lift up your hands in amazement.

We believe that people "go out with joy, and are led forth with peace"* *whenever* the Word is preached.

You know St. Peter, one of the first teachers of the Christian religion, and one of the first preachers of the Gospel, says: "Believing, ye rejoice with joy unspeakable and full of glory."† The first believers had no more to believe than you and I; they were only asked to believe the same Message as I have been proclaiming; and the results of the Gospel preaching in the first century were not one jot different from the results of Gospel preaching in the nineteenth.

* Isaiah lv. 12.   † 1 Peter i. 8.

And if you say how is it that we do not see more of these results in our churches and chapels, we must give as answer that the Word of God is not preached in its simplicity and in its entirety—it is either preached with a number of additions to it, or it is only preached in part and not in whole.

Some time ago one of the members of our Order went to hear a very noted preacher of the day, and, when he came back, I asked him what he had heard; had he heard the Gospel preached? He said, "About as much Gospel as would lie on a fourpenny-bit."

It is not fair when God sends a Message to the world, that is enough to satisfy all the poor, needy, hungry, aching hearts that hear the Word—I say it is a shame to give them a little only, and that little so covered up with a quantity of rubbish, called philosophy, casuistry, and metaphysical nonsense, that the Gospel itself does not do them any good—in fact, they hardly get any Gospel at all.

This is the reason why the promised results do not follow the preaching. Preachers do not preach the Word of God in its simplicity!

There are numbers of churches, in London, where people are gathered together and worship an imaginary being in whom there is no sensible kind of authority for believing at all. I recollect—I am only mentioning the names of public men, just the same as my name may be mentioned—that once I was passing the place where Mr. Voysey was announced to preach, and I made as though I were going in. But before going in I said to the man at the door, "Who are they worshipping in there?" The man said, "God, of course." I answered, "Is it the God of the Bible?" The young man's face looked a little long as he answered, "I cannot say that." "Then," I replied, "if it be a little private god of Mr. Voysey's I am not going to worship *that*;" and I went elsewhere to worship Him Who is a matter-of-fact, historical Reality, and Who has made Himself known in the Incarnation of His Own Son.

This is the God Who has been preached for eighteen hundred years; and, in spite of the world's opposition, has gathered out a people whenever His Message has been preached, by a force for which the world cannot account. The God Who not only says but does—That is the God Whom we worship; That is the God Whom we preach. And the results have been manifest.

I should like to read to you the letter to which I referred last night, written by, what the world would call, one of our "fallen sisters." What a mighty work it is, and what a mighty power that has washed her from her sin, and made her lay hold of Christ, with such rejoicing that her whole being is changed! And now she longs for opportunities to testify to the great things that God has done for, and in, her. And then numbers of others have written to tell of the satisfaction and the peace, that have come into their lives. Everything is like bright sunshine; it is a light, which they never knew before, that illuminates them; there is a Something that has filled up the aching void of years, and they have gone " out with joy." The Promise of the text has been fulfilled. They have been led forth in peace.

And, brethren, it is a joy that satisfies the wants of man and his compound nature. Man is a compound animal—a tremendously compound animal—and the more a man, with common sense, examines himself, the more he will discover what a wonderful combination of appetites and desires exists within him.

The unbeliever tells us that our higher appetites and desires are all rubbish; and that it is within the power of human nature to satisfy all its wants. And when we say there is such a thing as perfect holiness to be found, and perfect satisfaction, he tells us it is all a nonsensical dream—in fact, many of the materialists would have us believe that we are worse off than the dogs and cats at our feet. I cannot understand such a position as that. The materialist says there is no hereafter; no God; and that our nobler appetites and our spiritual cravings, which are more tremendously real than is our bodily hunger, are all folly.

I say the man is a fool who can say that these strong, imperious yearnings are not realities. But what, in the past, said such mighty minds as Zoroaster, Plato, and Virgil? Look at the magnificent energisings of Plato, his hungering after God; see how the fire of truth flashed from his heart, and threw into his words such might, that he won a hearing from the highest, till Plato's name became the rallying point for the noblest minds. Why? Because he pointed out that all were in sin, and he told how he had realised the reality of One Who knows no sin. Plato was waiting for Jesus.

Consider, too, how a Virgil could sing of the Golden Age, which the Gospel should bring to men (Virgil, Eclogue iv.), 40 years before our Saviour's birth. Also Suetonius, in his life of Vespasian, tells of the world's expectancy of the great ruler from the East.

One prophet calls Jesus the "Desire of all Nations;"* for all the noblest and best of mankind desired a knowledge of Christ, an atonement with God, a putting away of that sin, which is the tyranny and bondage of man.

And then Jesus Christ came and said: "I am the Living Bread which came down from Heaven"†—

* Hag. ii. 7.　　† St. John vi. 51.

"Come unto Me, all ye that labour and are heavy laden, and I will give you rest;"* and from that day forward there have been multitudes drawn out from the hungry crowds and fed; numbers have been washed in the Blood of Jesus. As Cowper's hymn says:—

> "There is a Fountain filled with blood,
> Drawn from Emmanuel's veins,
> And sinners, plunged beneath that flood,
> Lose all their guilty stains."

That is just what we believe and, although the world has laughed at us for eighteen hundred years; yet numbers to day "go out with joy and are led forth with peace."† We are at peace with God because faith in Christ has put away our sin, and brought us sinless to God, and we can look up into the Face of God and say "Abba Father."‡ Jesus tells us to pray and to say "*Our Father*, Which art in Heaven."§

This magnificent faith carries us through all trials and sorrows and storms of life; and, then, in the calm and gladness, that the world cannot touch, we confess: this is "the peace of God which passeth all understanding."‖ Oh! when we possess

---

* St. Matth. xi. 28.   † Isaiah lv. 12.   ‡ Romans viii. 15.
§ St. Matth. vi. 9.   ‖ Phil. iv. 7.

Jesus "we go out with joy." We do not want anything else because Jesus Christ quite satisfies those that accept Him, with simple trust and simple love.

But then the Promise is not only, "we shall go out with joy;"* it is also that "we shall be led forth with peace."* "They shall be led"—yes, as "My sheep." And He leads His sheep, for He says: "I am the Good Shepherd, and know My sheep;"† and He goes before them and leads them forth.

One of the letters which I am very happy to possess is from a poor young girl, who says: "Tell the congregation that since the mission I attended two years ago, when I accepted Christ as my Saviour, He has made me sensible of His Presence, at my side, and I have been kept from sin by His power; and not only that, but I find a joy in trying to glorify Him every day. Tell the people," she says, "they have been two years of happy experience."

We are sure that it is no human power which thus delivers these poor children from the horrible sin, in which for years they have persevered, and sets them free "into the glorious liberty of the children of God."‡

But we have more men converted at our services

---

* Isaiah lv. 12. † St. John x. 14. Rom. viii. 21.

than women! Some few Sundays ago we had a congregation of five hundred, and not more than twenty of this number were women; and the police told us that some of the worst men in the town were attending our services. Some of these had passed through the change of which we have been speaking. There is a power and a force that takes hold of us, and leads us about just like a shepherd leads his sheep: " He goeth before them;"* and the Good Shepherd says: "I will never leave them nor forsake them."† And He keeps His Promise!

I am talking of a real, practical, daily experience, which draws numbers of the human family out of the darkness of their sin-stained lives. I am talking of that which is as great a reality to-day, in the midst of us, as it was when it was first preached by Paul to the Greek philosophers, or by Peter in Asia.

Christian brethren, and especially you who have been converted to Christ this week; you are held up by One Who says, "He will never leave you," and that "no man shall pluck you out of His Hand."‡ And hear the Promise, all you that have come to Him, you "are kept by the power of God."§

And now I must speak to you, not only of those privileges, and the fulfilment of the simple Promise,

---

* St. John x. 4.   † Joshua i. 5; Heb. xiii. 5.   ‡ St. John x. 28.
§ 1 Peter i. 5.

but I must speak too of some of the difficulties with which you are going to meet; and it is very necessary that I should do so.

Directly a man is converted to Christ the world will make him *feel* that he is converted and no mistake; directly a man becomes a Christian the world is up in arms against him.

Perhaps the world will come to you in the person of your own children, perhaps it will come in the person of your own father or mother; directly you have received the love of Christ, and the peace of God, you become a man who is *in* the world but has ceased to be *of* it. Jesus Christ says: " Ye have not chosen Me, but I have chosen you,"* and He says: " Ye are not of the world, but I have chosen you out of the world."†

What a beautiful word that is used by the prophet Micah! He says: the children of God shall be "as a "dew."‡ Let me tell you an instance of what I mean. A young man came to one of my mission services. He thought it rare sport to hear a monk preach, and see what kind of a fellow a monk was; but it was not the monk who met him, it was the power of the Holy Ghost that met him; and, face to face with Jesus Christ, he heard the Voice of God plead with his heart

---

* St. John xv. 16. † St. John xv. 19. ‡ Micah v. 7.

Will you "come to Me that you may have life;"* "*whosoever* will," let him come. He told Jesus, "Lord, I will come."

Then, when he went home he had his family to face —a family of father and mother, and eleven brothers and sisters. Well, all sat down to the evening supper, the Sunday evening meal; but he could not sit still until he had told them that he had found peace in Jesus; and he said: "I want to tell you I have found Jesus to-night, and His Blood has washed all my sins away, and I can never be lost; and," he said, "I am not going to rest until everyone of you have obtained what I have obtained."

A year after I went to the same place, to hold a mission, and as I was leaving the hall a lady came to me and said: "Oh! Reverend Father, would you mind coming to our house? It is close by."

There was an earnestness in her voice that touched me very much, but I said: "I am sorry it is against our rule to pay visits, or to go to any house except that in which we are staying; but will you let me ask why you are so anxious for me to come?" Tears came into her eyes, and she said, "The last time you were here my second boy came to your mission service, and he found Jesus Christ, and has been the means of

* St. John v. 40.

bringing Christ to everyone in the family except the eldest son; and now we are a happy, contented family, with this exception, and he is utterly wretched and miserable; and we do not believe he will ever have peace until he accepts Christ as we have done."

Oh! then, the Promise is fulfilled. Some of you have very stormy lives to live, some of you have very uncertain lives to live, some of you have the seeds of some mortal disease in you, and it is only a matter of time how long you will live; some of you have some terrible domestic woes, some daughter perhaps whose name now can never be mentioned in the family circle; some children, perhaps, cast like wrecks upon the stormy sea of London life; maybe, some of you are bending under the load of some terrible affliction; and now I would solemnly ask you in the Name of One Who has carried me for nineteen years through troubles and persecutions, riots and storms, poverty and want, of every description (He has carried me and He has carried all His people)—I ask you, will you just do what we have done, accept Christ, in His fulness, as God's Gift to you?

If you say: "I would if I could *intellectually*," I say I do not care one rap about your intellect; it never fills your life with peace, it never brings calm and rest to the soul, and God never asked a man to believe with his intellect. "But," you say, "I am an intellectual animal, and I cannot accept what I cannot understand." That is not true; you accept a great many things you do not understand—in fact the things that infidels have to believe are a great deal harder than those we have to believe. It must be very hard to believe that we, human beings, came from nothing, with our intellects, our passions, our hopes, our magnificent moral, as well as physical, powers—to believe all came from nothing, because they say we came from a protoplasm; but how that protoplasm came into existence they do not know. I say the unbeliever has far harder things to believe than we Christians.

And not only that, but I say,—and here is an appeal to common sense—that the Gospel brings into play certain forces which operate always in the same way; and yet we are told this is all nonsense, a myth, and a dream. I say if this be a dream it brings into play forces that produce moral and physical results, which nothing else could produce; and if there be no reality in *it* then there is no reality in anything.

Other realities cannot produce what this so-called unreality does, and you cannot show me any force in existence which can evolve the results that the Gospel has evolved in this place this week. Therefore, if I cannot intellectually receive the Gospel, *common sense* must tell me that it is of God to exercise this unique power.

Common sense tells me that wherever there is a phenomenon there is a cause, and if the phenomenon be great the cause must be equally great; and if a man say that the Gospel is not a reality, I say he is a dolt and a fool, because common sense shows us, by practical results, that it is the most tremendous, magnificent reality that ever visited this life of storm and tears and pain and dying.

Jesus says: "I will give you rest."* "In Me you shall have peace,"† says Jesus. "I will feed you." "I will clothe you;" and He does all He promises.

Do not forget that you will have troubles and persecutions to bear. People will misrepresent you directly you tell them that you are saved and that you can never be lost. They will tell you it is great presumption, they will call you self-righteous, and say that you set yourself up as being better than other people; but this is just what you are not doing; and you can tell them that you came to Christ as a poor, lost sinner, and put yourself in the dust at His feet, and that *He* set you up and placed you among "the princes of His people."‡

And remember, also, brethren, the responsibility

---

* St. Matt. xi. 28.   † St. John xvi. 33.   ‡ Psalm cxiii. 8.

that is yours as witnesses, for Christ. Jesus Christ says: "Ye shall be witnesses unto Me."* Now, then, brethren, "go out with joy,"† go on "from strength to strength;"‡ and "you shall be led forth with peace"—"the peace of God, which passeth all understanding, shall keep your hearts and minds through Christ Jesus."§

* Acts i. 8.
† Isaiah lv. 12.
‡ Ps. lxxxiv. 7.
§ Phil. iv. 7.

X.

Jesus Christ and the Ark of Noah.

Mission Sermon.

Sunday Afternoon, May 3rd, 1885.

Jesus Christ, and the Ark of Noah.

Prayer before Sermon.

O, Jesus Christ the Ark of God, the Ark of Safety—we bless Thee for all here present who are safe within Thee—" Men in Christ ! " *—Amen.

* 2 Cor. v. 17.

"JESUS CHRIST AND THE ARK OF NOAH."

Mission Sermon.

"And knew not until the flood came, and took them all away; so shall also the coming of the Son of Man be. Then shall two be in the field; the one shall be taken and the other left. Two women shall be grinding at the mill; the one shall be taken and the other left."—St. Matt. xxiv. 39, 40, 41.

Has it ever struck you, my hearers, I wonder, how extraordinary it is that a very common mistake is made about the ark? People speak of the Church as being the ark. Now, you know, there is no sense in such a saying as that. The Church is *in* the ark. The Church consists of the people who have taken refuge in the ark. You might just as well call Noah and his sons and their wives the ark as call the Church the ark.

The Church is a company of faithful people who have made their escape and have got into the ark; and the ark of Christ's Church is Jesus Christ. He is the Ark. The whole force of the figure is lost unless you take it in this way. The Church cannot be the ark. The Church is made up of a number of poor sinners, and they cannot make the ark. God has made an ark for them, and all those that are Christ's Church get into this Ark, which is Christ Himself.

And so we find through the whole of the New Testament that expression used which is so familiar to the believer in Christ. St. Paul calls himself "a new man in Christ;"* and our Lord Jesus Christ speaks of His people as being in Him. It is "Ye in Me;"† and then He says we dwell in Him. I repeat, Christ is the Ark, and His people are the Church; therefore Christ is the Ark of His Church.

And, brethren, it is necessary that we should be very clear and very simple in our teaching to men now-a-days; for they are in such a great hurry that you can only get them to listen for a little while. It is therefore so much the best plan to shelve all the differences, and all the superstructures, and just first bring them on to the Rock of Ages, which is Christ Himself.

Our subject this afternoon, then, is "Jesus Christ and the Ark of Noah." I was thinking, as I drove through the streets just now to this hall—drove as a matter of absolute necessity or else I should not have thought of driving on Sunday, because a horse has as much right to rest as I have—I was thinking, as I saw streams of human life flooding the great streets, how sad it is to know that there is an Ark large enough to

---

* 2 Cor. v. 17. † St. John xiv. 20.

hold them all, but yet that so very few of them turn to the door and enter in!

In the old time God's mercy framed an ark, and He framed it, larger—much larger than it was necessary to frame it. There were only eight persons who availed themselves of the loving invitation of God! The others all made game of it; laughed at and ridiculed it—" until the flood came and took them all away."*

I am not now going to argue about the flood, whether it was local or universal. I believe it was universal, because I believe exactly the literal teaching of Holy Scripture; and therefore, as a Christian, I see no room for argument about the matter. I am perfectly convinced on the subject. God has convinced me of the truth of the Bible, by its power upon the hearts and wills and lives and minds of men.

The Bible can turn the vilest sinner inside out in a moment. It brings new life, new desires, new hopes, new appetites, new tastes to him; and I simply say that this Book could not do all that unless it were divine; and therefore I do not want to argue about it. There is plenty in the Bible which I do not understand, and which I have to accept with simple, childlike faith, as Christ says: "Thou hast hid these

* St. Matt. xxiv. 39.

things from the wise and prudent, and hast revealed them unto babes. Even so, Father, for so it seemed good in Thy sight."*

It can also be argued that upon the tops of the very highest mountains traces of the sea, such as shells, have been found; so that even from worldly teachings we have very great reason to believe that the waters passed over the highest hills. But that has nothing to do with our subject.

We have a very earthly and a very matter-of-fact description of the state of things before the flood. Men and women were then the same as they are now; with the same hopes, difficulties and interests. "As the days of Noe were, so shall also the coming of the Son of Man be. For as in the days that were before the flood they were eating and drinking, marrying and giving in marriage, until the day that Noe entered into the ark; and knew not until the flood came, and took them all away."† So that when Christ comes, those who have believed the strange story of God's mercy, in having provided a Refuge for humanity, against the coming sea of holy justice and wrath and judgment, *they will be safe in Christ.*

Now you know that, during all this mission week, we have been very clear in our preaching. We have tried, all we possibly could, not to mystify men's minds.

---

* St. Matt. xi. 25, 26. † St. Matt. xxiv. 37, 38, 39.

If you remember, during the week, one of the chief thoughts has been this: that there are only two religions in the world, God's religion and the world's religion. The world's religion is a religion that works to save itself. God's religion is that which offers salvation as God's free gift, and which hides in Christ, as a refuge, him who flees to Christ as the One Who satisfies all those who come to Him.

We flee to Christ for His righteousness to cover us, for His blood to cleanse us; for "His grace to abound within us,"* and for Him "to strengthen us with all might by His Spirit,"† according to His glorious power. We flee to Him as our atonement; through Whom we may find God's justice satisfied, and our debt to His Majesty paid "to the uttermost farthing." We flee to Christ, and in Him we find God's panacea for all the ills and aches and cravings of our being. Jesus Christ satisfies all who accept Him, and the weary and the heavy laden, and the sinner and the lonely, and the restless and the sad, and the sorrowful and the desolate—they all find a rest and a repose at His feet, Who says: "Come to me, I will give you rest."‡

So, then, those who come to Christ are sensible of intense satisfaction and rest; of a mighty protection. Jesus Christ is a mighty barrier between me and the wrath of God. Jesus Christ is to me the satisfaction

* 2 Cor. ix. 8.   † Ephes. iii. 16.   ‡ St. Matt. xi. 28.

for my sin. Jesus Christ is to me the cleansing of my sin. Jesus Christ is to me, as I said just now, all that I need; and, therefore, in the cleft of this Rock of Ages I have found refuge, security, peace, contentment, righteousness, salvation and repose. I am "a new man in Christ"* simply by accepting Christ as God's gift to me.

That is the message. "God so loved the world, that He gave His only begotten Son, that whosoever believeth in Him should not perish, but have everlasting life."† This simple faith is the only way that God has appointed for us to lay hold of the Gift He offers to the world; and if I have accepted Christ, God then accepts me; as St. Paul says, God accepts me "in the Beloved."‡

Now, brethren, you remember in the story of old, how men ridiculed and sneered at Noah as he proclaimed the coming flood. They sneered at him from day to day, and from month to month, and year to year; and the scientific men of the day, no doubt, regarded with ridicule the denunciations and prophetic warnings of Noah's sermons; for he was "a preacher of righteousness,"§ says the Holy Ghost.

Every now and then would the echo of the hammer and the workman's tool ring across the plain. The

---

* 2 Cor. v. 17. † St. John iii. 16.
‡ Ephes. i. 6. § 2 Peter ii. 5.

people looked from the villages and towns, upon the hills, and saw the rising ark, in its immense size, building on the plain. Still there were the voices of gaiety, laughing at the idea of such a gigantic vessel being built so far away from the sea. But although every species of ridicule and scorn was thrown at Noah and his ark, although he was doubtless proclaimed a madman, a lunatic, an enthusiastic bigot and a fool, he went steadily on, until at last the ark was completely finished.

There was echo *then* of hammer sounds no more; and many doubtless tried to stifle the premonitions and forewarnings that there might be some truth in Noah's story after all. Noah was a "preacher of righteousness,"* remember,—God's witness in the midst of a godless, faithless, noisy world. But, for all that, they all went on their way sneering and ridiculing Noah and his ark "until the flood came."†

Just picture the evening before the flood. The ark is quite finished. The door of the ark is wide open. It is *capable* of containing thousands, but its mighty chambers will not be wanted. There will only be eight persons who will there take refuge.

Now, think of the evening before the flood. Think of the hushful rest in the air, of the strange, slaty light in the evening sky. Think of the peculiar sound that

* 2 Peter ii. 5. † St. Matt. xxiv. 39.

there must have been in the lowing of the herds in the meadows; the strange bleating of the sheep. The noises of the song of the birds must have been more like a twittering of terror. All nature seemed as if it were on the verge of some mighty cataclysm, something like that which they tell us precedes an earthquake.

My brethren, the eve of the flood must have had something tremendously dreadful and weird about it! The rivers became encased in a black, thickening mantle of cloud; a strange movement passed over the sea, restlessness filled the air, a crash of wind followed—then utter stillness again—just such as we have experienced ourselves at sea, before some terrible storm comes on.

Then all the scientists of the day, I expect, were trying to comfort the timid ones by explaining these omens away. They could easily be accounted for. Calculations and arguments were forthcoming to show what occasioned it all. *But somehow the hearts of the people could not be comforted.* There was a terrible dread.

All at once, amongst them, gigantic drops of rain began to fall; these were followed by more, and still more, until at last there seemed almost to be a quiver in the air, and a quiver in the earth; then whole sheets of water fell; and the streamlets and the cascades in the hills, instead of leaping downwards with gentle spray-splashing showers, began to come tumbling down in tremendous volumes of water. The streamlets turned to streams, the rivulets to rivers, the rivers to rolling floods; and at last all the plains were covered with water. And as the day went by—and the next day—a day of terror and alarm—cottages on the plains were surrounded with water, and men were beginning to take refuge in the highlands and on the hills.

Still down, with crash on crash, came the streams of waters from the clouds; and the torrents from the mountains were terrific in their might and their noise; and the falling rivers, from the hills, leapt with a fearful roar into the majestic mass of water that was spreading on every hand; the plains were vast sheets of storm-tossed spray and water.

Then, my brother, all the scientific explanations went for nothing. Nobody listened to the scientific explainer now. They climbed to greater heights as they saw the water coming up the mountain sides in the tremendous convulsion of nature—thus working its tempestuous way.

And now, see the agony depicted in the young mother as she holds her little darling to her breast, and looks down with a sob of anguish at the ark reposing majestically upon the waters of God's holy wrath. She pictures to herself the wives of the sons of Noah *safe in the ark;* she remembers how but a few days before she saw them enter amid the sneers and jeers of the throng; AND THEN *the door was shut by* ANOTHER HAND, and the bolt was drawn OUTSIDE *by a mighty power!*

"The Lord shut him in!"*

Brethren, Jesus Christ is God's Ark to-day. Jesus Christ, as God's Ark, has been sailing through the waters of the ages, gathering out His Church amid the scoffing, sneering world. He has been gathering out a people of peace, as the angels sang when Christ was born: "Glory to God in the highest, and on earth peace to men of good will" †—only to them. But "whosoever will"‡—whosoever will—let him come, and those that come are the "men of good will." "Ho, everyone that thirsteth come!" § "Come unto Me, all ye that labour and are heavy laden, and I will give you rest!" ‖ "Him that cometh to Me I will in no wise cast out."¶ "He is able to save them to the uttermost that come unto God by Him."** Come! Come! "the Spirit and the Bride say come!"†† The Ark of Christ's Church is gliding on the waters still; still sailing on the flood surface of this changing, restless world.

Weary men, tired men, men whose nobler life is

* Gen. vii. 16. † St. Luke ii. 14. ‡ Rev. xxii. 17.
§ Isaiah lv. 1. ‖ St. Matt. xi. 28. ¶ St. John vi. 37
** Heb. vii. 25. †† Rev. xxii. 17.

not satisfied, the undercurrent of whose existence is storm-tossed and hungry and restless, there is food for you in Jesus Christ. He can satisfy your whole being. He can saturate your peaceless souls with peace. He can give to your restless minds the great calm of God, "the peace of God that passeth all understanding."*

During the past week, in this hall, men have been getting *into* the peace, *into* the Ark of God; and men have been realising what it is to have Jesus Christ for their bulwark. Oh, brother! it is no mere beautiful poesy of an imaginative mind; it is no mere pretty picture of a poet's song; it is no mere fancy of an excited brain; it is the most stupendous reality that God's love could produce for the relief of weeping, dying mortals.

See the results in the hearts and lives of those who have believed. See the drunkard reformed from his cups; see the impure man who loves purity now, and lives in the constant enjoyment of the presence of Jesus Christ, Who says to him: "I will never leave thee nor forsake thee." † See the mourner whose tears are dried by that love of Jesus which is the consolation of God. Oh, see the man of sorrow, see the man of sin, see the man of pleasure, see the man of business, see the man of excitement, see any man,—I care not in what position,

* Phil. iv. 7 † Heb. xiii. 5.

of what temperament, of what peculiar characteristic he may be,—Jesus Christ is God's Anodyne for each and all; and those who have received Him have entered into rest, as the Apostle says: "We which have believed do enter into rest."*

Brother, this Ark of Jesus is open now, this afternoon. You can go on rejecting Christ; you can go on explaining Christianity away, or if you do not condescend to do that, you can go on ridiculing Christianity as a myth; but remember, my brother, that it is a very mighty myth. *It works more stupendous changes in men's lives and hearts and wills than anything else.* All your Acts of Parliament put together cannot change a man's heart, *and you know it.* By Act of Parliament you could wash the bodies of all the poor, filthy ones in the East End in water; but you could not wash their hearts, and this is what Jesus Christ does do. Whoever accepts Jesus Christ "is a new creature; old things are passed away; all things are become new."† Thou shalt "wash me and I shall be whiter than snow."‡

Yes, brother! when a man is in Christ he is altogether renewed; he is created over again. He receives a new understanding, a new life. He is born of God, of the incorruptible seed of God; and so Jesus Christ says: "Because I live, ye shall live also."§ "*The*

* Heb. iv. 3.   † 2 Cor. v. 17.   ‡ Psalm li. 7.   § St. John xiv. 19.

man in Christ" is a changed man, a newly created man. "The man in Christ" is a divine man—as the Apostle Peter says in his second Epistle: There "are given unto us exceeding great and precious promises that by these ye might be partakers of the divine nature;"* and as St. John says: "As many as received Him, to them gave He power to become the sons of God."†

Oh! brother, for this we believe God created us. He has only put us in this world for a few passing days—school days to prepare us for the great eternity, which stretches out through the everlasting years, in the infinite domains of the Kingdom of God. This life is only the infancy of our existence. We are placed here to be nursed and trained for the great eternity.

The one object of life is to get *into* the Ark and find in the Ark salvation—the divine nature received; so that the old nature that is in us, which is so sinful, so weak, so wretched, so painful, so sorrow-stricken and sin-stricken, may be overcome; and that we may have the victory, and, as St. Paul writes, be "more than conquerors through Him that loved us."‡

This, my brothers and sisters, is what you look at when you see the happiness and the reality of the change which has taken place in the converted Christian man. You may laugh and argue as much

---

* 2 Peter i. 4. † St. John i. 12. ‡ Rom. viii. 37.

as you like; but this is a phenomenon that must be accounted for.

Now, can you show me such a thing as a changed heart by any other process or power than that of the Gospel? You may force a man, against his will, for a few days or weeks to keep pretty decent. You may have your chains and shackles of the law brought to bear on him; but let him loose and he is just the same man.

But bring him to Christ the great Reformer; bring him to Christ the great Healer; bring him to Christ the great Saviour; the Shepherd of our race, our Elder Brother and our Friend, and what does Jesus do with the man? He takes him to Himself, He takes him INTO Himself, He gives to him new forces with which to work, He gives to him a new vitality in which to live.

And so it is that Jesus Christ proves Himself to be risen from the dead, for He lives, He reigns in the hearts of all who have accepted Him in His fulness.

My brothers and sisters in humanity but *not in Christ*, before you go out of this assembly you may be men and women *in* Christ. Art thou in Christ, as thou sittest there? It is Christ or no—you are or you are not. If you are not you may be, and you may be this moment, this very instant; for the only way to be a man in Christ is to accept Christ, in His fulness as God's gift to you now; "he that believeth on Him HATH everlasting life."*

That is it, and there is no other way of salvation. You must accept it as a gift or not at all. Salvation is not to be purchased. It is not wages for good works. You can do nothing which God will accept until you are saved. The only step between you and death is that one step—taking God at His word, accepting Christ as the Gift of God; and directly you accept that Gift you are in the Ark—which is Christ; you are a "man in Christ;" or, as St. Jude puts it, "preserved in Christ."† And then, remember, when once you are in Christ, God's power keeps you in Christ; for as Noah did not shut himself into the ark, but *the Lord shut him in*, so it is with us when once we are in Christ. We are "kept (there) by the power of God,"‡ says St. Peter. We are "preserved in Christ,"† as says St. Jude. We are, as the Psalmist says, "kept as the apple of God's eye; hidden under the shadow of His wings."§ My brother, Christ is waiting to be to you what He is to me; He is waiting to be to you what He is to every believer in this congregation.

Now I should very much like, (if the Lord Jesus has any disciples here, which I believe He has) I should like them to confirm the truth of what I am saying before those who cannot receive Him. Will my

* St. John iii. 36. † St. Jude i. 1.
‡ 1 Pet. i. 5. § Psalm xvii. 8.

brothers and sisters in Christ, who know that they are in Christ, will they rise up? Thanks be to God, more than half the congregation—thanks be to God—living witnesses for Jesus! Thank you, brethren, for rising up.

Oh! what a strength that rising up has given to my heart and soul and brain in speaking for the Master! I am not standing alone like poor Noah was. You see I am surrounded by my brothers and sisters who know God as I know Him. Then, my dearest friends, you, who are not in the Ark yet, will you do what we have done? Will you get into the Ark in the same way as we have got into it, *for there is* no other way *of getting in but that?* "Whosoever will"* let him come. And Jesus says, "Him that cometh I will in no wise cast out."†

Sin need not keep you *away.* Oh no! That is the very thing to *draw you to Him.* The more sinful I am, the more I want to come to Him to cleanse me. The more I realise my weakness, the more I want to come to Him for strength. And, brethren, "now is the accepted time."‡ We are only invited to come "*until* the flood" comes. Then all those who have rejected the gift of God will be swept away. And, as we have the picture in our text, "so shall also the coming of the Son of man be. Then shall two be in

* Rev. xxii. 17.   † St. John vi. 37.   ‡ 2 Cor. vi. 2.

the field, the one shall be taken, and the other left."*

Now I will just comment upon these words and conclude. We who have risen up have done so, not for mere form's sake, but to testify to the fact that we are in Christ, and "that the Spirit of God beareth witness with our spirit, that we are the children of God."† As the Apostle John says: "He that believeth on the Son of God *hath* the witness in himself."‡

Well, then, the Spirit of God witnesseth with our spirits; and upon that witness we rose up. We that are Christ's, when Christ comes, " shall be caught up to meet Him in the air."§ St. Paul, in the Thessalonians, gives us exactly the programme of the taking up of the Church. The world is to be going on its way, just as it is to-day, when all at once "the dead in Christ rise."‖ No one sees them rise; but from the gigantic necropolis of the great city, from the little tiny hamlet churchyard, hedged among the trees, the dead in Christ rise.

No one sees, no one hears, them; but "the dead in Christ shall rise first," and " we which are alive and remain shall not prevent "—that is, not go before— " them."¶

* St. Matt. xxiv. 39—40.   † Rom. viii. 16.   ‡ 1 John v. 10.
§ 1 Thes. iv. 17.   ‖ 1. Thes. iv. 16.   ¶ 1 Thes. iv. 16, 15.

When Christ comes, at the conclusion of the Christian dispensation; when He comes to take the Church out of the tribulation which is coming upon the nations, He will come in the air, and "the dead in Christ"* shall rise first. "Then we which are alive and remain shall follow them, and be caught up together with them in the clouds to meet the Lord in the air."† Jesus says: "One shall be taken and the other left; two men shall be in the field; the one shall be taken and the other left. Two women shall be grinding at the mill; the one shall be taken and the other left."‡

This is the Christian's hope; this is what all Christian people are waiting for, "looking for that blessed hope, and the glorious appearing of the great God and our Saviour Jesus Christ."§

But he cannot come until the last of the people that the Father gave Him has been gathered in. Directly the Gospel has gathered in the last then shall He come to take "His elect from the four winds."‖ Jesus says: "Where the body is there shall the eagles be gathered together,"¶ and Jesus is the body and the saints are the eagles.

My brothers and sisters, directly we have taken our places, by faith, in the company of God's family of the

---

* 1 Thes. iv. 16.   † 1 Thes. iv. 17.   ‡ St. Matt. xxiv. 40.
§ Titus ii. 13.   ‖ St. Matt. xxiv. 31.   ¶ St. Matt. xxiv. 28.

saved, *then our attitude with regard to Christ is waiting for His coming.* As far as we are concerned personally we know it cannot be long, because death is so near to all of us. In one hundred years' time every one of us will have been called face to face with God. But when we speak collectively of the Church, the Church's attitude has always been " waiting for the coming of our Lord Jesus Christ."* This is our attitude now, and, my brethren, would to God that this afternoon's discourse might be the means of making you realise this. It is a very simple thing being saved, as simple as it well can be.

Salvation is a gift sent from, and offered by, God to an aching, bleeding, dying race of pain-stricken mortals. The Gospel is a message of peace, a message that all may understand; so there is nothing difficult about it. It is Jesus Christ, in His fulness, offered *now* to you, His righteousness, His love, His peace, His salvation; God's gift to you *now*, and NOW you can take hold of it with childlike faith. The unlearned and the ignorant may take it in before the wise and the prudent.

And, brethren, never mind this learned doctor or that learned doctor, this theologian or that theologian. We have had too much theology. There is no true theological teacher but the Holy Ghost; and unless

* 1 Cor. i. 7

the Holy Spirit takes of the things of Jesus and shows them unto me, I cannot have peace. I know Bishop Butler's Analogy, and Bishop Pearson on the Creed, Dr. Harold Browne on the Thirty-nine Articles, and all the rigmarole of theological education; but this has nothing whatever to do with salvation.

I never knew anything of Christ when I was passing through my theological course. I hope my tutors did, but they did not communicate it to me!

I could sooner learn from the old, experienced, though illiterate, Christian peasant of the country village. He knew that Jesus had come as God's gift to him, and the power of the Holy Ghost had convinced him that he was a poor, lost sinner, and that Christ could save him if he would only trust Him. I would like to learn my theology at that old man's feet. That is the theology that gives the peace which comes from God; of which the Apostle St. John speaks: "You have no need that any man teach you,"—"the same anointing teacheth you of all things."* You have "an unction from the Holy One, and ye know all things."†

My brother, *that is it*. This was what St. Paul referred to when he said "I know"—what? Astronomy? How many planets there are in our solar system? Oh no—not any rubbish of that sort—these things do not feed my soul; they do not give me

* 1 John ii. 27. † 1 John ii. 20.

rest and peace. "I know whom I have believed" says St. Paul, "and am persuaded that He is able to keep that which I have committed unto Him against that day."* He also says: "We which have believed do enter into rest."†

This is the knowledge for which the Church teaches us to pray in the prayer of St. Chrysostom: "Grant to us in this world knowledge of Thy Truth." It is *only* the Holy Spirit Who can give us this; and the Holy Spirit is inviting you now. He says: "Whosoever will,"‡ let him come. Come, then, and you also will be able to say: "I know Whom I have believed, and am persuaded that He" will "keep that which I have committed to Him against that day."* "I will fear no evil; for Thou art with me."§

Jesus has said: "I will never leave thee nor forsake Thee."‖ "I am with you always,"¶ and I believe it, *and I know it is true,* and He has satisfied my heart and my brain and my mind, fulfilling St. Paul's words to the Corinthians—"Christ is made unto us" (that believe) "wisdom, and righteousness, and sanctification, and redemption."**

Oh! then, brother, do come and be safe in the Ark. There is no reason why any of you should not be so.

* 2 Tim. i. 12. † Heb. iv. 3. ‡ Rev. xxii. 17.
§ Psalm xxiii. 4. ‖ Heb. xiii. 5. ¶ St. Matt. xxviii. 20.
** 1 Cor. i. 30.

Only come. You have set before you the open door of the Ark. I have come to you as a "preacher of righteousness," not by works, but that "which is of God by faith."* I have set before you this *open door*, and "whosoever will"† come, let him come. Jesus invites you—Come. The Holy Spirit invites you—Come." The Church of Jesus, in this world, invites you—Come. Will you come? Oh! "how shall you escape if you neglect so great Salvation?"‡

---

* Rom. iii. 22.   † Rev. xxii. 17.   ‡ Heb. ii. 3.

XI.

Jesus at Bethany: Scene at the End of the Mission.

Mission Sermon.

Sunday Evening, October 25th, 1885.

Jesus at Bethany: Scene at the End of the Mission.

Prayer before Sermon.

O Almighty God and Father, Who, by Thine Apostle Paul hast told us that Thou "choosest the weak things of the world to confound the strong,"* the wise, and the prudent; wilt Thou, for Jesus Christ's sake, take me and come with strength to my body and to my spirit, that I may speak Thy Word with Power. Bless everyone here with the outpouring of Thy Holy Spirit, that all here may be able to listen with attentive minds; and bless me, for the people's sake, and grant me power for the sake of Jesus Christ our Lord. Amen.

---

* 1 Cor. i. 27.

JESUS AT BETHANY: SCENE AT THE END OF THE MISSION.

Mission Sermon.

Then Jesus six days before the Passover came to Bethany, where Lazarus was which had been dead, whom He raised from the dead.

There they made Him a supper; and Martha served: but Lazarus was one of them that sat at the table with Him.

Then took Mary a pound of ointment of spikenard, very costly, and anointed the feet of Jesus, and wiped His feet with her hair: and the house was filled with the odour of the ointment.—St. John xii. 1, 2, 3.

What a wonderful supper party this was, brethren, which took place at the close of our blessed Lord's Mission here to earth! But it is not half such a strange company as the companies we gather together at the close of missions like this.

Let us just look, for a few moments, at the story in the Gospel—for I am talking as a Christian, who believes in the truth of the Gospel, and therefore I am not going to apologise for the miracles referred to in the text. Let us just picture this supper party at Bethany.

Our Lord's earthly Mission is nearly at an end—it

is to be finished in five days' time, from this supper here referred to.

Five days after this supper He is to be crucified; and the world is going to end its rejection of Him by the tragedy of Calvary.

The enthusiasm—call it the fanaticism if you like—of Jesus Christ is very shortly to bring Him to the Cross. He has opposed the world in its religious ideas, in its moral ideas, in its philosophical ideas, in its political ideas—to all the ideas of the world, He has run exactly counter. He has taught with amazing simplicity; but with a simplicity which possessed a unique power; such a power, in fact, that it silenced all who came to Him; "Nor durst they ask Him any more questions"* after they had received his answers.

Therefore, while He repelled the self-righteous and the self-satisfied, He drew around Him all the needy, sorrowful, heavy-laden, and despairing ones.

Very well then, this supper was the last social meeting of Jesus Christ, with His earthly friends, before the tremendous finale to His earthly history.

This supper party is a very typical scene. You will see what I mean in a moment. It is in Simon's house at Bethany, who is supposed to have been the uncle of Lazarus. Martha and Mary are present, and Martha is busily engaged in domestic offices.

* St. Matt. xxii. 46.

Mary is at the feet of Jesus, behind Him. Once, on another occasion, she was behind Him, at His feet, in another Simon's house—Simon the Pharisee at Capernaum.

Lazarus is lying on one of the couches at the table. You all know how, in the east, the guests lie resting on couches at table, whilst the servants minister to them between the tables.

Lazarus is lying at the table. What a weird thought! the man who has been in the grave—whose body was turning to corruption—is at the table, eating and drinking before the guests.

I dare say some of you have seen Ernest Renan's attempt to explain away this resurrection. He says that no doubt something wonderful did happen; but he does not believe that anything of the sort recorded in the Gospels occurred. But how he arrived at the conclusion that something wonderful happened, from any other basis but that of the Gospel history, I cannot imagine, for there is no other historical record of the fact; and if we do not take the Gospel narrative as *correct*, we must condemn it as a *myth*.

The Gospel tells us that Lazarus had been dead—had been stinking in the grave; but he is now alive at the table. Mary is at the feet of Jesus, anointing them with ointment, and wiping them with her hair.

Mary is a type of Christ's moral power; Lazarus a type of Christ's physical power.

If you ask me which I consider is the greatest miracle, which the greatest phenomenon of the two resurrections—that of Mary Magdelene, from her moral death, or the resurrection of the mortal body of Lazarus from material death—I say, without any hesitation, I consider that Christ's miracle of the healing of Mary Magdalene far exceeds in grandeur and magnificence the mere restoration of the material body of Lazarus.

My brethren, I may as well say, in passing, that the attempts, of the present day, to present to the world a Jesus Christ from Whose history the supernatural is entirely eliminated is a most extraordinary feat; and I do not think that any one, with common sense, can accept, as an historical character, a Christ Who is not the Christ of the Gospels.

There are no other historical documents in existence respecting Him than the four Gospels. They were public writings of the time, and these four Gospels were deliberately and systematically denounced by the Roman Government, who chased these books from town to town and from city to city, to destroy them; and one of the means taken to suppress the reading of the Scriptures was that the Roman Government made it a capital offence to possess the Scriptures;

and any Christian who refused to give them up was put to death.

We Christians, brethren, who have the light of the Holy Spirit illuminating our hearts have no difficulty whatever in rejoicingly and implicitly accepting the picture that I now bring before you, as a simple, historical truth:—Mary Magdalene, the harlot of Magdala, out of whom Christ "had cast seven devils,"* Mary Magdalene, the fashionable woman of sin among the teeming population of the western shores of the lake of Galilee; the admired and the courted in the ranks of the Roman society, in the district at that time; Mary Magdalene, with all her sins and all her beauty, utterly, thoroughly, and radically changed by the teaching of Jesus Christ!

I dare say some of you have seen Rossetti's picture of Mary seeking Jesus at Simon the Pharisee's house. Through an open casement Jesus is to be seen, and Mary Magdalene, in the street, is surrounded by her lovers. Her hair is trimmed with flowers; one young fellow has his hand upon her arm, and another stands beside her, and the gossips are seen standing watching, with the greatest curiosity, to see what will happen—whether the chains of sin and sinful, earthly love will prevail; or whether there is a power that

* St. Mark xvi. 9.

will accomplish her deliverance from the life of sin. In Mary's eyes there is a far-away look, she does not seem to feel the clutch of the young man upon her arm, she does not seem to heed the earnest entreaties of the young fellow on her right; she seems to look right away, just as though she were seeing on through the spanless infinity of the everlasting years; just as though she were hearing the voice, in her soul, which was raising her from the death of sin in time, to lift her into a life of infinite righteousness in eternity. Her gaze seems to go right on, and up through the ether of our planet, to the mystic kingdom of the Eternal, and again she hears Jesus Christ preaching on the quiet summer evenings, by the Galilean lake.

We know what the result was. She did enter the house, and we know that in spite of all the paraphernalia of Jewish ecclesiasticism which surrounded the Pharisee, in spite of the scoffs through which she was sure she would have to pass, in that just man's house, without hoping to meet with a word of sympathy, she made her way, with amazing courage, and startling impertinence, into the very *canaculum* of the Pharisee's house.

Then, oh! how her eye glanced round the room, until she caught sight of *that* Face, Whose eyes had beamed upon her with such a mystic majesty; Whose lips had uttered sounds which had taken her out of herself, out of death and sin, and had lifted her into the joyful gladness of undying hope. Then, we know, how Jesus was not ashamed of her gaze; He did not shrink from the sinful woman's touch, as she bathed His feet with her tears and wiped them with her hair.

And Jesus Christ is not ashamed of His lost sheep to-day! He came to seek them out; and, therefore, He has given to His Gospel Message the self-same power that it possessed when it was spoken in the ringing words of Divinity Incarnate, on the Syrian lake-side.

Yes, there was a mighty resurrection from the death of sin, and from the taint of a sinful world, in Mary Magdalene's story—Mary Magdalene "out of whom He had cast seven devils."*

So, brethren, it seems to me, that Mary Magdalene's resurrection is certainly the nobler, grander, and more sublime picture and proof of Christ's infinite power upon which to gaze, than the resurrection of Lazarus.

The close of Christ's Mission presents to us then a very strange gathering. Simon the leper; Martha the busy, loving, devoted disciple; Mary Magdalene, whom Christ had raised from the darkness of earthly corruption; and Lazarus, whose body had stunk in the

* St. Mark xvi. 9.

grave of death; Lazarus, whose spirit had fled away through infinite fields of space—Lazarus, whose spirit had gone into the regions and realms of infinite mystery; but who never dared to utter a word of what his spirit had seen and heard in the mystic land; for there was a hush mantling over the soul of Lazarus, and he could not tell what he had seen.

Like St. Paul he had heard things "which it is not lawful for men to utter;"* and there he is as a picture showing Christ's power over matter; while Mary shows Christ's power over spirit. Yes, Mary Magdalene is reformed—as the Apostle says: "If any man be in Christ, he is a new creature; old things are passed away; behold all things are become new."†

Supposing, brethren, you were to see in the height of fashion and sin, and youthful beauty, one of the most sinful denizens of the fashionable world, with all her enamel, paint and smiles, and giddy laughter; supposing you were to see her in the midst of sin and guilty pleasure, and a week hence you were to find her in sober mourning weeds of penitence, utterly transformed, from within, and preaching the Crusade of love and purity, in the Name of Jesus Christ, Who had won her from sin to holiness, from Satan to God; what would you say had produced such amazing, startling results?

* 2 Cor. xii. 4. † 2 Cor. v. 17.

And again, if you watched that woman, year after year, climbing to greater heights of holiness, drawing numbers from sin and causing them to receive the self-same power that she had received, so that they should be able to realise the reality of what they professed, what would you say was the cause of this radical and sudden change? Some, no doubt, would say it was a delusion and caused by excitement.

But what was it that had been at work in Mary Magdalene? What was the power, what was the moral force, that had brought about this gigantic change?

And, remember, Mary Magdalene is only a type of a whole race of sinners who, from that hour to now, have been drawn out by Jesus Christ's love and the Gospel of His Cross.

And yet this Gospel which did, and which does, such moral wonders, which produces such startling moral phenomena, that there is nothing like it—this Gospel has been shelved even from our schools!

One young woman, who has been attending our services, has the misfortune of being in a board school, where infidelity and atheism surround her; and she came and told me that she was just on the point of beginning a life of sin in London, when the power of the Gospel entered her heart, and Jesus Christ took her under His care. I asked her last night, "Is Jesus Christ really holding you up, and do you realise His power at your side?" and, with a smile of gladness, the girl said: "Yes indeed."

I could tell you of many other instances to show you that the story of Mary Magdalene is no exaggerated picture upon which you are called to gaze. The Gospel of Jesus Christ is reproducing works of love, holiness, power and grace every day, in spite of the sneers of nineteenth-century enlightenment. Jesus Christ is doing for men and women what all our Acts of Parliament, and all our rationalistic doctrines and philosophies, cannot do. Jesus Christ is renewing, and is changing lives; Jesus Christ is transforming souls and bringing them into harmony with His holy Will, and that of the eternal Father God.

Jesus Christ is going on doing precisely what He did when He was here on earth; is doing precisely the same thing, by the power of His Own Word, in the mouths of His ministers.

It does seem to me a terrible piece of cruelty, from a social point of view, that Christianity should be treated in the cool fashion that it has been treated by our politicians and statesmen. They must give a sop to the tone of unbelief in the nineteenth century, by giving religion a blow here and a blow there. Our politicians are under the thumb of popular opinion— the god that is set up in our midst.

But popular opinion is not always infallible; it is not an opinion that brings calm and rest and joy and gladness to the weary, tired hearts of men.

I dare say if popular opinion were consulted upon a great many points, it would be very tender with vice of the worst description, vice that is really eating into the very core of humanity's existence. Popular opinion would deal very tenderly with fashionable vices, and with that scepticism and unbelief which exists in every stage of society.

But Christianity is still God's hallowed anodyne for weary souls; and the Voice of Jesus is the love-note of God to poor, friendless, weary, lonely souls.

Oh! those who carry Christ's Message see the results. No matter whether it be in the garret of the poor starving sempstress or in the palace of the noble and the wealthy—wherever the Gospel finds its way it brings peace and love and satisfaction and new life. And, you know, it is no beautiful dream about which I am talking. "As many as received Him," St. John says, "to them gave He power to become the sons of God."* Simple faith in Christ lifts a man up, and makes him a sharer in Divine nature; and he proves his conversion by his new life.

We ask our unbelieving friends to examine this renewed life, and to explain the marvellous change

* St. John i. 12.

that takes place in the minds and in the wills, in the hearts and in the lives, of the successors of Mary Magdalene.

Jesus Christ " did not come to call the righteous but sinners to repentance;"* and I ask you to look at the picture which the Gospel gives us of Jesus and His outstretched arms. I ask you to look on that dying Saviour's Blood and to listen to His words : " I came to seek and to save that which was lost."† "There is joy in the presence of the angels of God over one sinner that repenteth."‡

And so the result of a mission now is just the same kind of thing as we see at this supper at Bethany. How many are restored to home and to society at a Gospel mission ; how many are arrested just upon the threshold of a life of sin ; how many are drawn out of the cesspools of the world's iniquity and brought into " the peace of God which passeth all understanding !"§

How many parents, at missions like this, get back their children—a whole family of eleven were converted at one of our services !

Yes, the results of these missions are the bringing back of wanderers home, bringing back daughters to

* St. Matt. ix. 13 ; St. Mark ii. 17 ; St. Luke v. 32.
† St. Luke xix. 10.   ‡ St. Luke xv. 10.   § Phil. iv. 7.

their mothers' arms; restoring sons that are breaking their widowed mothers' hearts.

Where Jesus Christ is preached this is the result that follows the utterance of His mighty Word.

My brethren, this is the Word of Life. There is nothing but love in the Gospel. We are not to tell people to give up their sins. Christ did not say to the publicans that gathered around Him : " You infamous wretches, you ought to be ashamed of yourselves." No, He told them there was "joy in the presence of the angels of God over one sinner that repented."* He told of the great love of the Father God ; how He gave His Son to become Incarnate, to seek and to save. He told how He came to be a Shepherd to the lost sheep; and He showed how long He would seek for the lost—" until He find it."† He will never give up the search until He shall find His sheep.

There have been spiritual resurrections in our midst this week; the light of the Holy Ghost has revealed Jesus Christ to the souls of many.

If you say to me : " You ask me to give up my sin," I answer : No, I do not. All I ask of you is to receive Christ and to trust in Jesus. Directly you trust in Him His love fills you, and you will not care for sin ; you will not wish for the things of this world. Ask

* St. Luke xv. 10. † St. Luke xv. 4.

the man, whose heart is now renewed, and whose feet are securely planted upon the Rock of Ages, if he would like to go back to the gaming table and other pleasures of this world. He will tell you, "Certainly not!"

And I am sure the Lord Jesus never asked you to give up anything that is worth having, or that would do you good.

I wonder how many of you will reject the Message to-night. Of course there will be some, and they will make all sorts of excuses. But those excuses will not do in the end; you won't be satisfied with them yourselves in the end. At all events, whatever excuses you make you cannot deny that you reject something that has a most marvellous power for restoring the hearts and lives of men. And so, brethren, at the "End of the Mission" this is what we have to offer to you—the love of Christ. Literally, this is to-night a moral supper party, and the Gospel table is spread in this hall, at this moment; and numbers have sat down and partaken, and have risen up to newness of life; and they will go out from this place new creatures.

God grant that everyone gathered in this place to-night may sit, at last, at "the marriage supper of the Lamb,"* in that Glad Land, " where the wicked cease from troubling and the weary be at rest."† In that

* Rev. xix. 9.   † Job. iii. 17.

happy time, in that day, when the weary shall have rest, when the toils of life and the weary strife of earth shall be over, God grant that not one of you may be missing. If you shall be missing, if you shall fail to hear the Word of Jesus "Come, ye blessed!"* it will be your own fault—you will have rejected the offer of life.

God grant that everyone of you may meet me in the glory land of Heaven and say: "Here I am, I have been gathered out from the captivity of restlessness and tears and sin, and I am among the redeemed ones—the children of God. You may meet me, perhaps, in the golden streets of Jerusalem, when some magnificent procession is sweeping up to the mighty temple where "the Lamb that was slain"† is adored for ever and ever; and, perchance, you may touch me on the shoulder, in the throng, and say: "You told me of Jesus; I accepted Him, and He has brought me here."

And then the refrain of the heavenly anthem shall swing backwards and forwards, in the courts of gold, rejoicing with Him Who shall be singing: "I have found My sheep which were lost—rejoice! rejoice!! rejoice!!! I have found my sheep."‡ I have gathered them out from the filth and misery and tribulation of earth and sin; from the homes of poverty and woe,

* St. Matt. xxv. 34.   † Rev. v. 12.   ‡ St. Luke xv. 6.

"out of every kindred, and tongue, and people, and nation."* These are my sheep, and "of them that the Father gave to me have I lost none."† Rejoice, rejoice, rejoice. And oh! oh!! oh!!! as the decachordic strains die away they shall be echoed by the white-robed choirs, in a song of wondrous sweetness; but that song shall not be half so sweet as the one you and I shall be chanting when the angels' notes of welcome are hushed and the Church is singing: We have come "out of great tribulation, and have washed our robes, and made them white in the Blood of the Lamb."‡ "Blessing, and honour, and glory, and power be unto Him that sitteth upon the throne, and unto the Lamb for ever and ever."§

---

* Rev. v. 9.   † St. John xviii. 9.   ‡ Rev. vii. 14.   § Rev. v. 13.

XII.

The Lord's Day.

An Address to Christians.

Tuesday Afternoon, October 20th, 1885.

The Lord's Day.

Prayer.

Lord Jesus 'Christ, we are gathered, at this time, in Thy presence, as Thy believing people, and we desire to sit at Thy feet and to be taught of Thee. Thou seest our hearts, each one of us, and Thou knowest how we long to hear Thy voice because Thy voice is sweet and soothing to our souls, in the midst of life's terrible pilgrimage, through a world of sin and unbelief, of sorrow and pain.

Oh Shepherd, speak to Thy sheep; Oh Master, speak to Thy servants; Oh Saviour, speak to Thy redeemed. Oh Thou, our righteousness, speak to our inmost hearts. Build us up at this time in Thee. Cover us with the shadow of Thy wings; let us nestle among Thy feathers and be safe, and let Thy faithfulness be our shield; let Thy truth be the buckler to buckle it on.

And also, let us realise, at this time, how glorious it is for the Lord's people to dwell in the quietness of the Lord's Day. Make us to realise indeed that it is the Lord's Day. Make us to realise the brightness of the Lord's Day, the quietness, the light, the privileges thereof, for we are not of the darkness, but of the light, for a true light hath shone on us, and "the Sun of Righteousness has arisen"* for us who dwell under His wings. Oh, then, dear Lord Jesus, speak to Thy people in such wise that they may go forth from this place so fitted and comforted, instructed and clothed, that they may be stronger in Thy strength, to resist sin, the world, and the devil, and to continue "Thy faithful soldiers and servants unto their lives' end." Grant this, O Jesus, Who hast redeemed us with Thy most precious Blood, for Thine unending love and mercy's sake. Amen.

Malachi iv. 2.

THE LORD'S DAY.

An Address to Christians.

"And in *that day* thou shalt say, O Lord, I will praise Thee: though Thou wast angry with me, Thine anger is turned away, and thou comfortedst me."—Isaiah xii. 1.

I wonder how many of us here have ever said " Praise the Lord ! " to anybody. I wonder how many of us care whether people do " Praise the Lord ! " I wonder how many of us have really said, with our whole hearts, " Praise the Lord ! "

We are told further on in this chapter : " In that day shall ye say, Praise the Lord, call upon His name, declare His doings among the people, make mention that His name is exalted. Sing unto the Lord, for He hath done excellent things : this is known in all the earth. Cry out and shout"*—" Oh no, don't do that, don't do that, don't be like the Salvation Army people and make a noise about it."

But we just *will* make a noise about it, and I should be glad if I could get all of you to go down Ratcliff

* Isaiah xii. 4, 5, 6.

Highway, in a procession, singing and shouting "Praise the Lord!" It would be a good thing indeed if we knew a little more about the shouting: "Cry out and shout."

Some people cannot shout. They do not want to shout; they have nothing about which to make a noise. But here it explains itself. "Cry out and shout." But who is to cry out and shout? "Thou inhabitant of Zion."*

It is only these who have anything for which to shout. It is only the "inhabitants of Zion" who have cause to raise a loud shout. And why! let us see why! There is no doubt about the reason.

If we are *once* inhabitants of Zion we have a reason for shouting. "Cry out and shout, thou inhabitant of Zion; for great is the Holy one of Israel in the midst of Thee."*

When Jesus is in your heart, when His Blood has washed your soul, when His righteousness has clothed you; when He is your life and your salvation, when He is your strength, you will not be able to keep quiet; you will be so enthusiastic, so indiscriminate in your zeal, that you will not care about what people think. "I cannot help shouting, and they know for what reason I am shouting."

I want, this afternoon, to speak on the first words

* Isaiah xii. 6.

of this chapter. "In that day." I want to talk to my brothers and sisters in Christ about "that day." There are a great many people who talk about Christ's salvation, and the knowledge of Christ, and the peace of Christ, as if it were a thing that was *to come*. They say we cannot expect peace *here*. We never can be sure of being saved *here*. It is a thing to which we are to look forward.

I should think that a person who has his doubts as to whether he will spend eternity in heaven or hell, cannot be very happy. He is toiling among the shadows of night. He cannot see what's what, and he does not know anything for certain. There is a gloom and a shadow hanging over his very existence. It is just like a man on a strange road. He knows nothing precisely as to his whereabouts. He does not know what is the danger before him; he cannot see the pitfall here or the barrier there. He is all in the midst of darkness. It is night.

But I am talking now to people who are in Christ and for whom "the dayspring from on high hath visited"* the earth. I am talking to those now who are able to say, "through the tender mercy of our God."* "We are the children of light, and the children of the day: we are not of the night, nor of darkness."† St. Paul says that those who have believed, who have

* St. Luke i. 78.   † 1 Thess. v. 5.

accepted Christ; those who know Him, as their Saviour—those who have come to Him—they have been turned from darkness to light; and they have received forgiveness of sins. They are sanctified. They are not in the darkness but in the light. They are "children of light and of the day."*

Now "the day"—"*that day*"—the day of the Lord; the Lord's day. There was a time when God's dispensations, with regard to man, were like the evening twilight. You know the patriarchal and prophetic dispensations. They tended, like the shadows of the preceding evening and night, towards the brightness of the morning star, and they all pointed to the day. Now the day alluded to, in our text, is the day of the Gospel dispensation; the day when "the Sun of Righteousness shall arise with healing in His wings," † the day of which the Apostle says: "Now is the day of salvation." ‡ Salvation!

I repeat that people who are in the dark say that salvation is a thing to which they are to look forward. They say salvation is a thing for which we are to pray, and seek, at some *future time*. They talk as if salvation were a thing that we were to obtain at the judgment day.

The Apostle tells us *now* "to make our calling and election sure." § May I very lovingly put the question

* 1 Thess. v. 5.   † Mal. iv. 2.   ‡ Cor. vi. 2.   § 2 Pet. i. 10.

—are you, each one of you, and am I, quite sure that we are in this Gospel day?

I suppose we all belong to a *visible* Church. I suppose I am speaking here to people who are very good Roman Catholics or very pious English Catholics, or very devoted orthodox Protestants. I am doubtless also speaking to some very zealous, strict Dissenters. May I ask one and all, the Roman Catholic, the English Catholic, the Low Churchman, the Dissenter, may I ask each one—have you realised that Christ has come to you and given Himself to you, and that you have accepted Him, as God's covenant for *you* in the Gospel? If so, the knowledge that Christ really has arisen for you, "with healing in His wings;"[*] the knowledge of His great care for you, His promises made to you; His presents bestowed upon you—this knowledge gives to your life a *brightness*, and a *certainty* and an absolute *peace*, that enables you to say, you are "in the day." You are safe as safe can be. There are no shadows now to hide from you the salvation of God.

You are able to say that "you know that you have eternal life."[†] You can say this because you see Christ by the illuminating power of the Holy Ghost. You are able to say that Christ is your own, individual salvation, and, that you shall see the King.

---

[*] Mal. iv. 2.   [†] John v. 13.

You are able to say that you see in Christ your perfect protection from sin; yes, you see in Christ your " robe of righteousness."* You see in Christ " grace sufficient to help in time of need;"† and you are able to say, " In the Lord have I righteousness and strength."

If you are able to say all this, oh! is it not the most manifest spreading out of the Day of God on your soul ? What can crush out the brightness of this Sun that never sets when once He is risen ? What can crush out the brightness of that Day ? Nothing—and you take the words of my text and say, " Lord, I will praise Thee."

Jesus Christ has turned away God's righteous anger from me. Jesus Christ has reconciled me to God, and washed me whiter than snow‡ and has given me grace " to help me in every time of need."‖ " Thine anger is turned away, and Thou comfortedst me."§ You are safe in the "everlasting arms"¶ of that Shepherd, out of which "no man shall pluck you." Yours are the blessed " promises of Christ, which are all yea and amen;"** with you is His very presence. " I will never leave thee."†† " I am with thee always."‡‡

" Thine anger is turned away and Thou comfortedst

* Isai. lxi. 10. † Heb. iv. 16. ‡ Ps. li.7.
§ Isai. xii. 1. ‖ Heb. iv. 16. ¶ Deut. xxxiii. 27.
** 2 Cor. i. 20. †† Heb. xiii. 5. ‡‡ St. Math. xxviii. 20.

me."* Oh! the blessing of God's Incarnate love, so strong, so tender, and so kind! "I can lay me down and take my rest, for He maketh me dwell in safety."† There shall no evil happen to me, "neither shall any plague come nigh my dwelling,"‡ for it is in the cleft of the rock I have hid myself—in the "Rock of Ages." "Rock of Ages cleft for me" *I have hid myself in Thee.*

"In that day thou shalt say, Oh Lord, I will praise Thee; though Thou wast angry with me, Thine anger is turned away, and Thou comfortedst me."* Satan and sin rise up against me; Satan reminds me of my infirmity and weakness, and then a voice at my side assures me: "Whiter than snow."§ "The Blood of Jesus Christ cleanseth us from all sin."‖

Oh! when I remember the days that, in agony of mind and terror of conscience, I looked forward to a righteous judgment to come, and when my conscience told me that God was just, and I deserved an everlasting hell for being a rebel against so good a God; it was in the shadow of night, and under the conviction of sin, that I was yearning for the "Dayspring" to arise, that I might see the goodness and loving kindness of God for me. *And He wiped away every single spot upon my soul.* "O Lamb of God, I come;" but

---

* Isaiah xii. 1.   † Ps. iv. 8.   ‡ Ps. xci. 10.
§ Psalm li. 7.   ‖ 1 John i. 7.

to the feet of Jesus I can only come by the power of God's Holy Spirit convincing me of my sin and of Christ's love.

And I say I was convinced. Oh! then "the dayspring from on high"* rested on my soul, and I entered into the day of God, and day took the place of the dark, stormy night of pain, and I could look up to Him with joy because I was reconciled to Him.

And He led me forth right up to the Father's throne; and I was accepted in the blessed Son. Peace, like a river, streamed into my soul then. The Blood of the Son has cleansed me, and the love of God, in Christ, has received me, and I am comforted with "the peace of God"—"the God of all comfort." †

It is the Lord's Day for me now; and the Lord's Day has no sunset, the Lord's Day has no ending. It is one perennial day of everlasting happiness begun in time, never to be ended. "In that day thou shalt say: Lord, I will praise Thee: though Thou *wast* angry with me, Thine anger is turned away."‡

"I have blotted out thy transgressions;" § "Thy sins and thy iniquities will I remember no more." ||

"And Thou comfortedst me." "Comfort ye my

---

* St. Luke i. 78.   † 2 Cor. i. 3.   ‡ Isaiah xii. 1.
§ Isaiah xliv. 22. || Heb. viii. 12.

people, saith your God."* "*Now* is the accepted time; *now* is the day of salvation."† Supposing there be anyone here who has not entered into this day yet, who is still in the night and shadow of formalism; supposing there should be anyone listening to me here who has a church, but has no Saviour!

Supposing there should be a person here who has plenty of ceremonial, and plenty of church, who is a very devoted member of his own church, but still he does not belong to that Church of which it has been said: "Upon this rock I will build My Church, and the gates of hell shall not prevail against it."‡ Such an one cannot make anything of what I am saying. "This bright day that delights the souls and the minds of the children of God, with the brightness of its beauty and its light: to him it seems only like the singing of a beautiful psalm; and he will go on his way and say that he has heard a fanatic who speaks of a kind of Arcadian religion, a Utopian scheme of religion, where everything has brightness, gleam, and light.

Supposing such an one be here: I ask you, would you like to come into this day of which I speak, provided it be a reality? You answer me: "Yes," because you know, brother, that you are not satisfied with your religion — your churchianity. You

---

* Isaiah xl. 1.   † 2 Cor. vi. 2.   ‡ St. Matt. xvi. 18.

know that your Church does not satisfy you, and give you peace. You know, many a time, when your priest has turned round from the altar, at the end of the Holy Communion Service, and has said: "The peace of God which passeth all understanding, keep your hearts and minds,"* &c., you have not felt peace. You know that you have not.

You exclaim, perhaps, "The peace of God keep my heart and mind! I don't know what it is to be at peace. How can I be at peace while there is a chance of an everlasting hell?"

Yes, you are uncertain about your eternal salvation. How, then, can you be at peace? But Jesus says, "Come unto Me, and I will give you rest."† Jesus says, "In Me ye might have peace;"‡ and the Apostle to the Roman Church says, "Therefore being justified by faith, we *have* peace with God."§

How can you get into *this day?* Jesus Christ is the Morning Star. "I am the bright and morning Star."‖

Will you just look up into His face for a moment? He is in the midst of us now; for He has said: "Where two or three are gathered together in My name I am in the midst of them."¶ He is in the midst of us now.

---

* Phil. iv. 7. † St. Matt. xi. 28. ‡ St. John xvi. 33.
§ Rom. v. 1. ‖ Rev. xxii. 16. ¶ St. Matt. xviii. 20.

Will you close the eyes of your body and look up, with the eyes of your soul, into the face of this present Saviour, and then say: "Lord Jesus, may I trust Thee; will it be safe for me to trust Thee?" He says: "Trust ye in the Lord for ever." "Dear Lord Jesus, may I trust Thee now?" "Whosoever will, let him come."* "Him that cometh to Me, I will in no wise cast out."† "He that believeth on Me—not may have—*hath* everlasting life."‡

"Is it safe to take Thee at Thy word? Won't it be presumptuous for me to believe and trust in Thee?" "Oh! soul, for whom I died, is it presumptuous to say that you *know* that you have eternal life?"

The instant you can speak to Jesus like this the dayspring begins to dispel the clouds of night, which give place at length to Jesus, "with healing in His wings"‖ for you, Who enables you to know that you believe and have eternal life.

"He that hath the Son hath life."§ By the witness of the Spirit you can thus lay hold of Jesus with all your soul, and then it is the "Lord's Day" with you. In your soul it is "the Lord's Day," and in your mind it is "the Lord's Day;" and you are out of the darkness of the children of night.

I have revealed Thy light to them that "sit in dark-

---

* Rev. xxii. 17. † St. John vi. 37. ‡ St. John iii. 36.
‖ Mal. iv. 2. § 1 St. John v. 12.

ness."* "A light to lighten the Gentiles, and the glory of Thy people Israel."† "Now lettest Thou Thy servant depart in peace, according to Thy word: for mine eyes *have* seen Thy salvation."‡ "My soul doth magnify the Lord, and my spirit hath rejoiced in God *my* Saviour."§

In that day you shall say: "O Lord, I will praise Thee: though Thou wast angry with me, Thine anger is turned away, and thou comfortedst me."‖

Perhaps, brethren, there is a soul here that is just coming into the day. Listen to what the Holy Spirit says to him. "As one whom his mother comforteth, so will I comfort you; and ye shall be comforted in Jerusalem,"¶ the Church of the Redeemed, the Holy City of Refuge; the people purchased by the Precious Blood, the people of whom Jesus says: "All that the Father giveth Me shall come to Me; and him that cometh to Me I will in no wise cast out."**

"Cry out and shout, thou inhabitant of Zion: for great is the Holy One of Israel in the midst of thee."††

In conclusion, you have expected me to speak about Sunday. True. By the words "the Lord's Day" we mean Sunday. We can call the day a Salvation Sunday. But the Christian's life is a continual Sunday. "There remaineth a sabbath-keeping for

---

* Psalm cvii. 10.   † St. Luke ii. 32.   ‡ St. Luke ii. 29, 30.
§ St. Luke i. 46, 47.   ‖ Isaiah xii. 1.   ¶ Isaiah lxvi. 13.
** St. John vi. 38.   †† Isaiah xii 6.

the people of God."* The Christian's life is a sabbath life, but in what sense? In this sense. God, on the Sabbath, rested from His works.

What is the Gospel sabbath? We who have entered on the Lord's Day, rest from our works. But Christ's people do not remain in their beds all Sunday, although they stop their work. They have ceased from work, but they rise earlier on the Sunday morning than ever; and if they were to meet a worldly friend out in the street, he might say to them, "I thought you looked on this as a day of rest." "Oh, yes," the answer would be; "but I am going to the Lord's work."

He ceases from his own work, and then the Lord begins to work in Him. He ceases from all strivings to buy salvation. He has done with that. "He ceases from his own works, as God did from His,"† and then God begins to work *in him*, "to do of his good pleasure,"‡ and the Christian's works are works from, not for, salvation. They are works which spring from love, out of gratitude. So many of our Catholic friends misunderstand us here. They say we do not preach "good works."

What we say is this. It does not matter to what church you belong, or what you do, before you have come to Christ and are saved. God tells the sinner, you are a poor lost soul, and you can do nothing to

* Heb. iv. 9.   † Heb. iv. 10.   ‡ Phil. ii. 13.

help yourself; but I have provided in My Son a full salvation for you; *and if you will accept it, by the hand of a simple faith, it is yours.* Have you received it? If you have, you will manifest it. You will show forth His glory. You will strive to do the works of the Spirit, and they will be done out of love for Him who first loved us.

So the believer is in the Sabbath. He has done with working for salvation. His works now are the works of love and gratitude towards Him who loved us.*

The Christian's life is a continual sabbath life. Yet it is full of works that are done in a spirit of loving gratitude and active rest.

But how shall we keep the literal Sunday? Very determined attempts are now being made amongst us to bring about a sort of continental observance of the Lord's Day. You hear people say to boys: "If you go to mass in the morning, you can have a game at cricket in "the afternoon." I would say to these, I am certainly "not under the law, but under grace,"† and Christ is in my heart, and you will try in vain to get me to give *half an hour* of Sunday to the devil!

The Church, by unanimous consent, has given Sunday to Jesus. I would just as well commit any other theft as play a game at cricket on Sunday. Why do

* St. John iii. 16.   † Romans vi. 15.

I keep Sunday holy? Because I am afraid I shall go to hell? Oh, no. We Christians keep the Lord's day holy, as the freewill offering of our hearts to Jesus.

It is all our precious Saviour's Day. Every hour belongs to Him; and all His people praise Him every hour of the Lord's Day, from very love of Him.

That is the spirit in which the believer keeps the Lord's Day. They tell me I need not keep the afternoon for God if I keep the morning for Him. It would be no enjoyment for the believer to keep away from the Lord's House on the Lord's Day. We want to get nearer to Him. The six days of the week are long enough, and when Sunday comes it is "the Lord's Day," every hour of it; and I would not rob Him of half a minute of that day.

This is the view that the true Christian believer takes of the Sabbath; and it is a very happy view.

When we go early in the morning to meet our Lord in the mystic Feast of His dying love, we come home with fresh oil poured into the lamp of the soul, and then comes the solemn midday act of worship of the King Who so loved, and loves, us. Oh! the blessedness of enjoying the Lord's Day—with Jesus and for Jesus.

And then, when we see the sun gradually getting into the west, and Sunday evening shadows falling, we regret to think that the Lord's Day is nearly over —Sunday is gone!

A Sunday well spent with Jesus gives such strength to the soul for the coming week; and we may look back with gladness on the Sundays of our lives that have been like golden steps leading right up to the Throne of God.

Oh! prize your Sundays, Christian people; treasure up the holy hours: and we shall be "in the Spirit on the Lord's Day";* and those who live the Lord's Day best on earth are those that have entered into the Lord's Day of salvation.

On Sunday let us leave the world in the distance; the roar of the storm is lulled, and we are in spirit near the calm land, the other side of the sea; where the wicked cease from troubling and the weary are at rest."†

---

* Rev. i. 10. † Job. iii. 17.

XIII.

The Lord's Cross.

An Address to Christians.

Friday Afternoon, October 23rd, 1885.

The Lord's Cross.

Prayer before Sermon.

Oh! Blessed Lord Jesus, Who didst feed us yesterday at the Gospel Feast, and didst help Thy people to realise what was the full provision that our Father's love had made for us in the Gospel Feast; we now come and gather round Thee to be taught about Thy Cross. Thou hast taught us about Thy people, Thou hast taught us about Thy supper; and now we would have Thee teach us more about Thy Cross at this time than we have ever known before, if it be Thy Blessed Will.

Be mindful of Thy promise that, if we "take no thought what we shall speak it shall be given us."* Oh! Shepherd of the sheep, show us Thy face and Thy riches, and we shall be glad; and Thy words will be, in very deed, sweet to our taste, for Thy people live by every word that proceedeth out of Thy mouth.

We know that Thou art in the midst of us, and that Thy presence is hallowing our assembly. Oh! let us, each one, realise that Thou art indeed here to teach, to comfort, to strengthen and to guide Thy sheep in the way of everlasting life; and Oh! Blessed Saviour Jesus! make each separate one here present to realise that Thou art here for him, as though there were none here but Thee and himself—*Jesus* and *me*.

And then, with eyes and hearts closed to all sights and thoughts and sounds but Thy voice, let us, in the quiet of Thy presence, sit in the school of the Holy Ghost and be taught at Thy dear feet.

Our hearts cry out, "Speak Lord, for Thy servant heareth." Glorify Thy Name by answering our supplications; and then, whilst Thou art glorified in us Thy people, we shall be blessed in Thee our living hope, for Thy loving mercy and Thy truth's sake. Amen.

* St. Matth. x. 19.

THE LORD'S CROSS.

An Address to Christians.

"Save in the Cross of our Lord Jesus Christ."—Gal. vi. 14.

Now, beloved brethren, it is very easy for us to repeat over those words. Here we are quietly and calmly sitting in this room, afraid of no disturbance, afraid of no suffering for believing these words to be true and right and real. But before I attempt to uncover the Cross of Jesus, by the help of the Holy Spirit, I want to ask you to look at St. Paul's position when he spoke those words.

All St. Paul's troubles and persecutions arose from his preaching Christ crucified and glorying in the Cross and in nothing else. St. James, Bishop of Jerusalem, did not care much for St. Paul; and when St. Paul came to Jerusalem, after begging money in all the churches for the poor saints at Jerusalem, although he came with all the offertories he had collected, James never invited Paul to his house.

St. Paul had to stop somewhere else; and he was taken to see St. James one day, but there was a tremendous disturbance brewing in Jerusalem. The Jewish Christians hated St. Paul.

If it had not been for the destruction of Jerusalem the Church of Jerusalem would have been a hindrance in Christendom, for they in Jerusalem wanted to mix up a Jewish ceremonialism with Christianity. They wanted to teach a sort of half-and-half Christianity. Yes, believe in Jesus; but go to the temple, offer sacrifices, join in the Jewish ceremonies, and make it a *sine qua non* that people should be circumcised!

So taught a very strong and powerful school among the Jewish Christians, and we know perfectly well that St. Peter, although he knew it was wrong, was very much inclined to side with them at Antioch; and although he was very good and sound on the principles of the Gospel, until "certain came from James,"* he then turned his coat—his teaching—for fear of the Jewish element, working in the Church.

But St. Paul withstood all opposition. St. Peter wanted to strain a point for popularity's sake. St. Paul stuck to the one point, "I am determined not to know anything among you save Jesus Christ and Him crucified." †

Then followed riots in the temple (for they used to fight in churches in those days as in ours), and on one occasion there was a riot in the north-west corner

* Gal. ii. 12. † 1 Cor. ii. 2.

of the temple near the fortress of Antonia, where the Emperor of Rome used to keep his soldiers; and these soldiers had to go, in great numbers, and take Paul by main force out of the hands of the Jews, because they wanted to kill him; and that because St. Paul would know nothing but the Cross. You know the meaning of the word *nothing*. "God forbid that I should glory save in the Cross."* Nothing else. In the Cross of Jesus Christ.

I just want, with the help of God's Holy Spirit, to ask you to follow me in the question : What does this Cross mean? Perhaps some who are listening to me do not approve of figurative interpretations of Scripture; but I must allude to one now—the widow woman picking up sticks. If the widow woman had not gone to pick up those sticks she would never have met the Lord's messenger; she would never have had her vessels filled with oil. The English Church, for many hundreds of years, has taken this act of the widow woman as a typical act of faith in the Cross.

The Cross was made of two sticks; and the doctrine of the Cross is made up of two parts; and both of them are so full of insult to the pride of the heart and the intellect—that the doctrine of the Cross will never be popular, and was never meant to be popular.

* Gal. vi. 14.

What is the doctrine of the Cross? The first part of the doctrine is that we must give up all idea of human merit as having anything to do with salvation. That is the first part of the doctrine of the Cross. It is no good mincing matters; and my hearers know that I never do mince matters.

This must be taken hold of firmly, as the first part of the doctrine of the Cross. If you go to Christ for salvation, there must be a thorough putting aside of all works of righteousness that you have done. As St. Paul writes: "Not by works of righteousness which we have done, but according to His mercy He saved us."* There is no such thing as human merit apart from Christ, and God will accept nothing whatever apart from Christ.

Come to Christ as a sinner, or not at all; and our Lord very emphatically puts this. He tells us clearly that He did not come for the righteous—but for sinners. "The Son of Man is come to seek and to save that which was lost."† Therefore until a man realises that he is utterly lost, and is yearning to come to Christ as a lost sinner; until the Holy Ghost convinces him of sin, and he is in absolute need of Jesus—until the Holy Ghost convinces him that his very "righteousnesses are as filthy rags,"‡ there is no doctrine of

---

* Titus iii. 5. † St. Luke xix. 10. ‡ Isaiah lxiv. 6.

the Cross in his heart, and there is no salvation by the Cross in his soul.

This is the first part of the doctrine of the Cross, and St. Paul used to affront people very much about it. When he writes to the Roman Church he says: "Not of works, but of Him that calleth."* Apart from Christ the most moral sinner and the most immoral sinner are alike before God.

Very often, when I am preaching this, people get up and walk out. They will not be told: you cannot do anything to save yourself; you must go to Christ, and Christ alone, for salvation; and that salvation is a free gift. It is of faith and not of works. All we have is of the free gift of God.

You know how fond I am of putting two chairs on the platform side by side. I am going to do it now. There are two chairs. *There* is the most religious person in Westminster; the most religious, philanthropical Church professor. He would not do any bad action for the whole world. And *here* is the most immoral, licentious, wicked villain that London can produce. St. Paul says to them: "You are both sinners." Then this gentleman gets up and says: "Oh, no. That is the most immoral person in the world. You cannot class him with me." I say to him, "Are you saved?" "No," he answers, "I cannot say

* Rom. ix. 11.

that I am; but I hope to be saved." I then ask the other, "What do you say, my friend?" "Oh! I say that I am a poor lost sinner, and I know it; there is no one in the world worse than I am." Then I say to that poor lost sinner: "You are likely to enter into the Kingdom of God before that man; and, until that man will take in the truth, that 'there is no difference'* before God, because they have both sinned, and his 'righteousnesses are as filthy rags,'† just the same as your immorality, he cannot be saved." The two men are both sinners in God's sight.

This is the doctrine that brings the sinner very low in the dust. Every one "that humbleth himself shall be exalted; and he that exalteth himself shall be abased."‡ A sinner comes to salvation, is washed in the Blood of the Lamb; the righteousness of Christ clothes his soul, and the sanctification of the Holy Ghost conforms him gradually to the likeness of his Lord. He is greatly exalted. The self-righteous one comes down to a great abasement. This is the first part of the doctrine of the Cross.

What is the other part? The first doctrine took away from me my own righteousness; the next gives me the righteousness which is of God, by faith. The arms of the Cross hold out to me the righteousness which is the righteousness of God—a perfect righteous-

* Rom. iii. 22.   † Isaiah lxiv. 6.   ‡ St. Matt. xxiii. 12.

ness, which enables the sinner to be holy before his God. How can I be holy, in the holiness of God, unless God clothe me with that holiness by a free gift?

The arms of the Cross hold it out to me; it is a free gift. "The righteousness of God, which is by faith,"* The Cross holds out to me Jesus in His fulness, and gives me "wisdom, and righteousness, and sanctification, and redemption."† This is the other doctrine of the Cross. Put them together, and then you have the whole truth that Paul preached, and for which Paul suffered.

Brethren, the human heart rebels against the Cross, because it is counter to itself. The holy doctrine of the Cross takes away, and crushes, self and exalts Christ; those who are believers in Christ know that they are justified through faith in Jesus; but in no other way.

So it is "not by works of righteousness, which we have done, but according to His mercy He saved us."‡ Now, who amongst our congregation, this afternoon, can say my text from their hearts? "God forbid that I should glory, save in the Cross of our Lord Jesus Christ."§

When the believer knows that the Blood of Christ has cleansed him, washed him "whiter than snow;"‖

---
* Rom. iii. 22. ‡ Titus iii. 5.
† 1 Cor. i. 30. § Gal. vi. 14. ‖ Psalm li. 7.

when the believer, safe in the arms of Jesus, realises that he is "justified freely"* from all sins, that God has put away his iniquity, that he is one of those that are "blessed, to whom the Lord will not impute sin;"† whose "transgression is forgiven;"‡ then the believer rests in the finished work of the Cross—then the believer can trust Jesus. He has finished the work for us, and as His work *for* us was perfect, so His work *in* us will be perfect, until the day of the Lord: for He will present every one of us perfect before God.

"Waiting for the coming of our Lord Jesus Christ: Who shall also confirm you unto the end, that ye may be blameless in the day of our Lord Jesus Christ."§ He has promised that we shall be blameless in the day of His coming. The Cross is very precious to the believer; "to us which are saved it is the power of God."‖ To us, who are invited to this believers' meeting, this picture is indeed precious, because we have found Him to be our individual, present salvation, life, righteousness, grace, strength.

We believe that He cannot leave us because He has said that He will "never leave us."¶ We believe that our Shepherd's hand is a strong and safe one, and holds us; and He says that "no man shall pluck us out of His hand."** We believe He is

---

* Rom. iii. 24. † Rom. iv. 8. ‡ Ps. xxxii. 1.
§ 1 Cor. i. 7, 8. ‖ 1 Cor i. 18. ¶ Heb. xiii. 5.
** St. John x. 28.

Almighty. We are "kept by the power of God;"* and "being justified by faith, we have peace with God;"† and we can cry out, from our hearts, with the blessed Apostle of the Gentiles: "God forbid that I should glory, save in the Cross of our Lord Jesus Christ."‡

Dear brethren, do not let us be afraid of the true, dear old message. Do not let us think that it cannot take care of itself. Do not let us think that the nineteenth century will not stand it. None of the centuries have ever stood it. They have always been against it. It is a doctrine which the world will always reject; but nevertheless it is the doctrine that *draws out* the people of God. It is God's fishing-net; and it is a net which never breaks, in which no bad fish can ever be. It is not the fishing-net of the visible church. It is the net of the Holy Cross, which gathers in for God those of whom Jesus says: "I know my sheep."§

As I was coming through that door, the other day, and passing on to that one, a gentleman sitting here would not let me pass, and taking hold of my hand, he said: "Oh, Reverend Father, I must speak to you, and tell you how thoroughly I enjoy what you say and endorse it;" and I said, "I see you belong to Christ, and therefore, as you realise my words, you

* 1 Peter i. 5.   † Rom. v. 1.   ‡ Gal. vi. 14.   § St. John x. 14.

enjoy them." I thought at first that he belonged to the Plymouth Brethren; but it turned out that he was an Evangelical Roman Catholic; and he said to me that many Protestants actually deny that there is any such thing as an Evangelical Roman Catholic. "They do not know," he said; "and if they only knew the true teaching of our Church they would see there is nothing to prevent our saying with St. Paul: 'God forbid, that I should glory, save in the Cross of our Lord Jesus Christ.'"* Oh! when the believer says, pointing with extended finger "to the martyrdom of the Cross" (that is the Death of Jesus, the Martyr of Humanity), *there* is the beginning and ending of my salvation, he has indeed received the power, the glory, the salvation and the love of Jesus Christ Himself.

Catholic or Protestant, it does not matter half so much about the external worship; as long as you worship God lovingly, and with a child-like faith, you are both saved in Jesus. And I say, from my heart, if the Roman Catholics set forth Jesus, in His fulness, with a greater simplicity and love and reverence than the Protestants, I hope they may be paramount; and if the Protestants do so more than the Roman Catholics, I hope they will influence the children of God.

Whatever we are let us see that we are under the banner of the grace of God, by manifesting love to

* Gal. vi. 14.

the brethren; for "by this shall all men know that ye are My disciples, if ye have love one to another;"* and you will be better able to go through the persecutions and sufferings that God calls you to endure from an unbelieving world.

When I find that I am allowed, by the Master, to gather round me a company of believers in Jesus, who are Roman Catholics, High Churchmen, Low Churchmen, Dissenters, &c. (for we have such strange unions at our missions)—of all who call Jesus *Lord* in sincerity and truth—I say with the blessed Apostle: "God forbid that I should glory, save in the Cross of our Lord Jesus Christ;"† for this "is the Power of God unto Salvation to every one that believeth."‡

---

* St. John xiii. 35. † Gal. vi. 14. ‡ Rom. i. 16.

XIV.

The Lord's Mother.

An Address to Christians.

Saturday Afternoon, October 24th, 1885.

The Lord's Mother.

Prayer before Sermon.

Lord Jesus, Thou art here now, in the midst of us yet again, to bless us and to teach us; and we are gathered around Thee, at this time, once more, as Thy believing people, to whom Thou has made Thyself known, and who are known of Thee, as Thy sheep, whom the Father has given Thee. We have also the comfortable assurance that we belong to Thee and that Thou dost, as the Father's gift, belong to us.

We wish now to enter into the quiet of Thy presence and into the calm of the Holy Ghost. Oh! blessed Lord, grant that true words and wise words may be heard at this time; words that shall glorify Thee and give blessing to our own souls. Open up to us the mystery of Thy Mother. Help us to think aright concerning the tremendous mystery of Thy Incarnation; and if there be here present, in our midst, any of Thine own dear people, who have been taught, through any prejudice, to feel aught against her Who brought Thee into the world, Oh! wilt Thou grant that the presence of Her Son, Thyself, may make their thoughts silent and still while the Holy Ghost, Who overshadowed her, and made her Thy Mother, shall interpret to us more of the mystery of that wonderful love of God, that gave Thee to take our nature from Her, in order that Thou mightest redeem Thy people and bring them back, as reconciled children, to God.

And oh! help me, Blessed Jesus, that no words of over-zeal or over-love for Thy Mother may cause me to grieve the hearts of any of those now before Thee. Let the words that shall be given us to speak, and to hear, be indeed for Thy glory—be indeed well pleasing to Thee and for the profit of Thy people here present. Grant, dear Lord Jesus, our supplications, and favour us with Thy blessing, now and for evermore. Amen.

THE LORD'S MOTHER.

An Address to Christians.

"Mary, the mother of Jesus."—Acts i. 14.

Well! These few words go right into our hearts, because we are the people of God. Let me say them over again; because there is such a wonderful charm and such a wonderful power in them. "Mary, the Mother of Jesus." What! Do you believe, and do I believe, that Jesus had a Mother? Do you believe and do I believe that Jesus has a mother now—at this very moment? Do we believe that there is such a being in existence, at this very moment, as the Mother of Jesus? It seems blasphemy, at first sight, to say that Jesus had a Mother, and has a Mother. But we do believe it, and, at this very moment, while our blessed Lord Jesus is in our midst, and while we are now enjoying a sense of His presence, we believe that He has a Mother.

It is an awful thought, but it is a true thought. Our blessed Lord and Saviour has a Mother; and if He had not we should all be damned for ever. Why?

Because it is the Blood of the Lamb that has saved us, and there is no pardon except through the human blood of Jesus. If Jesus had no Mother He would have no blood! What an awful mystery is this!

I am speaking to Christians only now. But I am also speaking to men and women who, all, every one of them, have mothers. The greyest-bearded man, listening to me now, has a mother either here or in the spirit world; and most of us love our mothers; most of us love them with a love with which we have never loved anyone else.

There is a peculiarity about the love for a mother which there is in no other love. It is nothing like (if I may use the words reverently) the selfish love of the husband towards the wife. It is not the love which we have for a friend, or for any other relation. The love of a mother is something that seems to be one of the initiatory mysteries of our existence. The very first sensation of our hearts was love for our mothers. We can almost recall the time when we could only just put our arms round our mother's neck with tenderness, in giving her the first kiss.

My mother! There is no other relationship that touches the heart like the one expressed by these two words! "My mother!" Of course I am not speaking now to those who, unhappily, have had very bad, wicked mothers. Though, even then, there is something in the thought of "my *mother*" that would make it agonising to think anything that was bad of *her*.

But now we are only thinking of the general run of Christian mothers, and of the charm there is in the words "my mother."

Do I not recollect, myself, how proud I used to be of my mother? I remember when a boy at school, and the Apposition Day came round, when the boys had to make speeches, and their parents used to come to the school to hear them—I remember when my mother came into the room, how proud I was of her; and I used to like to point her out to the other boys. I did not think there was anybody in the world like my mother.

And I am sure that is what Jesus thinks about His Mother, with His human heart; for He is very Man as well as very God. And Jesus knows one Being to whom He can look up and say, before the angels, before devils, before men, "My Mother!"

There is to me, as a man, and as a Christian, a charm that is unutterable in the thought; "Mary, the Mother of Jesus!"* Oh! to speak her name is, to me, such a bringing of Jesus to my heart, as man to man. If Mary be His Mother, I can realise that Jesus is my Brother.

He has the flesh and blood and bones of man

* Acts i 14.

though He be God of Heaven! "He came down from Heaven, and was Incarnate, by the Holy Ghost, of the Virgin Mary, and was made man."

"Mary, the Mother of Jesus!"

Why, if anyone pointed out to me the mother of a very great statesman, or the mother of a very great orator, or philanthropist, I should feel a kind of reverence for the woman for her son's sake. Supposing, when the Duke of Wellington came back from the wars, during which he had sustained the honour of the British Empire, and in which he had, a thousand times, risked his life, for dear Old England; supposing, when he came back from the last of his wars, that the first person whom he had met was his mother: do you not think that the people would have said: "Look, that is the mother of Wellington"? And they would at once have made way to let the mother pass to her son's side.

But she was not half so much the mother of Wellington as Mary was the Mother of Jesus. Mary is the Mother of Jesus in a far deeper, intenser sense. Jesus had no human father. Mary was the centre connecting Jesus with humanity. When Jesus thinks of Mary, there His thoughts must rest; for Mary is the beginning and the end of His humanity.

I cannot give utterance to one-millionth part of the feelings, in my own heart, when I think of Mary, the

Mother of Jesus; and it does not seem to me to matter, one single iota, what people say to me about this, for I feel that I have Jesus on my side; and that I have the Father on my side, Who, from all eternity, elected Mary to be the Mother mystic of His Son Incarnate!

The words "Mary, the Mother of Jesus" have a sound that makes me feel quite at home with God; because God, through Mary, became very Man.

Do you not all feel this? Are there any listening to me who think that I am exaggerating? If so, let me just refer them to one verse, in the 1st chapter of St. Luke, and let me ask them to listen to these words. They are in the 35th verse of St. Luke i.; and it is a verse the like of which there is not, in all the Bible, for mystery tremendous—for marvel unutterable and ineffable.

"*And the angel answered and said unto her, The Holy Ghost shall come upon thee, and the Power of the Highest shall overshadow thee; therefore also that Holy Thing which shall be born of thee shall be called the Son of God.*"

Nazareth was busy in the fields, for it was spring time—the corn was beginning to grow, the birds were singing in the trees, and the farmers and the labourers were hard at work preparing for the planting of the earth—all nature's toil was going on its way; but, in a little cottage, on the hill, there was a mystery of eternity being enacted between the Archangel of Heaven and the lowly maiden Mary.

No eye but the eye of Mary saw the tremendous glow of the gleaming light, when the Archangel came to her and said: "Hail, thou that art highly favoured,"* and told her that she was to be the Mother of the Son of God. Then Mary asked him: "How shall this be, seeing I know not a man?"† And now listen to the Angel's answer: "The Holy Ghost shall come upon thee, and the Power of the Highest (that is of God the Father) shall overshadow thee: therefore also that Holy Thing Which shall be born of thee shall be called the Son of God." ‡

My brethren, "the Holy Ghost shall come upon thee:" that is the Third Person. The Power of the Highest shall overshadow thee:" that is the First Person. "The Holy One born of thee" is the Second Person. There is the whole Trinity.

How awful, how blasphemous, if it be not true! Is it true? Is it true that Mary became the Mother of Jesus, by this tremendous and overwhelming revelation of mystery and truth? Is there, in existence, a Being who was the Mother of God the Son by the overshadowing of God the Father, and by the conception of the Holy Ghost?

It cannot be true! It is an utter impossibility!

* St. Luke i. 28.   † St. Luke i. 34.   ‡ St. Luke i. 35.

It is the stumbling block in the way of Christianity! People who would believe in Christianity are turned from believing through the mystery of the "Mother of Jesus." Really, to take in the mystery of Christ's Incarnation is to be wading in the depths of the waters of mystery.

Oh! brethren, need I urge any argument to convince my present hearers that really and truly Mary became the Mother of Jesus, the Son of God, by the overshadowing of God the Father, and by the Holy Ghost coming upon her? No, because I know that you all believe it quite as much as I do. Mary, the Mother of Jesus, is a mystery; but we do believe in this mystery of the New Testament; it is the *foundation* of all the other mysteries of Christianity; and they would be nothing but for this. Of course the outside world does not believe it; and a great many in the visible Church do not believe it either.

I was once travelling from Marseilles to Genoa, when a gentleman, and fellow-traveller, on board the steamer, entered into conversation with me; and a question that he asked me was whether I believed in the Virgin Mary. I said: "What do you mean?" He said: "Do you believe that Mary, while a virgin, was the Mother of Jesus?" I said: "Of course I do; I should not be a Christian if I did not." "Well," he said, "I cannot."

And he was a Roman Catholic, and said his prayers most devoutly; but he told me that he could not believe in the Virgin Mary. He said it was perfectly impossible that she was the Mother of Jesus by the Holy Ghost.

But if he did not believe in the miracle of the Mother of Christ he could not believe in the Divinity and in the Incarnation of Christ, nor in the Atonement of the Cross; for if the Blood that Jesus shed on the Cross was not that of the Son of God, It could not save us any more than any other blood.

Protestants would not seem to believe it by the way they speak of her; but they do, in their hearts, believe it as much as we Catholics do. All Evangelical Christians believe it as a revealed, divine mystery, a most tremendous mystery, of God.

We cannot prove it by argument; no logic can prove it; it cannot be proved by any other means than the Holy Ghost convincing the heart of the reality of this awful, and unutterable, mystery.

Of course if there be any individuals here who do not believe this mystery, my words must seem most blasphemous to them.

Can you feel how sweet it is to call Mary the Mother of God? I say I should not be a Christian if I could not believe that she was. What! God have a Mother! Certainly. And yet people, who call themselves Christians, scarcely acknowledge that Mary is the Mother of God.

Mary is not the Mother of God in the way in which my mother is my mother. She is not the mother of the Godhead. Mary is the Mother of the humanity of Him Who was God—of a Divine Person who, though He took human nature upon Him, was still very God. And this is a mystery that all must believe.

May I ask you, first of all, is it not tremendously necessary, in these evil days of rationalism and materialism, that we should be sound on this fundamental doctrine of our holy religion? Is it not necessary that we should know what we believe on this point, and why we believe it? Shall I, because I am afraid of the ridicule of an unbelieving world, say I do not believe that Christ is really God; and that Mary is only the Mother of a God-*like* person? Shall we say this? No; to settle the matter, we give the title to " Mary, the Mother of Jesus "* of " Mother of God."

And now, my brethren, consider how comfortable it is to be very clear on this point; because, when we are clear on this doctrine of Christ's Mother, it brings Jesus so very close to us. We see Him, and we realise that He is our High Priest. If this mystery

* Acts i. 14.

be not true, Christ is either not God or not man. If Mary be not the Mother of God, Christ is not God; and if Mary be not God's Mother, God has never taken our nature and never redeemed us.

Therefore we cling pertinaciously to the truth that "God so loved us" that He came down from Heaven, took our nature upon Him, and "bought His Church with His Own Blood."* He so loved the Church that He gave Himself for it. Oh! my brothers and sisters in Jesus, this truth brings home to me so plainly that Jesus is the "Friend that sticketh closer than a brother."† Jesus is the true friend—born for adversity. It makes me to realise that I may cast all my sorrows on Him, for once He bore our sorrows; once He was "in all points tempted like as we are."‡

How could He have been tempted like we are if He had not become "very man?" God could not be tempted. Therefore He came down and was Incarnate, and "was made man," that He might be able to "be touched with the feeling of our infirmities."‡

When you, yourselves, are nearly overcome with grief, when tears stream down your cheeks, then comes the thought to you that He suffered, that "Jesus wept,"§ that Jesus was weary! Oh! what calm it

---

* Acts xx. 28.   ‡ Heb. iv. 15.
† Prov. xviii. 24.   § St. John xi. 35.

brings to the soul to know that He is able "to be touched with the feeling of our infirmities," because He "was in all points tempted like as we are."* It makes life so different to go through it with Him on our side. He once was like us, because He was "very man," "born of the Virgin Mary."

I have touched on the doctrine, at great length; and now I want you to ask yourselves the question: "What can we think,—knowing what we do of the feelings of the best sons, among men, towards their mothers,—*what can we think our Lord's feelings towards His Mother are?*

My love for the Blessed Virgin is one of the chief things for which I have been persecuted for twenty years, and misrepresented, and for which I have had to suffer a very great deal. I was about to preach a mission in a church, where I should very much have liked to have gone; but, all at once, the clergyman drew back because of my great love for the "Mother of God."

There are plenty of people in the Church of England who do not believe it right to love her; and if there be any such people here present, may I ask them not to let their party spirit prevent their listening patiently to what I say. Do they think we can grieve our Lord by loving His Mother?

* Heb. iv. 15.

Instead of loving her too much, I feel that I cannot love her enough.

The answer to my question would probably be: "Look at our Roman Catholic brethren, how they exaggerate the honour due to the Mother of Jesus." But there is no argument in that, for if we are not to use a thing because of the abuse of it, there would be an end to using the Bible itself. The Blessed Virgin could not have been saved without the merits of her Son; and to make a goddess of her would be heretical and ridiculous. I have "heard of" Roman Catholics who do make a goddess of her; but I have never yet met one, myself, who did.

Brethren, I ask you quietly to put this question to yourselves: is it pleasing to our Lord that His people's hearts should dwell with love on the remembrance of His Mother, or is it not? If it be pleasing that His people should love and reverence His mother, what a sad thing it is to think that, in the majority of the churches of our land, the Blessed Virgin may scarcely be mentioned. If a clergyman happen, from his pulpit, to eulogise our Lord's Mother, people rise, stamp their feet, and walk out. But they do not mind the mention of the devil. They have not the least objection to hearing about Satan himself.

Once I was catechising a little girl in school, and I

asked her if she knew who our Lord's Mother was. She said, "Please sir, she was Mary Magdalene, out of whom He cast seven devils." That is the idea she had of our Lord's Mother. It is no wonder. That child had been taught how shocking it was to give honour to the Virgin Mary; and so it got into her head that the Mother of our Lord was some monster of iniquity. I only just mention this little incident in passing.

The very name of the Virgin Mary is "like a red flag to a bull" to some people; and as I have this week chosen these subjects for our meditations—viz., "The Lord's People," "The Lord's Day," "The Lord's Prayer," "The Lord's Supper," and "The Lord's Cross," I determined that, on this Saturday, I would speak words very clearly and emphatically about "our Lord's Mother;" because if we do not hold right views about her, the atonement of the Cross is invalidated; for if Jesus be not divine the Blood on Calvary would be of no use.

I am here, therefore, to speak now of the Lord's Mother; but I do not speak dictatorially; and I know that you have quite as much right to your opinions as I have to mine.

But the feeling that I have is, that the more we revere the Blessed Virgin Mary the more we please her Son.

If you were to go to Margate Cemetery, at the end of July, where my own darling mother's mortal remains are lying, till Jesus comes and "the dead in Christ rise first," you would see her grave covered with beautiful flowers. Pounds and pounds are lavished on my mother's grave, and this by people who have never seen her; but they have a love for her for my sake; and they will spend money on her grave, for my sake, out of gratitude for what I have done for their souls. And for Jesus' sake we do honour to the memory of the Mother of Jesus.

It is for *Jesus Only* that I love the Virgin Mary. She would be no more than any other woman to me if she were not His Mother. Therefore, all the glory that I pay to Mary is for love of her Son; and I am sorry that anybody should think this wrong.

The next point is "praying to the Virgin."

You ask your wife to pray for you, and you teach your child to pray for you, and in the same way I can understand our asking the prayers of those who are departed. I do not believe in asking the prayers of *dead saints;* but *I* never heard of a dead saint! I do not believe in dead saints. *I believe that Jesus lives; and because He lives they live also;* and that is the reason why we ask their prayers. I believe that they are "alive for evermore."

The Apostle Paul says of the departed, "We are

compassed about with a great cloud of witnesses."* While we are "running the race" they are the witnesses looking on. So that when a person speaks of "dead saints," and says that they cannot hear, he has no authority for his assertions from the Word of God.

So, my brethren, I not only believe that it is not wrong, but that it is right, and very helpful, to ask the prayers of my fellow-believers; and you will have to prove to me that the Blessed Virgin is not among the Living "Cloud of Witnesses" before condemning me for asking the prayers of her who is our Lord's Mother.

Perhaps some of you do not believe with me; but I feel taught of God to ask her prayers; and I do not think that the faith with which I ask her prayers, and with which I long to exalt our Lord's Mother, grieves Him.

If you say: "where are we told in the Bible to give all this honour to the Virgin Mary?" I would answer: "if Queen Victoria were to walk into this room now, should I sit still and say: 'I am not going to rise, I shall not get up, I am not told anywhere to do so when I see the Queen'?" No. I should rise instantly, as an Englishman, because I believe the Queen is the Lord's Anointed over us, in

* Heb. xii. 1.

civil matters; and I should wish to show her every honour that I could. I should not require to be *told* to rise; and therefore all that I want to be told is *that Mary is the Mother of Jesus*, and nothing else; and I must give her the honour that is her due.

There is the Mother of your Lord—treat her as you please; but, for myself, I say that the more I love my Lord and Saviour the more I shall reverence the Mother, whom "all generations are to call blessed.*

On the Cross Jesus said to His best loved disciple "Behold thy Mother;"† and in these words He speaks to me, "Behold thy Mother;" and therefore I say: "Holy Mary, Mother of God, pray for me."

Do not let prejudice cause us to misunderstand a simple thing like this.

If this belief should not commend itself to you personally, do not rush into the persecution of those who do think that it does glorify our Lord; and let us Catholics be very tender towards the tenets of our Protestant brothers on the subject. Let us be joined one to another in love; and if the Holy Spirit teach you that it does glorify God to pay reverence and devotion to our Lord's Mother, *pay the reverence;* if you do *not* believe it right to do so, do *not* pay it, as in that case it would be wrong.

But again I say, I believe it to be right; and I have

* St. Luke i. 48. † St. John xix. 27.

received very many blessings through the prayers of my Saviour's Mother. Therefore do not condemn me.

And I ask you, before I conclude, does my love to the Blessed Virgin hinder me from enjoying Christ in His fulness? Do I mix up the mystery of the Virgin with the message of the Gospel to sinners? Certainly not; and I think that the more I love and reverence the Lord's Mother, the more I realise what her Son is, and the more I long to proclaim what He is to a world that is " dead in trespasses and sins."*

* Ephes. ii. 1.

XV.

Jehovah-Jireh.

An Address to Christians.

Wednesday Afternoon, May 19th, 1886.

T

Jehovah-Jireh.

Prayer before Sermon.

O! great and loving Father, Who hast seen to it for Thy people, who hast been Jehovah the Provider in Jesus, and hast not only Provided but hast provided abundantly for all our needs in Him, We beseech Thee grant us to speak and to hear, at this time, a word that shall enable us to set up a *Jehovah-Jireh* in a sense that some of us have never set up such a memorial before. Let none go out from this place without being able to set up, once and for all, such a *Jehovah-Jireh* that the rest of their lives, here below, may be lives of simple rest and trust in the Lord. Unfold to us, by the wisdom of the Holy Ghost, our most wonderful subject, and make it so lovely in our eyes that our hearts and minds may feast upon its loveliness, until we shall be so satisfied with Jesus that we shall be able to "set to our seal" that He is indeed the "Alpha and the Omega"* of His Church; that He is indeed "the author and finisher of our faith."† O! dear Lord Almighty, and glorious Father, we pray Thee glorify Thy Holy Child Jesus, in our midst, on this occasion; and let our subject unfold itself to our hearts, like a beautiful flower beneath the genial dew and rain and sunshine of Thy love; and we ask this that each one of Thy people here present may be profited, and fed, and comforted; and that Thy Son Jesus may be magnified, exalted, glorified and admired in every heart here present. Grant this for His sake, Who liveth and reigneth with Thee in the unity of the Holy Spirit, God for ever and ever. Amen.

* Rev. i. 8. † Heb. xii 2

JEHOVAH-JIREH.

An Address to Christians.

"Abraham called the name of that place Jehovah-Jireh."
Gen. xxii. 14.

Yesterday we were looking at Abraham's patient, restful faith with regard to God's promise, that Sarah should have a child. Yesterday we were looking at the extraordinary faith of Abraham, who, at the call of God, had come out from his own household and family and country, and had followed the leading of God's Spirit into a strange land; and how he became perfectly convinced that God would fulfil His promise in blessing all the nations of the earth, through a child that Sarah should bring to him.

And we watched Abraham go down the hill of life; we watched the grey hairs mantling on Sarah's brow, and we watched the wrinkles coming over her once beautiful face; we saw the shrinking of her beautiful, womanly form into the decrepitude of old age; and yet we saw that Abraham was quite strong in faith that Sarah would have a child.

And so, as we watched the family of Abraham, and saw the son of the bondwoman received by all the servants in Abraham's encampment as the heir of Abraham, we saw how Ishmael was the admired of the tribe, how full of youth and animation and strength the boy seemed to grow; and yet he was not the one.

It was from the haggard, wan, wrinkled, grey-haired Sarah that the real boy was to come, through whom God would bless the world, by drawing out, from all the nations, that beautiful brotherhood of the Christian Church, which should be a family of peace in the midst of the nations of war; a family of rest in the midst of the nations of toil; which should be a family of light in the midst of the world of darkness; a family of eternal life amidst the nations that were dying and "sitting in darkness and the shadow of death."*

And then we saw the strange amazement and the marvellous wonder of Abraham's tribe, when it was heard—" Sarah has brought forth a child at last, and little Isaac sleeps in Sarah's bosom, and Sarah's withered breast is filled with the fruitfulness of Heaven; and she nurses little Isaac in order that he may produce Mary, who shall nestle Jesus, the Son of God, in her bosom." If there had been no fruitfulness in the aged Sarah there would have been no

* Psalm cvii. 10.

fruitfulness in the Virgin Mary to produce that Child through Whom salvation and righteousness have flowed throughout all the nations.

And so we were constrained to admire exceedingly the faith of Abraham, who "staggered not at the promise of God through unbelief,"* on account of Sarah's age.

And then we went on to consider how Isaac and Ishmael differed. Ishmael was Abraham's son; but God did not promise Ishmael to Abraham; and therefore he went for nothing. He was counted for nothing; and not only that, but he was "cast out." He was cast out of Abraham's house. Ishmael was a mistake. Isaac was the true child, through whom the blessing was to come.

And so we made Abraham's household a symbol of the visible Church. The visible Church contains the "children of promise"; but it also contains those who shall be cast out: and we saw how very useless it was to belong to the visible Church unless we "made our calling and election sure"† by faith in Jesus Christ.

Unless you and I know that we are the seed that the Father has promised to Jesus, it is very little use belonging to the visible Church. The visible Church is quite as full of Ishmaels as it is of Isaacs; but

* Romans iv. 20. † 2 Peter i. 10.

Ishmael shall be "cast out;" for he is "the son of the bondwoman."

When the time comes for the Isaacs to inherit the glorious inheritance of light, then shall Ishmael be cast out. It is only those who are chosen of God in Christ; it is only those who are given, by God, to Jesus, who shall inherit the inheritance of Isaac. Ishmael shall be cast out. Ishmael shall grow more and more strong and powerful; Ishmael shall triumph over Isaac; but he shall be cast out at last. So the worldly professing Church persecutes the spiritual Church. The worldly Church is getting the upper hand. The world's religion, Ishmael, is far more uppermost now than Isaac and his seed; but the time is coming when, from the tent of Abraham shall Ishmael and the bondwoman be cast right out into the deserts of everlasting darkness; out into the abyss of the flames of the eternal world; and Isaac only shall inherit the promised land.

No wonder, then, the Apostle says to each one, "make your calling and election sure."* He also says, "for in Christ Jesus neither circumcision availeth anything, nor uncircumcision, but a new creature."†

My brothers and sisters,—you who come to these meetings in the afternoons,—I address you as the "children of promise;" I address you as those who have

* 2 Peter i. 10. † Gal. vi. 15.

taken hold of the promise of God, and appropriated it to your own souls. And I showed you yesterday afternoon how that God's great Promise is Jesus Christ. There are no promises of God except in Christ, no promises of God out of Christ; just as there is no righteousness out of Christ, no pardon out of Christ; just as it is said, "he that hath not the Son of God hath not life,"* he that doth not possess Christ hath nothing to do with the promises of God.

It is only those who are "born again"† who are children of the Promise. Christ is God's great Promise, in Whom all His other promises are summed up. The promises of God are all in Christ; they are all hanging upon this one point, that we have accepted Christ. No promise of God, in that Book, is made to any except in Christ; therefore, until we have taken hold of the great Promise of God, which is Christ, the promises of Christ are nothing to us; for they "are all in Him, yea, and in Him, Amen."‡

I think now I have been very clear and very plain about the "children of promise," although a clergyman here yesterday said he did not know what I was driving at. It was because he was not accustomed to our services; but my own hearers know, oh! they know, with the heavenly inspiration, and divine illumination, what I mean. They know what I mean,

* 1 John v. 12.   † St. John iii. 2.   ‡ 2 Cor. i. 20.

in very deed and truth, that it is "Jesus Only," and nothing but Jesus. They know that no one can be a "child of promise" except a man in Christ; and therefore I did not expatiate very largely on the fundamental truths which pave the way for the full enjoyment of the subject. He, this clergyman, did not know "what I was driving at." May God bring him to the rest of the services, and he will soon find out what we are driving at.

We have now another picture of Abraham, and it is the picture of Abraham setting up an altar on which to inscribe the words *Jehovah-Jireh;* and will you allow me to draw just a little picture of the place, because there is something so intensely interesting and marvellous about it? Abraham has come from Hebron, to the mountain country of Judea, guided by the Spirit of God, accompanied by his servants and his son Isaac.

He is to go and worship upon the mountain that God will point out to him. He is to worship in a most horrible, revolting manner. The worship that Abraham has to give to God is the most monstrous and hideous, which it is possible for human nature to gaze upon or contemplate. He is to kill, in cold blood, the "Child of Promise" Isaac; he is to kill him and burn him on a hill that God will show him.

Dear people, we must not judge this horrible scene

from our Christian point of view. If we judge this scene from a Christian point of view it is monstrous and abominable; and we should hate the picture and the idea that the picture conveys; but we must remember that in Abraham's time human sacrifices were very common—in fact, among the Hindoos, if it were not for the British Government putting them down, by main force, there would be many human sacrifices to this day.

It is the beautiful, softening influences of the Gospel of Christ, which is the highest class in God's school, from which *we* judge this scene. But you must put aside your heavenly education; and you must also remember that people, in those days, were in the first class—not in the last; so that in Abraham's time they were only beginning their education, and God had to educate the human race up to Christ.

Abraham did not know so much of the mind and will of God as Moses; and Moses did not know so much as the prophets; and even the prophets themselves, in their magnificent enlargement upon the evangelical idea, very often spoke things that they did not understand.

And do you not remember how, when Daniel had those splendid visions given to him, he turned round to the angel, and said: "I do not know what they mean." "No," said the angel, "nobody will know what they are until Christ comes."* And so it was left for Jesus Christ to speak of the Book of the prophet Daniel in this wise: "When ye therefore shall see the abomination of desolation, spoken of by Daniel the prophet, stand in the holy place, (whoso readeth, let him understand)."†

Alleluia! It has come at last; the Book is unclosed; the prophecy is made known; we may understand it; and if we take Jesus Christ and St. Paul together, the whole of the Book of Daniel is explained. Now, "let him that readeth understand."‡ It was hidden at the time, till the end of that age—till the bursting forth of the Christian dispensation.

So you must not judge Abraham, and the modes by which God instructed and led him, by those ideas with which God leads and instructs us now, in the full blaze of the Gospel day. You must judge the scene as a cotemporary. In Calcutta, perhaps some of you know the temple of the goddess Kali. If it were not for the British Government there would be human sacrifices offered to that goddess, because her devotees believe that a human sacrifice makes atonement for the sins of men for two hundred years.

Was it not a human sacrifice that was rendered

---

* Daniel xii. 8, 9. † St. Matt. xxiv. 15; Daniel xii. 11.
‡ St. Matt. xxiv. 15.

absolutely a *sine quâ non* by the immaculate, spotless purity of God when they nailed *The Man* to the Cross?

No other real man has ever existed from the beginning of time but Jesus Christ. All others are only defiled, ruined creatures: Jesus Christ is *The Man*. Did not Jesus Christ Himself say, when He stood on the stairs of Pilate's palace, and the raving multitudes were shrieking at Him in the streets—did not He say to them: "Behold The Man"? He was crowned with thorns then. Perhaps some of the very spittle of the soldiery was trickling down His sacred face. We have it in our English versions: "And Pilate said, Behold the man;"[*] but in the original it is, "Pilate brought forth Jesus, and He said,—'Behold the Man.'"

So there is the final object of the whole ritual of sacrifice fulfilled in the human offering of the Child of Mary on the Cross. We must, therefore, be very careful how we allow our Christian sentiments of horror to burst forth as we contemplate Abraham leading about his tender child, of only sixteen years, over the mountains of Judah, first to cut his throat and then to burn him as a victim of love to God.

When Abraham came so near to the hill that he saw it afar off—when he saw, right far away, in the distance, the spot appointed for his sacrifice, he

[*] St. John xix. 5.

said to the servants: "Abide ye here with the ass; and I and the lad will go yonder and worship."* It might have been a journey of four hours. Abraham has the fire, and Isaac carries the wood. You can almost see the form of the boy, with the wood on his shoulders, as he walks along with his father, who carries the fire. Isaac, holding the wood upon his shoulders, with his hands outstretched to hold it, seems to speak of that true Isaac, the Son of the great Father, Who "so loved the world "† that He sent His Son to die for us.

Isaac walks along bearing the wood and, poor old Abraham!—his poor old anxious face, every now and then, turns to look at his worshipped, idolised child. He looks at young Isaac; he thinks to himself that the promises of God are centered in this boy; he is to be the child from whose loins shall spring a nation that shall produce the great Restorer of the human race; but now his God seems to forget the promise. He looks at the boy and his lip quivers, his eyes moisten with bitter tears; but still the grand, sacred old father walks on, confident in the strength of that faith which has made Abraham "the father of all them that believe." ‡

The Lord has given him a spiritual posterity in the Catholic Church of Jesus, the magnificence of which

* Genesis xxii. 5.   † St. John iii. 16.   ‡ Rom. iv. 11.

shall abide for ever, and go on extending and growing in beauty and strength, until the spiritual Israel shall be presented, as the bride, before the throne in Heaven, " not having spot, or wrinkle, or any such thing."*

Oh, beautiful faith of Abraham! Let us all bow down and kiss his feet as he pauses on the road, for we are sharers of his faith; and we are participators of the promise.

When he reaches the " place which God had told him of,"† it is a hill standing somewhat by itself. In after years the great Altar of the temple of Solomon was built on the spot.

There, on the spot where Abraham built the altar to sacrifice his son, God's providence built the Altar upon which all the sacrifices were to be offered that were to point to Jesus Christ, "the Lamb" that was to " take away the sin of the world."‡ This spot, where Abraham was to offer his son Isaac, became so dear to God! The passion in the heart of God seemed to pour itself out on that spot. Abraham's faith was so wonderfully dear to God that He has consecrated that spot with a tremendous consecration. The shadow of the Cross of Jesus fell on that spot, where Abraham's love and faith to God were so great as to offer Him his " well-beloved son." Oh! the faith of Abraham has given to me Jesus and His salvation; and it is by

* Ephes. v. 27.   † Gen. xxii. 9.   ‡ St. John i. 29.

the faith of Abraham, on that mount, that you and I are eternally redeemed.

Oh! how God loved that spot, and God said in after years, "I will not accept any sacrifice unless it be offered on that spot. I will not accept a sacrifice anywhere else; it must be on that spot where Abraham's faith was tried. That is the only spot in the world upon which I will accept a sacrifice."

Dear people, are we not drinking in the intense sweetness of the dew of faith in God's sight? Oh, how a simple trust lays hold of God! Abraham's magnificent faith, the pertinacity of that faith, was so great that it took God captive; and Abraham is called by a most blasphemous name if God had not given it to him. He is called "the Friend of God."* And those who trust in Jesus, with the faith that Abraham trusted, these are God's friends, for He says Himself, "I call you not servants: but I have called you friends."†

So the "friend of God" comes to the spot. He builds the altar of stones. He puts the wood on it; and little Isaac says: "My father: behold the fire and the wood; but where is the lamb for a burnt offering?"‡ Abraham says to Isaac, "*Jehovah-Jireh.*"§ That is Abraham's answer. He said it

---

* St. James ii. 23. † St. John xv. 15. ‡ Gen. xxii. 7.
§ God will provide.—Gen. xxii. 8.

with a quivering lip, with a moistened eye, with a trembling hand; but still he said it. "Jehovah-Jireh." And the little boy bowed his head in trustful, childlike faith, and followed at his father's side, until they came to the spot "which God had told him of."* Then, all at once, Abraham turned and looked at the boy, and no doubt he kept on repeating in his heart the words "Jehovah-Jireh"—that is, the Lord will provide.

"But there was no voice, nor any that answered."†

And then Abraham's faith is strong enough; he seizes Isaac by the throat, he flings him on the altar; he takes his murderous knife and raises the dagger in the air, ready to plunge into the boy's breast—and then—stay now thy hand, "lay not thine hand upon the lad, for now I know that thou fearest God, seeing thou hast not withheld thy son, thine only son from Me."‡ The angel of the Lord then points to a little "ram caught in a thicket, behind him, by his horns."§

Jesus Christ is God's Lamb. They put on His head a crown of thorns, and He was caught a willing victim because of Abraham's faith in offering his child. And on the very spot—"Jehovah-Jireh!" Abraham's heart burst forth with a whole ocean of joy, and sent

---

* Gen. xxii. 9.   † 1 Kings xviii. 26.   ‡ Gen. xxii. 12.
§ Gen. xxii. 13.

forth streams of gladness and thanksgiving. Oh, how good it was to leave the altar there and to write on it "Jehovah-Jireh!" "He called the name of that place 'Jehovah-Jireh.'"*

Oh! did Abraham know one-half the meaning of the Jehovah-Jireh? Did he know, when he wrote those words, that they should only be fulfilled when God gave Christ to be the life, righteousness, peace, salvation of His people? Did Abraham know that God would provide *such* a righteousness as He has provided for us? Did Abraham know that God would provide such a salvation as He has provided in Christ? When Abraham said "the Lord will provide,"† did Abraham know how much, how gladly, how beautifully, how fully, how eternally He would provide for His people, the true children of Abraham in Jesus?

Oh! when Abraham wrote "Jehovah-Jireh," "the Lord will provide," did he know that the Lord would provide an everlasting righteousness, a divine righteousness for all believers? Did he know that the heavens would be rent and God Himself, in His own Incarnate Son, would come down to redeem and save, and take out of the captivity of sin and the prison-house of the world, a people amply provided for in all grace, all strength, in all good works; so that all those

* Gen. xxii. 14. † Gen. xxii. 8.

U

who could say " Jehovah-Jireh " could say " the Lord is my Shepherd, I shall not want ? "*

"Jehovah-Jireh !" The Lord *has* provided.

Dear people, is it not unutterably sweet to think that we are able to say " Jehovah-Jireh ?" Don't I remember when first I was able to write " Jehovah-Jireh " upon a certain day in my life ! Do you think after Abraham had put up that altar, and called it " Jehovah-Jireh," that he ever forgot it in all his after troubles, in all his countless difficulties, in all his sorrows and tears ? Do you not think that " Jehovah-Jireh " was, as it were, the mother of a thousand lesser " Jehovah-Jirehs ? "

How many Jehovah-Jirehs have you put up since you put up the great " Jehovah-Jireh " that you found in Christ, God's provision for your eternal life ? All our daily blessings, all our little passing deliverances, all our consolations in times of earthly trials—these are only tiny shreds of the great " Jehovah-Jireh " that you and I set up, when first we received Christ, in His fulness, as God's gift to us.

Oh ! when I accepted Jesus as God's gift to me, and I put up " Jehovah-Jireh," on that day and in that place, the thought came to me, " shall He not in Christ also freely give us all things ?"†

If He loved me enough to enable me to write up

* Psalm xxiii. 1.   † Rom. viii. 32.

"Jehovah-Jireh" as to my eternal needs, and everlasting needs; if, in Christ, I saw "Jehovah-Jireh" for my everlasting wants; if I saw in Christ "Jehovah-Jireh" for my eternal inheritance among the elect; if in Christ I saw "Jehovah-Jireh" for my eternal righteousness, for my eternal pardon, for my lasting peace; oh! can I not trust Him, in days to come, in the smaller necessities of time?

If my everlasting necessities have been met,—have been completely answered in Christ; if I set up on the Cross of Jesus the words in letters of flaming, fiery love, "Jehovah-Jireh;" if, when I look at my crucifix, I can read "Jehovah-Jireh" there, and know that the Lord has provided on that Cross everlasting salvation, everlasting righteousness, perfect pardon, grace sufficient "to help in every time of need,"* "an inheritance incorruptible that fadeth not away"† —if God has provided in Christ what He has, will He not provide, in Christ, for me, for my daily wants, my worldly necessities, my earthly needs? Will He not, in a Father's love, supply a gracious proof of "Jehovah-Jireh" when I need it most? Will He not provide a hand to soothe my aching brow and throbbing heart, when dark, cloudy days lower on my heavenward way?

When desolation and abandonments, when troubles

* Heb. iv. 16.   † 1 Peter i. 4.

and disappointments, come, may I not contentedly expect that each one will be a fresh opportunity for me to set up another " Jehovah-Jireh " ? Oh ! there shall nothing happen to those that are Christians but which shall be a " Jehovah-Jireh " on each occasion !

This is what our Lord means us to understand when He teaches us to pray " Give us this day our daily bread."* This is what He means when He tells His children to ask of God to supply their needs for the day, according to the necessities of the day—not the daily bread of the body—that is a mere nothing, but the daily bread of heaven, which is Jesus Himself, the living " Bread which came down from heaven."† For it is *in* Christ, from Christ's eternal and Divine fulness and all-sufficiency, that " Jehovah-Jireh " takes place ! It is *from* Jesus and *in* Jesus that all our needs are supplied ; and that we are enabled to say, under all circumstances, and on all occasions, " Jehovah-Jireh ! "

Oh ! dearest brothers and sisters in the love and in the life of Jesus, is not your life and mine a constant setting up of " Jehovah-Jirehs ? " Can you not look back to days of cloud and mist and doubt and fear, when it seemed as if it were all over with you ?

Sometimes sin had seemed too strong for us, the world's persecution and influence too mighty ; and we were sinking in the strife, and were almost fallen to the

* St. Matt. vi. 11.   St. Luke xi. 3.   † St. John vi. 41.

ground; when, all at once, there came a mighty influx of Divine consolation, and spiritual strength, and spiritual illumination; and we were sustained by the fulness that comes forth from the heart of Jesus.

He delivers us. *He* comes to soothe, to pacify and to save; and you put up another "Jehovah-Jireh"!

Oh! the Christian's life is a continual repetition of "Jehovah-Jirehs." There is scarcely a place in the Christian's house where he might not put up a "Jehovah-Jireh" of some sort!

And, beloved brethren in our precious Jesus, let me ask you, shall we trust Him for the days that are left, for the stormy times that we have yet to pass, for the tempestuous waves that we have yet to brave? Shall we trust Him when all we love the most shall be gradually taken out of our hand? Shall we unclasp the hands that grasp the dear one to our breast, and shall we say: "Let Jesus have him or her if He wishes—'Jehovah-Jireh' "?

Only a few days ago a Christian mother and father, whom I happened to meet, interested me very much. They had a wonderful little boy of seven years old; and this little boy was so filled with the Holy Ghost that he used to gloat over his Bible like an ordinary child would gloat over a box of sweets; and when he found out a particular promise, he would positively dance for joy, and hug his Bible in his arms. His mother told me how delicate he was; she said she hoped he would live, but yet she said: "If Jesus wants him let Him take him."

There had been so many "Jehovah-Jirehs" in her Christian life that she knew there would be a very beautiful "Jehovah-Jireh," if Jesus took the child. Oh! shall you and I trust Him, when He comes to test and prove us? God loves to try those He loves the most, because it is through much temptation that our faith is proved, and God is glorified. The Apostle Peter says, our faith is very "precious"* to God; and so is "the trial of our faith precious"† to Him.

Will you let Him, dear brethren—Will you say, let Him—"do that which seemeth Him good;"‡ and will you trust Him for the "Jehovah-Jireh"? Oh! do, for you *shall not* trust in vain!

May I give you a passage from David in the sixty-third Psalm, which seems to bring out very sweetly and very harmoniously, and very gently this beautiful thought? David says: "Because thou *hast* been my help, therefore in the shadow of Thy wings will I rejoice."§

Because, in the days that are passed, my Jehovah-Jirehs have studded my way, I will go forth and trust in my Lord God, in the days that are coming, and in

---

* 2 Peter i. 1.   † 1 Peter i. 7.
‡ 2 Sam. x. 12.   § Psalm lxiii. 7.

the love of Him " Who loved me and gave Himself for me;"* and I know that to the end of the journey "Jehovah-Jirehs" shall be mine, until, in the land where "the weary be at rest,"† and the weepers in Jerusalem rejoice for ever, I shall set up my eternal "Jehovah-Jireh" beside the Throne; and I shall cry out with the hosts of the redeemed: He hath "done all things well;" He was faithful to the promise.

Oh! what "Jehovah-Jirehs" we shall have in Heaven! Oh! what "Jehovah-Jirehs" we shall sing to the angels; and when we say our "Jehovah-Jireh" psalms, the very angels will be ashamed of their chants and anthems of praise, for our "Jehovah-Jirehs" shall have a sweeter harmony for the ear of the most High, than all the songs of the angels—"Jehovah-Jireh!"

My brethren, perhaps next month, perhaps before the season is out, you will want to look out for a "Jehovah-Jireh." Remember, when everything seems darkest, when your heart is all of a quiver, when your whole outer man is trembling, as you stand on the threshold of some great sorrow; remember the days of light and the loving-kindness in the past; and trust in Jesus and get ready to write, with the hand of your soul—"Jehovah-Jireh;" and the deliverance is sure to come to the "child of promise."

How many of us, lastly, will set up a "Jehovah-Jireh"

---

* Gal. ii. 20.   † Job iii. 17.

at the foot of our dying bed ? I have to die soon—so have you. Have any of us a natural fear of death; have any of us here a physical horror of that strange passage out of the body ? Oh, that will be the last opportunity for setting up a Jehovah Jireh ! Won't we set it up ? Oh! won't we, when tears are falling quietly around us, and our eyes are closed to all that is going on of weeping and grief; won't we set up a "Jehovah-Jireh," with that song of the heart, when our lips are too faint to articulate the words: "Yea, though I walk through the valley of the shadow of death, I will fear no evil: for Thou art with me"? *

Brethren, if there be anything for which I most long for myself, it is that when I come to die I may set up such a "Jehovah-Jireh" as shall glorify the "God of Abraham," † and shall prove the faithfulness of His loving-kindness to them that believe.

---

* Psalm xxiii. 4. † Exodus iii. 6.

XVI.

Validity of Orders and Sacraments in the Church of England.

Oration.

Monday Afternoon, May 24th, 1886.

Validity of Orders and Sacraments in the Church of England.

Prayer before Oration.

O Almighty God, Who hast given to the disciples of Jesus, a desire, in their inmost hearts, to glorify Him, and to show forth His praise, grant to us that words may be spoken, at this time, which may glorify Thy blessed Son, and be in harmony with His will, and in obedience to His word. And let Thy blessing rest upon us, at this present time, through the same Jesus Christ our Lord. Amen.

THE VALIDITY OF ORDERS AND SACRAMENTS IN THE CHURCH OF ENGLAND.

Oration.

"And they continued steadfastly in the Apostles' doctrine and fellowship."—Acts ii. 42.

I want this afternoon to speak very respectfully to my hearers, and in a very undictatorial spirit. I only want just to give my own reasons for believing that the Church of England possesses real Orders and real Sacraments; and I hope that I shall say nothing offensive, or disrespectful, to our Roman Catholic brethren; or words either which may wound the hearts and feelings of Protestant Christians.

But I want my hearers, who have been following me during the past week, in my mission here, to understand why I think I am right in holding the position that I do, and that I desire always to keep, as a member of the Church of England.

Having made these remarks, by way of preface, I am sure that my kind hearers will forgive me if I inadvertently, in the heat of extempore speaking, say anything contrary to the feeling that I have just expressed.

It seems to me, then, that the Church of England is in a most painfully peculiar position before the eyes of all Christendom.

On the one side we are ignored almost entirely by the Western Church, and also by the Eastern Churches. They do not authoritatively, at any rate, or corporately, acknowledge either that we possess a valid Christian ministry, that we are "in the fellowship of the Apostles,"* or that we possess valid Sacraments.

Now, it is no use closing our eyes to this fact; and it is of no use making light of it; because it is a terrible and important fact, that neither Eastern Christendom nor Western Christendom acknowledge our position as a part of the visible Catholic Church of Christ.

And then, on the other side, consider those who are zealous and earnest Protestants; for here again our position, in the Church of England, prevents us from holding any intercommunion whatever with Protestants. We are, by virtue of the assertion, in the preface of our Ordinal, debarred from holding intercommunion with any Protestant Church at all. We are not allowed to admit to our altars any Presbyterian, Lutheran, or Calvinistic clergy. We are compelled to ignore utterly and entirely the ordination of ministers of all the Protestant Churches.

* Acts ii. 42.

So, just see—on the one hand the Catholic portion of Christendom denies the validity of our Orders, denies our credentials, and disputes the assertions that we make as to our Catholic position; while, on the other hand, we, by our Catholic position, on the subject of Sacraments and ministry, debar ourselves utterly and entirely from communication with all Protestant sects; so that even our Protestant brethren ought to take the matter up from their point of view.

We are therefore an isolated Church in the centre of Christendom.

It seems to me to be a most painful, and a most sad, pitiable, and discreditable position, which the Church of England occupies. Can nothing be done to remedy this state of affairs ? Surely the truth of our claims ought to be investigated by lawful authority, as to whether we are what we say we are, or whether we are not. Would you and I rather that the matter were not ventilated; or do you not think that the time has come when the matter should be authoritatively, and in a Christian and bold spirit, investigated to the very bottom ? It seems to me that this time has come.

Surely our present Archbishop of Canterbury has some very grave interest in the question as to whether he is an archbishop at all, and whether he rules over any true, vital, living, historical, animated portion of the one visible Church of Christ! Surely it is a question of which he cannot afford to make light, when the whole of Christendom is separated from us, and denies the validity of our claims!

Surely also Bishop Ryle, and many of his school, ought to take the matter up from their point of view. Bishop Ryle would be compelled to accept a Roman Catholic priest as a real minister of the Church of England, if he made his submission to the Church of England; whereas, if the Presbyterian clergyman of Blair Athol, in whose church he (Bishop Ryle) himself officiated, desired for Christian communion, he would have to treat his friend, the Presbyter of Blair Athol, as not ordained at all. This is a very difficult position for Bishop Ryle and his school; and it seems to me, from both sides of the question,— Catholic and Protestant alike,—that this subject ought to be brought forward, very determinately, by men of spirit, position, influence, and education. Do you think, for a moment, that the question is so unimportant with regard to Christendom generally that the authorities of the Church of Rome would refuse to look into the matter?

Our Roman Catholic brethren say that the thing has been decided once and for all. I cannot see that it has. I have never heard of such a thing as an authoritative definition upon the subject. I know speaking generally, that the Roman Catholics ignore our Orders; but Dr. Lee has put into our hands a book which all English churchmen ought to read. He has put before us, in a popular form, facts which make it certain, beyond a doubt, that there have been considerable acknowledgments respecting our Orders from men of authority in the Roman Church, who were highly competent, by their learning and position, to express an opinion on the subject; and I should like to say, before I go further, that I am much indebted to Dr. Lee and his book for what I am going to say in regard to this portion of my lecture.

There are very many tractates issued by the Roman Catholics to disprove the assertions that are made in favour of the validity of the ministry of the Church of England; one particularly by a Roman Benedictine monk, Father Breme, full of very interesting facts; but still, at the same time, full of a very great many assertions that are really valueless.

I should like to give you an instance of what I mean. Dr. Lee gives us very clearly, in his book, the letter of Bishop Bonner with respect to the reinstatement of Bishop Scory to his office in the Church of England, in the time of Queen Mary. Bishop Scory had been ordained by the new Order, which our Roman Catholic friends say is totally invalid, and incompetent to confer Orders.

Dr. Lee gives us this letter; but Father Breme says

that there has been a misuse made of this letter—that Bishop Bonner was not authorised to reinstate Bishop Scory, of Chichester, in his episcopate. He was only permitted to reinstate him as a priest in the diocese of London, to celebrate the divine services; and that he only called him bishop out of courtesy. I really think, with all due deference to such a superior person as Father Breme, that if we take into consideration the circumstances under which Bishop Bonner wrote, he would have been the very last person, for courtesy's sake, to have told a lie of that sort; for if Scory were not absolutely a bishop of the Christian Church, it was, under such circumstances, a lie to call him so.

I shall be able to give but a very imperfect lecture; for, owing to my state of health, and the very heavy work of the mission, I am sorry to say I have not been able to think over the subject half as much as I had wished to have done.

But I want to place before you some objections for your consideration; and then to give you my very simple, commonplace answers as a mere common-sense Englishman.

Our Roman Catholic brethen, then, fix us entirely upon the question of the consecration of the first, so-called Protestant, Archbishop of Canterbury, Matthew Parker. He was the first archbishop of the new régime, and our Roman Catholic brethren say that he was no

w

archbishop at all; and that, as we derive our Orders and Sacraments through him, they are entirely invalid, for the following reason :—who was it that consecrated Matthew Parker Archbishop of Canterbury? It was William Barlow, Bishop-elect of Chichester; but not *actual* Bishop of Chichester.

Now, before I enter upon this subject, I would remind you, with all due respect, that our Roman Catholic brethren have not been very particular about their methods of attacking us; because, if you remember, for a very considerable time they used to urge the "Nag's Head" story. They have given that up now; but it *was* used very determinately by men whose names really would render them worthy of our esteem in most matters; but our Roman Catholic brethren, on the other hand, have been so shamefully treated, from our side, that it is really no wonder that they have resorted to any amount of animosity to retain their position.

We had brought them to such a pitch, and had robbed and treated them in such a diabolical manner, that it is no wonder they were full of very bitter human feelings against those who had treated them in this way.

But still, violence is not argument, and we must take, *cum grano salis*, the very weightiest argument used against us; and it is a very important point if they are able to prove that we are no Church and no Catholics at all.

The first statement is, that Barlow was not consecrated, as we say he was, in the year 1536, in the reign of Henry VIII., by the old English Catholic ritual; for, remember, Barlow was consecrated, as bishop, at the time when no other ordinal but the old English Sarum ordinal was used.

Before the Reformation there were no such things as Roman Catholic books used in the Church of England at all. The first ones were introduced in the reign of Queen Mary. Barlow acted as bishop in the reign of Henry VIII., who, no matter how bad a creature, how great a tyrant, and how immoral a man, he was, was a a great stickler for everything Catholic; for Henry VIII., so far as his conscience (if he had any) was concerned, was an out-and-out Catholic; and *he* would have taken pretty good care that nobody should have acted as bishop without being properly consecrated.

Another argument used is that Barlow was no bishop at all, because there was no record of his consecration. That is a fact. There is no record of it in the Lambeth Register of Archbishop Cranmer; but, brethren, if there be any argument in that we shall be able to show that other consecrations are not to be found in the Lambeth Register.

Archbishop Cranmer's register was kept in a very

slovenly manner; and it is not in one whole, but consists of several different parts sewn together; and therefore there is nothing astonishing in the fact that Bishop Barlow's consecration is not to be found.

There are other omissions, and among them is Bishop Gardiner's. *That* cannot be found, and yet we have had no question, from the Roman side, of Bishop Gardiner's consecration, because he was one opposed to the "reforming" party!

So that I think the fact of Bishop Barlow's consecration not being found in the Lambeth Register is no evidence whatever to prove that he was not a lawful bishop. It is ridiculous to suppose, for a moment, that he would have been allowed to act as a Catholic bishop unless he actually had been one; for Henry VIII., I repeat, would have been the very first to have brought such a matter to book.

Then we find him acting in concert with other Catholic bishops, and being styled by one of these bishops, his "brother Bishop of St. David's." Therefore, the Catholics would be themselves to blame for acknowledging a bishop who had never been consecrated!

Then another argument is that Barlow was no bishop at all because such very loose ideas, at that time, were held about the necessity of consecration. That is a most absurdly ridiculous statement. Who held the loose ideas about the consecration of bishops? Who? Certainly not the pope of the Reformation, Henry VIII., for he held the most determined ideas upon Catholic matters ; and do you mean to say that Cranmer, who was such a pitiable tool of Henry VIII., would have gone against the violent prejudices of Henry VIII. in the matter?

No matter how loose Cranmer's ideas were upon the subject of the consecration of bishops, he would not have dared to allow such a grave irregularity as this. Cranmer did not mind chopping off other people's heads, but he took precious good care that he did not jeopardise his own!

Then we are told that when Parker was consecrated, Barlow only, of the four consecrators, used the words of consecration. Now, I do not see how our Roman Catholic brethren can make a point of this, because they have not at present settled what *is* the formula of episcopal consecration ; and if we come to consider that many of the popes have settled that much of the ritual is unnecessary to the validity of Orders, I think that our Roman Catholic brethren are living in a glass house themselves, in these minor points ; and before they throw stones at the Church of England, they should remember that we could throw stones at them with great effect.

I do not know whether I am correct in saying that

it is only five hundred years since the Roman Church had the word *dicentes* in the rubric. If so, according to their own argument, the validity of the consecration of the bishops, previous to that time, was questionable!

But our Roman Catholic friends have not proved that Barlow alone said the words of consecration! It is an open question whether the other bishops did not say the words—our records go to prove that they *all* did—but that is so unimportant that I need not deal with it.

Another argument used is, that the form of the ordinal of Edward VI., which was used in the consecration of Matthew Parker, was invalid. Now, here is a very difficult question for them. What constitutes the invalidity of the form of ordination?

If the whole of Christendom were appealed to on the subject, I cannot believe they would go further than this. They would say: all that is necessary for the validity of the consecration of a bishop is imposition of hands and prayer. Now, if they could prove that there is no imposition of hands, or that there is no prayer for the special purpose of the consecration of bishops, in the ordinal of Edward VI., then, I say, they have materially shaken our position; but if the whole of the service, and the whole of the prayers and ceremonials, are proved to be for the express purpose of consecrating a bishop; and the bishops put their hands on the one to be consecrated, saying: "Receive the Holy Ghost," it is perfectly sufficient according to the testimony of the universal visible Church of Christ.

Then, if the Roman Catholic brethren say that that ordinal was invalid, without any further reason, we must say: "very well, your popes were willing to sanction it, for Popes Pius IV. and Paul IV. both agreed to sanction the Prayer Book and the ordinal." I think I am correct in saying this; if I am not, can anyone tell me?

If Queen Elizabeth would only have accepted the authority of the Bishop of Rome, he was prepared to accept the Prayer Book in its then condition, which included the ordinal; so that our Roman Catholic brethren must find fault with the popes of that day for being willing to accept the ordinal. Either the Roman Catholics of the present day or the popes of that day are wrong; both cannot be right.

Therefore, if the present Roman Catholics are correct in asserting the invalidity of the form of our ordinal, the popes of that day were both wrong, and very far from infallible, in their judgment on the matter.

Another argument that has been used is, that the consecration of Archbishop Parker was challenged by the Catholic party five years after the event took place; and as we follow the arguments of the Roman Catholic party we cannot help acknowledging that it was challenged. But then there was another Roman Catholic party that did *not* challenge it; and if we follow Dr. Lee's work, which I feel we are very safe in doing, some of the greatest Catholics of Europe examined the subject and stated that Parker's Orders were absolutely valid. I refer to the decision of the great theological faculty of Paris in particular.

The last argument used is, that because the consecrating bishop did not deliver the chalice and patten, the ceremony was invalid; but that is too silly to talk about. It is such a modern ceremony; and if our priests are not consecrated, then the Roman Catholics were not consecrated either, for hundreds of years. That is, comparatively speaking, a modern ceremonial.

One question which has troubled a great many Church people is this—that baptism has been so carelessly practised in the Church of England that fears have been expressed, very often, whether some of our bishops have even been baptized. Well, we cannot deny this fact, unfortunately, that baptism, in our churches, has been very carelessly administered, and very often very imperfectly performed; and as the Sacrament of baptism is the initiatory Sacrament to all the other Sacraments, a man who is not baptized cannot be a lawful bishop; and a young friend the other day at "——" came to me and said that he felt that he must become a Roman Catholic because Archbishop Tait had never been properly baptized.

Do you know, brethren, I may be very wrong here,

and I may be very much mistaken; but in a question of such solemn moment as this I am so exceedingly comforted by my faith in our most loving God. I feel most perfectly restful on the matter, because I feel perfectly assured that the providence of our loving Father would overrule a matter like this present one. He knew that that young child was to be Archbishop of a great Church—the instrument through which the fellowship of the Apostles would flow, for our part of the visible Church; and do you not believe that He would, in His Fatherly love and providence, secure the validity of the initiatory Sacrament? In such a case, if I could doubt God in this matter, I could doubt Him in everything; and I was so thankful, when this young man put this before me, that I was able to lift up my own heart to God, and his heart too; and I felt perfectly content in the matter.

But "what is sauce for the Church of England goose is sauce for the Roman Catholic gander"; and we find that such things as careless Roman baptisms, in the Roman Church, are possible.

Why, as we see in Dr. Lee's book, the present great learned divine Döllinger does not know whether he has been baptized for certain; and then he tells us of a bishop of Spain who was baptized without the formula being used at all; and it was found out after he had been made bishop!

So that I really think that a point like this is an argument which would cut both ways; and unhappily there are in the Church of Rome, as well as in the Church of England, priests who do not believe in Christ. They are quite as broad in the Church of Rome as in the Church of England; the only difference being that the exercise of Roman discipline keeps them silent about their belief, whereas our Broad Church school speaks out without any fear.

But what about the baptism performed by a man who does not believe in the divinity of Christ in the Church of Rome? Do you think that his intention would be to do what that Church, of which he is priest, intends, when he does not believe the very fundamental doctrine on which it rests?

Therefore, I say, this argument would cut too far; it would cut both ways with equal force; because the validity of the Sacrament would be dependent on the intentions of the priest, according to Roman doctrine.

Then another argument used is: the Church has so often added to the ordination rites that it is not safe to tamper with any of them. I am too stupid to see the argument of that.

Our present ordination service is made use of as a very powerful argument against our Orders. The ordination services, which we now use, date from 1662; and there have been several improvements made in this service. Things that were omitted in the ordinal of Edward VI. were added to the present ordinal in 1662; and our Roman Catholic brethren acknowledge that they were a great improvement; but that they came one hundred years too late. But the improvements of 1662 were non-essential, just the same as the improvements which the Roman Church has been continually making are non-essential.

In our ordination services there is no difference in the essential rites, in the laying on of hands, and prayer; and this is all that is necessary, by the consent of the greatest teachers, and even popes of the Church of Rome.

Then our Roman Catholic brethren say: "You Church of England people try to make a great point of the fact that in your reformed Prayer Books you retained the word "priest;" and as you retained the word "priest" you say it shows that the Church of England intended to continue the true priesthood to which the reformers were opposed." But the reformers used the term "priest" in a non-Catholic sense.

But we say this is not so; and I think that the whole of this question is settled by an appeal to the preface in our ordinal.

What are the two things which the Church of England, since the Reformation, has not allowed a deacon to perform? The very two things which constitute the essence of the Christian priesthood, as acknowledged by the Church of Rome, viz: the Consecration of the Eucharist and the giving of Absolution. Those are the two things that a deacon is not allowed to perform, as functions peculiar to the Priest.

Therefore, I say, the Church of England then uses the word "priest" in its own, original sense, as the Church of Rome herself uses the word. The Church of England thus shows that she holds the word "priest" to mean what the whole of Catholic Christendom holds it to mean.

I shall conclude now by just a short reference to the question of "jurisdiction." Many Roman Catholics now say that we have a valid priesthood. They are quite willing to acknowledge that. They are willing to follow the opinions of those Roman Catholics of last century, and the century before, who examined into the question, and pronounced in favour of our Orders; but they say: "although you have a valid ministry, you have no jurisdiction." Why? Because the Bishop of Rome is the sole source of jurisdiction.

We know that when a man has been made a bishop he has a special territorial locality allotted to him, in which he is to exercise the office of a bishop.

He must not go into the diocese of another to exercise it. This jurisdiction, say our Roman Catholic brethren, can be allotted by the pope only.

If this be a fact our Roman Catholic friends must blot out from their calendars the names of a great many old Celtic saints. I want you to be very attentive to this, because there is a large Roman Catholic school which acknowledges the validity of our Orders, but denies our jurisdiction.

If jurisdiction be from papal authority only, they must expunge from their calendars all our old Celtic saints; for from whom did St. Aidan and St. Colman receive their jurisdiction? I should think they received it (we know certainly they did not receive it from the pope) from their abbot, who very likely was only a layman—the Right Rev. the Lord Abbot of Iona—who arranged the matter between the Northumbrian *kings* and themselves. He had bishops under him as monks; and he sent these bishops out to exercise the episcopal function in Northern England, in harmony with the express desire of the Northumbrian kings; so that these bishops received their jurisdiction equally from the kings and their own abbots by agreement.

May I ask also, from whom did our own magnificent patron saint of Wales, St. David, receive his jurisdiction? From whom did our old British bishops receive their jurisdiction? We know perfectly well that they repudiated—with rather an ebullition of temper, I must confess—the authority of the Pope.

It was not their fault. It was St. Augustine's bumptiousness, if I might use such a word of so holy a man, that caused them to utterly refuse any foreign interference with their ancient Churches.

I think then that the question of jurisdiction can be very easily settled, for there were bishops of the ancient British Church, long before St. Augustine's visit, who certainly never received the jurisdiction from the Pope, and yet are accepted by the Roman Church as canonised saints. I refer especially to St. Dubricius, St. Cadoc, St. Illtud, St. Sampson, and many more of the canonized British bishops.

We find that Pope Eleutherius never attempted to exercise any papal supremacy over our island when he sent missionaries here. There always was a very strong, determined feeling in our land of holding our national independence as a *bonâ fide* portion of the one Apostolic Church of Christ.

I have spoken very lengthily, and perhaps to some very uninterestingly; but I have thrown out some of the thoughts that seem to be very powerful in my own mind on this subject; and I think that if some of our chief men of the present day, both Roman and Anglican, could form a committee of investigation on the subject, a very great work, for the glory of our Lord Jesus Christ, would be done; for the painful position in which the Church of England stands ought to be regretted by all Protestants and Catholics alike.

XVII.

The Protestant Church: What is It?

Oration.

Tuesday Afternoon, October 27th, 1885.

The Protestant Church: What is It?

Prayer before Oration.

O Lord Jesus Christ, who seest and knowest the hearts of all men, and especially the hearts of Thine own people, we beseech Thee grant that our meeting together at this time, in this place, may be for Thy glory; and that the subject before us may be so treated that Thy name may be glorified in the hearts of everyone here present. Oh! let us learn, more and more, what Thou art, to each one who believes, and how Thy Church is made up of all who put their trust in Thee.

Grant to us the help of Thy Holy Spirit, at this time, that this meeting may not be in vain, as far as Thy glory, and our own good, and our own spiritual education are concerned. Grant our petitions, O Jesus Christ, the common Saviour of all who believe, for Thine own precious Name's sake. Amen.

THE PROTESTANT CHURCH: WHAT IS IT?

Oration.

"Simon Peter answered and said, Thou art the Christ, the Son of the Living God."—St. Matth. xvi. 16.

Now, here we see a most wonderful confession of Christ's Messiahship and of Christ's Divinity! Here we see, in the midst of public opinion to the contrary, a very distinct and clear declaration of that wonderful Incarnation of Christ, about which men knew nothing.

Peter declares Christ to be the Son of the Living God, and "The Christ." Our Lord then says to Peter, "Thou art Peter" (*i.e.* rocky); and on this rock—of which thou art now a part, by thy confession of Me, "The Rock of Ages"—I will build. *I*—Christ only —will build on this "Rock of Ages"; of which the Apostle St. Paul, in another place, taught of God, says "That Rock was Christ."*

But think how Peter had received the knowledge to confess Jesus to be God Almighty and "the Christ." He here confesses Christ to be that very

* 1 Cor. x. 4.

Rock of which the Psalmists and Prophets sang. He declares Christ, in spite of all the contrary public opinions of the day, to be "The Rock of Ages," even the Living God; and then, when he declares this faith, our Lord tells him whence he obtained it. It was not from flesh and blood—from any human teacher; it was not through any human means. He received his knowledge straight from the teaching of the Holy Ghost. "Flesh and blood hath not revealed it unto thee."*

And it is just the same now. Flesh and blood cannot reveal Christ to the sinner. It must be the distinct revelation of the Holy Ghost, teaching and convincing the heart of the individual man. So it is on this *Rock*, which Peter, by the inspiration of the Holy Ghost, confessed Christ to be; it is on this Rock that Christ will build. He is the Architect. No one can build Christ's Church but Christ Himself; He calls it "*My Church.*"† He says that "against this Church," which He will build on Himself, "the gates of hell shall not prevail." And the gates are a figurative expression for "the powers;" the powers of hell shall not prevail against Christ's Church.

Therefore Christ's Church is an indestructible Church. It is a Church not one part of which, by

* St. Matt xvi. 17 † St. Matt. xvi. 18.

any possibility, can be lost. If one single part of Christ's Church can perish, the gates of hell *have* prevailed against it. Therefore the Church which He has built on "the Rock," the Church which Christ Himself builds on Himself, stone by stone—as St. Peter tells us in his 1st Epistle, "Lively stones are built up a spiritual house"*—cannot be prevailed against by the gates of hell. This is the mark of Christ's Church.

And now, having taken this short view of the Church of Christ, as to Who is its Builder, how it is built, wherewith it is built, and what promise the Builder has made with regard to it, we will proceed to the subject of our address this afternoon.

Those who have been attending our mission during the past week will be fairly saturated with one idea, and so saturated with this one idea that none of them will misrepresent what I have taught. Some people, however, who do not follow us, go away with very false and incorrect impressions, and they misrepresent us (though not intentionally, I am sure) for the simple reason that they will not give us a full and fair hearing. Now you, who have followed me during the whole of the past week, will be filled with this idea, *that it is no use whatever belonging to any visible Church UNTIL we believe in Christ.*

* 1 Peter ii. 5.

Unless a man has come to Christ, unless a man has a personal trust in Christ, as his personal Saviour, it is of no use his belonging to any visible Church; and the question of Church is, therefore, an after question.

When a man has sought Christ, and by a saving, living faith has received Christ in His fulness, as God's gift to him, then is the time for him to look about to see to which Church he should belong.

And, having settled that first matter, we yesterday considered the position of the Church of Rome in the nineteenth century. This afternoon we are going to consider "The Protestant Church, and What is it?" You see I ask the question, "What is it?"

In no part of our Prayer Book is the word "Protestant" used, and we have no right to apply that term to the Church of England.

I am here this afternoon, not to speak of the Church of Rome—we spoke of that yesterday;—and I am not here to speak of the Church of England, but of the "Protestant Church." And I repeat that, in the first place, you will see, by our notice, that I ask the question, "What is it?"

I confess to myself that this is a very difficult question to answer. We shall not have time for much argument; but I should very much like some kind Christian Protestant present to give me the fixed definition of "the Protestant Church." What is the Protestant Church ?

If you will allow *me* to answer it, I should say, as a matter of history and fact, knowing as I do the original use of the term "Protestant," that a Protestant is simply a member of the German Lutheran Church; and that all other Churches, which call themselves Protestant, are not Protestant in an historical sense; because we know, perfectly well, that it was Luther, and those who followed him, in his part of what was called "the Reformation," who first adopted and applied the word "Protestant."

Therefore, to answer the question at once, it seems to me we must say that the German Lutheran Church is the Protestant Church.

But then this is simply answering the question from an historical point of view; it is not entirely correct, for we know that the word has been extended beyond its proper limits. We know very well that there are very many bodies of Christians in London who would call themselves Protestants, but who would deny that they were Lutherans. I do not think they would wish for the term if they realised the teaching, —on Sacraments for instance,—which is one of the chief peculiarities of Lutherans.

Therefore, all such are entirely separate from the term Protestant in its historical meaning.

The word "Protestant" is not merely used in a technical sense either; but it is also used in a popular sense. And I think that the word Protestant means, in a popular sense, all those who have protested against the Catholic Church; including the whole of those communities who protest against the general Church of Christendom,—for that is the meaning of the word Catholic.

It is not only against the Church of Rome that the word "Protestant" is used, for Protestants also clearly protest against, what they call, the corruptions of the Greek Church and of the Russian Church. To show you that it does not mean only those who protest against Popery, you know perfectly well that these same people would not apply the term "Protestant" to the Greek Church. And both the Greek and Russian Churches protest most emphatically against the Pope!

So we find that the word Protestant does not mean all who protest against the Church of Rome. Protestants would consider it an indignity to be classed with the Russian, the Abyssinian, and the Armenian Churches; yet all these Churches protest against the Pope.

It seems to me, therefore, that the correct definition of the term Protestant is a person who protests against the general Church of Christendom.

Protestants are a body of persons who have joined, in some shape or form, with the great helpers of the revolution, against the general Church.

I have been accustomed, during the last ten days, to so much politeness and charity and patience from my hearers, that I feel I shall be heard with the same patience and kindness this afternoon; and I wish to say, in passing, that I do not set up my opinions as infallible any more than you would set up yours; but I am only just giving you my own, when I shall leave you to judge of them according to your own light and conscience. You may be quite right on this point, and I may be quite wrong; but I am very anxious for my general congregations to know my opinions on such points.

We see, then, that the Protestant Church, historically, is simply the Lutheran Church of Germany; but we put aside the historical idea of the word, because it is not conterminous with the use that is now made of it, when Protestants are supposed to consist of all those who have separated from the doctrine and from the discipline of the general Church of Christendom.

To make this idea still more clear, I would ask this question: would Protestants feel themselves any more at home in the worship of the Russian or Greek Churches than with the Roman Catholics? They would not find nearly as much satisfaction in worshipping in those Churches as they would in the Roman Catholic Church; for they would find much in the Roman Catholic service that is in their own service. They would, in point of fact, be more at home in the Roman Catholic than in the Greek Church.

Take, then, the word "Protestant" to mean all those who protest against the general doctrine, the general government, and the general worship of general Christendom; and I shall show you to-night that the Church of England has never done this. And that is why the Church of England always uses the term "Catholic" in her creeds; and the Greek Church, in her services, also uses the word "Catholic."

I like that old English honesty of the farmer, who, when he repeated the creed and came to the words "I believe in the Catholic Church," instead of saying these words, used to stamp his foot and say, "I believe in the Protestant Church;" and when his friends asked him how he could do that in church, answered that we called ourselves Protestants *out* of church, and he wasn't going to call himself anything else *in* church! He did not believe that he was a Catholic, and he wasn't going to say that he was! Of course it was an uneducated man who spoke in that way; but at the same time there is a great deal of plain English common sense in his behaviour. That man had been taught to believe he was a Protestant, and he was determined to use the term always.

The Protestant Church, then, I have defined to be made up of all those who reject the worship, the doctrine, and the government of general Christendom. Now this Church (I call it "Church" at present for the sake of convenience, but I shall show you that I gradually dissolve the word into its real sense before I end,) you will all agree is "*the Church of the Reformation.*"

And here I meet with a very great difficulty. When we speak of reforming, we generally speak of something that comes about from within. Supposing I talk of reforming my household, I do not mean that I am going to leave it and set up another; and yet this is what was done at, what was called, the "Reformation." The reformers did not stop in the Church and reform her, by waiting upon God, and trusting to His promise; but all kinds of different persons broke away from the old Church; *and they all broke away in different directions!*

They none of them agreed among themselves why they separated from the Church. If Calvin and Luther had, in a patient, Christian spirit, stayed in the old Ship, and by faith and patience, resting on the promise of God, had tried to touch the errors that were in the Church with the magic wand of Christ's love, we should not have had the disgraceful exhibition of heathenish cruelty, that we find practised by the people who broke away from the old Church under the pretence of " Reformation." We should not have had Luther abusing Calvin with the horrible epithets he does. We should not have had the vulgar insults that the reformers flung at one another, had the spirit of Jesus been regulating their hearts.

We all know that many of Christ's own believing people also fell in with the movement; and they fell in with the movement from the purest motives. Many a Christian, yearning for greater nearness to God, tortured by the doctrines of error, yearned for better things; but he very soon found out that it was out of the frying pan into the fire that he was leaping.

If I am asked, however, to examine into the lives of most of these persons, who first broke away from the old Church, I should say that it seems to me that the spirit of the love of Jesus had left their hearts.

God forbid that I should say a word to hurt any of the Lord's people among the Protestants of to-day; but I may say this, that I am perfectly convinced that they would no more agree with the practices of the reformers than I should myself.

When we think of the horrible treatment that the people of the new doctrine inflicted on those who still conscientiously held to the old—how they used fire and faggot to put a stop to liberty of conscience—we shall see that all the stories that have been told of Catholics have been more than equalled by the Protestants; and I feel, in my own heart, that the period of the Reformation is a period that must pain the hearts of all true believers in the Gospel of love and peace, whether they be Catholic or Protestant. Catholics and the Protestants ought to form together a *protest* against the conduct, under the cloak of religion, that was so rife, on both sides, in the sixteenth century.

I touched on the fact of there being scandals in the Catholic Church. Brethren, no Catholic, possessed of the commonest of common sense, would deny that there were scandals; but then this new Church that was formed was as bad or even worse. Just look at the writings of the reformers themselves, and the terrible wholesale murderings which the teaching of the reformers produced! We must not be prejudiced on one side more than on the other, if we wish to view the subject with Christian fairness.

Too long have we, in England, been accustomed to believe that all the wickedness, and all the fire and killing, were on the Catholic side; and that the Protestants were all men of God, doing God's work, in God's own way.

Now, we know, from history, that it was nothing of the sort; and we have even more opportunities to ascertain the facts connected with the Protestant Reformation now than we had fifty years ago; and although we know that there were scandals in the Catholic Church, before we have a right to use the word "*reformation*" we should be able to prove that we have in *Christ's way*, and by *Christ's methods*, tried to bring about a cleansing of abuse in the Church in which we are placed by God's Providence.

That would be a "Reformation" in very deed and truth; but to go and separate entirely, and set up a new Institution, with new scandals, seems to me very incompatible with the term "reformation."

We are very often told that in the forming of the Protestant Church there was a great deal of murderous cruelty on the part of Catholics; and we have all sorts of instances of Catholic cruelty brought before us; but do you remember this word of Jesus: "Woe to that man by whom the offence cometh?"[*]

What was it that provoked the Catholics? What was it that stirred them up to such determination for revenge? Look into the cause well; and when you find that the creed of 1,000 years was being made an occasion for capital punishment; when you find that any man professing to be a Catholic was killed in the most barbarous manner, *e.g.*, witness the drawings and quarterings at Tyburn Gate; when

[*] St. Matt. xviii. 7.

Protestants would insult Catholics during their worship, rifle their tombs, rob their altars, as the Huguenots did in France and Belgium; and could take human beings and torture them, as the Calvinists of Holland did the Catholic martyrs of Gorcum; can you not imagine how human nature was human nature, and how the Catholics, when they got the upper hand, were glad to revenge themselves on the spoliators and persecutors of their own Church?

We must look at both sides of the question; and if we do, I will tell you what will be the consequence; we shall break down the horrible barrier that separates Catholics from Protestants.

That for which we long is to bring sinners to acknowledge Jesus as their personal Saviour,—to bring them to God; next, to bring all believers in Jesus together; and if we could only be fair, on both sides, I am sure that the bitter strife that has been waging between Catholics and Protestants would terminate.

Both parties must confess that wrong has been done on both sides.

I fear I have occupied too much time upon this part of my subject; but I must just refer, in passing, to the strange inconsistencies and extremes in which the Protestants of what is called "the Reformation" period indulged. I would remind you of the Protestants of Holland. Some of these good people took it into their heads that it was wrong to wear any clothes at all; and respectable old ladies took to walking about with nothing more on than a pair of spectacles, or perhaps an umbrella. This is very ludicrous, but it is true. One Protestant party went into one extreme, another into another; till they became a perfect Babel in every respect. If each party had gone in for liberty of conscience, it would have been all right; but they did not, as a matter of history, do so. I think it is Mr. Blunt who says, in his "History of the Reformation," that none of the reformers had the least idea of granting liberty of conscience to their opponents; and they proved it by the way in which they killed those who did not agree with them.

They had all separated from the old Pope, and they all wanted to be their own popes. This is what it was. Calvin wanted to be pope, and acted like a pope at Geneva. He utterly rejected the teaching of Luther in very many points, and spoke in very harsh language of him. Luther, on the other hand, did the same; for he was determined to be pope himself. Everyone thought himself right, and everyone else wrong; and all this was brought about by, what was called, the work of God; and styled the "Glorious Reformation."

There is another point. When once you break

away from constituted authority it takes a long time to put any other authority in its place. When once you open the flood-gates of rebellion, either ecclesiastically or politically, it is a very difficult thing to say where the rebellion will stop. The reformers broke away from the regular uniform jurisdiction of bishops; so they lost the regular order; and therefore no minister had any right to administer the Sacrament. I say that when they broke away from the old established, authorised ministry of the Church, and set up new forms of church government, they had no authority whatever for what they did, except from the *vox populi*, which is liable to as many changes as the weather.

There is one thing to be taken into consideration, which is, that wherever the reformers went *they* did not think anything of walking into a Catholic's house, and taking his things and furniture, and settling themselves in it. Now if a man were to walk into my house, turn it inside out, throw the furniture out of the windows, and then say to me: "I have reformed you;" I should say that that was very cool impudence.

The Protestants drove the Catholics out of their own houses and churches; and if this were all right and correct in the Protestants, it would be all right and correct in the Catholics. But the Catholics ought *not* to have retaliated. They forgot our Lord's words: "If any man will take thy coat let him have thy cloke also"*; and perhaps some of *us* might have forgotten them too!

They should have stood by calmly and not have said a word, but they retaliated when they had the power; and so Jesus was dishonoured and forgotten.

It is after going through the consideration of all these facts (and that they are facts you can ascertain for yourselves) that the question, "The Protestant Church, what is it?" becomes so very difficult to answer and define. I do not think there is a single sect in Christendom that does not call itself by the name of Protestant, in the general sense of the word.

I asked a Christian just now how he would define a Protestant; and he said: "All those who confess Christ, and know Him as a personal Saviour." That is a very novel definition of the term "Protestant"; but the definition will not do.

If you look at the Protestant Churches of France, Switzerland, or Germany, you will find that rationalism is the most decided tendency of them all; so I do not think that the word "Protestant," from a Christian point of view, is one which I should like to apply to any of my own Christian brethren. I think if they would give up the word "Protestant," and

* St. Matt. v. 40.

adopt that of " Christian " instead, it would be a great deal better.

May it please our Lord to grant that I have not said a word to hurt the feelings of any Protestants here present. I have far more enjoyment of spiritual communion with a converted Christian Protestant than with a dozen unconverted, unchristian Catholics.

Jesus is more to me than the ridicule of the world, and Jesus is more to a Christian Protestant than the outward form of Protestantism.

Jesus, and " Jesus only," is the common Saviour; and we must all belong to His Church, which He built on Himself, and " against which the gates of hell can never prevail"; and of the members of which He says: "No man shall pluck you out of my hand."*

" *The Protestant Church! What is it?* " is a question, then, that it is impossible to answer, even from the Protestant side itself; and I am sure *I* do not know what it is, nor would I take upon myself, the difficult—not to say impossible—task of answering the question or attempting to define the indefinable—Myth!

There is really,—as a matter of FACT—no such thing as " The Protestant Church " !

* St. John x. 28.

XVIII.

Ritualism: The Good it has Done, and the Harm it has Done.

Oration.

Wednesday Evening, October 28th, 1885.

Ritualism, the Good, and the Harm, it has Done.

Prayer before Oration.

Grant, Blessed Lord, we pray Thee, that the words to be spoken, at this time, may glorify Thee and benefit Thy people, here present, and may help to increase, and not diminish, Thy love in our hearts, for Jesus Christ's sake. Amen.

RITUALISM: THE GOOD IT HAS DONE; AND THE HARM IT HAS DONE.

Oration.

"Let all things be done decently and in order."—1 Cor. xiv. 40.

In the more literal rendering, from the Greek, this passage reads, "Let all things be done according to a good scheme, and according to order or arrangement."

St. Paul had been dealing, in the chapter from which the passage is taken, with the public worship of the Christian Church; and we, who know the circumstances of the early Church, may feel quite sure that it would have been utterly impossible, at that early period of the new Christian religion, to have made any settled arrangements *in details* respecting Christian worship. I say "in details" because we know that the early Christians worshipped in such a hurry, and under such circumstances of terror, danger, and alarm, as to render it impossible for them to conduct their worship "according to a good scheme," and according to prescribed arrangements.

The subject of this address is "Ritualism: the good it has done; and the harm it has done;" and this is a subject which has caused a vast amount of scandal. In one way or another, Ritualism has, from outsiders, brought a great deal of ridicule upon Christianity in general.

Many of you will remember that, when the revival of ritual began in the Church of England, the smallest trifles were made a reason for great riots, disturbances, and manifestations of violence. Many of us can remember the surplice riots at Exeter; but now, even our dissenting brethren, in some cases, preach in surplices. I think I am correct in saying that at Mr. Newman Hall's magnificent high-church-looking place of worship, the preacher wears a surplice.

Certain points of ritual which, at the commencement of the revival of ritual in the Church of England, were made the cause of considerable rancour and hatred, are now taken as a matter of course. People do make a fuss so often, not only about nothing at all, but about things which, in a few years, they get to like very much indeed themselves.

Now, I want to treat my subject in a matter-of-fact, and, therefore, in a fair and honest way. But may I ask one question before I proceed? It is: "*Can we do without ritual of some sort or another?*"

The universal answer, of all thoughtful Christian

men, to this question will be, "Certainly not." Every single class of professing Christian worshippers has a ritual of its own.

I remember the ritual to which I was accustomed when I was a child, and certainly I cannot say that it was very edifying.

If we take Ritualism in the sense in which I wish to apply it—and I would ask your kind consideration of the question as I bring it before you—it does seem to me that, as far as man is concerned, Ritualism is an appeal to the mind and the sense, in public worship, through the medium of the eye. Whether Ritualism be beneficial, or the opposite, is an open question.

On God's part, and with reference to Him whom we worship, it does seem to me that Ritualism is offering the best natural gifts to the Creator in the solemn worship of His Church. I know that some people would discard art altogether from the worship of God, as being distracting to the mind rather than helpful. All I would say to those who feel that an artistic ritual is distracting to their minds, is, "Let them not use it;" but let them not condemn others, who feel persuaded, by practical, and almost daily, experience, that it is an assistance to them; for we are not all constituted alike; our temperaments, characters, and idiosyncracies are totally different. Therefore we should make allowances for one another.

I think, on a subject such as the one we are now considering, we should first ascertain, as a matter of fact, what is generally understood by "Ritualism," seeing that every one uses, in worship, ritual of some kind or other. When I was a child how I used to wonder what was the meaning of certain acts of Protestant ritual that I used to see!

A Roman Catholic, when he goes into church, takes the holy water, signs himself with the cross, makes his reverence to the altar, kneels, and takes his seat; and although this seems to many of our Protestant friends a sort of mummery, because they do not view it, and appreciate it, from the same standpoint as does the Catholic, they (the Protestants) have also *their* ceremonials.

I remember, when I was young, that the Protestant gentlemen all had their very decided ritual upon entering church, and the ladies had theirs also. They generally doubled themselves up upon their seats, in their high-backed pews: but numbers of the gentlemen had a peculiar piece of ritual which consisted of standing up and looking into their hats. Do you know, really and truly, when I was a child I was so puzzled to know what it all meant! I really thought it meant something, but what I did not know.

I could draw other pictures of Protestant ritual to which I was accustomed; but of course this is all a matter of taste to a great extent, and I should be very sorry to tell a gentleman that he has not a right to double himself up, or look into his hat; but I do not see why he should object to my kind of ritual when I enter church; for we both follow our own tastes; and perhaps, if we were to examine the case, we should find more conscientiousness in the Ritualist's, than in the Protestant's, case; because I do not think there is any conscientious motive in practising the very peculiar ritual to which I have just alluded.

Have you not often been at really devoutly attended Protestant meetings? I have, very often; and I have found that, while nearly all agree to kneel down at private meetings, they do not kneel in public; and I have often wondered why our Protestant Christian brethren have such an objection to kneeling; and why we so seldom see, in "a low church," people really on their knees! They have a way of sitting and bending over; and this, recollect, is an act of ritual!

But I cannot say that I enjoy such kinds of ritual.

For instance, you may see one devout old gentleman turn his back upon everybody, and face the wall; and you will see a perhaps equally devout old lady facing in another direction. You will see one looking in one way, a second in another, and still another sitting with his back to the rest; all in different positions and attitudes, and all equally devout.

That ritual, to my mind, is something very ludicrous.

All this, however, is a matter of feeling, taste, and opinion; though, as far as I am concerned, I must say that I do not think the ritual arrangements of our Protestant friends are always as solemn and edifying as they might be.

You see, then, that it is a fact that all of us, to a certain extent, practise some form of ritual in our attitude, and in our mode of worship; that ritualism, in some shape or other, cannot be dispensed with; and that it is universally practised in a greater or lesser degree.

But now we have to ask another question: " is an ornate ritual, such as we associate with the word 'Ritualism,' in harmony with the mind of God; and is it in accordance with God's revealed will?" If such ritual be not in harmony with God's Word; if it be not in accordance with His Holy Will, as revealed to us, no matter how I may admire it, I should think that I was wrong in practising it.

What answer can we make to the following question? Has Almighty God ever revealed His Mind as to the manner in which His public worship should be conducted? Has God ever prescribed definitely the mode and method of Divine Worship among His people?

We know that He certainly did so for the Jewish Church, by the mouth of Moses, His prophet; and we know that the Mosaic Church was symbolical, and very minute in detail—so much so that the very colours of the embroidery on the curtains in the Temple were prescribed by the Holy Ghost Himself; and we are told that the Holy Spirit enabled the workmen to carry out the embroidery which God had commanded.

We cannot, therefore, call this trivial; we cannot call this childish; for God Himself expressed His mind and will in the matter.*

Now our Protestant brethren may say that that was a prescription for worship in the Old Testament religion, when everything was shadowy and emblematical; but that it was done away with in Christ. But when they say all this was done away with in Christ, it does seem to me that they are begging the question, unless they can give chapter and verse in the New Testament for the statement.

I do not see any authority in the Scriptures that a beautiful and ornate offering to God was done away with in Christ. But then they may say: "oh! but God said, 'God is a Spirit: and they that worship Him must worship Him in spirit and in truth.'"† But that has nothing to do with the question, for the religious Jews worshipped God "in spirit and in truth."

So now the question comes as to the authority and practice of an ornate ritual.

* Exodus xxxvi. 1, 2, 3, 4.   † John iv. 24.

Do we find any definite, rubrical arrangements in the New Testament, as in the Old? We do not. But then, we must remember, that the circumstances surrounding the early Christian Church were totally different from those that surrounded the Jewish; and it would have been utterly impossible—humanly speaking—for the early Christians to carry out any fixed code.

The early Christians had to flee from town to town, and their worship was often broken in upon by the presence of persecutors, who would discover them, at their night services, in caves of the earth. For some time the Church of Christ practised no particular order of ritual in their worship. At the beginning there was no settlement for Christians; nor were there any churches for them wherein to worship. In those early days we do not read of a single fixed place of worship being built—I believe we have no testimony of such; and the Christians met in all kinds of places, by river-sides, in caves of the earth, in upper rooms; they met secretly at midnight assemblies; and we read of St. Paul preaching till midnight and administering after-midnight Sacrament.*

But, it may be asked, after the Christian Church became settled, and was able to act out St. Paul's

* Acts xx. 7, 11.

instructions, as stated in the text, how *did* they act out those instructions? Have we, in our possession, at the present day, copies of any liturgies of the ancient Churches of God to give us an idea whether their services were "ritualistic," in the modern acceptance of the term, or not?

As a matter of fact, we have very ancient liturgies in our possession: we have the liturgies of the Egyptian Church, the liturgy of St. Mark, the liturgy of St. James, and we have also the liturgies of St. Chrysostom and St. Basil, showing the method upon which they acted in carrying out St. Paul's instructions: "Let all things be done decently and in order."*

At the first commencement, and during the subsequent development, of Christian worship, a high ritual, and ornate symbolism, were used by Christians in their worship of God; and it does seem to me that we find a really more ornate symbolism *then* being used, than is used now in the worship of our blessed Lord and Saviour Jesus Christ.

Then, what about English Church ritualism? I suppose most of my hearers know that *the English Church never used the Roman Catholic ritual;* I suppose my hearers also know that, from time immemorial, the English Church had her own national

* 1 Cor. xiv. 40.

service, peculiarities, and ritualistic arrangements; and if you compare the old ritual of the English Church with that of the Roman Catholic Church (I do not wish to offend any one, but I do say, without fear of contradiction, if you compare the two), you will find that the ritual of the old English Church was, if possible, far more stately and ornate than were the ceremonials of the Church of Rome!

This ritualism was put in form by St. Osmund, of Salisbury, and received the sanction of nearly the whole Church of the British Islands; so that the Sarum Ritual became the authority of the British Church as far as Aberdeen in the north, and St. David's in the west.

When I was at Dunkeld in Scotland, I found out that the Sarum Ritual of the Church of Britain was used there; I also found, two years ago, at St. David's in Wales, proof of the adoption, even there, of the Sarum Ritual.

The ritual of the English Church was always peculiar to herself; and if the liturgical scholars of the day applied to any foreign Church for assistance, they went to the Gallican Church—and *not* to the Roman—because there always existed bonds of unity between the Gallican and the Anglican Churches from earliest times.

It would take more time than I could afford

to give you the intricate history of, and enter into details respecting, English ritual; but, as a matter of fact, the British, Saxon, and Norman elements in English ritual were consolidated into one form by St. Osmund in the twelfth century.

But there came, in the sixteenth century, a great change in the matter of "Ritualism." Remember, it is distinctly British ritual of which we are speaking.

In the time of the Tudors we see the ritual of the Church of England receiving a tremendous blow; when the Sarum and other books of British Church authority were, as far as they possibly could be, collected and destroyed.

When Edward VI.'s short reign terminated, and Queen Mary came to the throne, she desired to restore the old British ritual; but the books had been nearly all destroyed! The magnificent manuscripts and the vast libraries, where the learning and researches of our British forefathers had been stored with the industry and perseverance of generations, were sent in cartloads to be burnt, or in shiploads to be used as waste paper in foreign lands. Our libraries, ecclesiastical works, rare and wonderful manuscripts, ritual books, and copies of the Scriptures, which had been collected together in the various monastic libraries, were brought forth and destroyed; and in Queen Mary's reign it was impossible, under the circumstances, to have an English rite practised as it had been practised before.

Then the first introduction of the Roman Breviary and Missal into the English Church took place; and that only lasted a few years, and its introduction was brought about by the universal destruction of the Church of England service books.

In Queen Elizabeth's reign matters changed again. "Good Queen Bess" we are accustomed to call her, although the more we look into that lady's character the more ground we find for supposing her to have been savage and very cruel; and if we call Mary "Bloody Queen Mary," I think we should call Elizabeth "Bloody Queen Elizabeth;" for if we must use hard names we ought to be equal and fair in the distribution of the nomenclature. We find that Queen Mary was called "bloody," because her council spurred her on, against her will to a great extent, to kill nearly five hundred Protestants; while Queen Elizabeth goes scot-free, although she caused the death of *more* than five hundred Catholics, and positively had them chopped up, and drawn and quartered! I think that treatment was equally as cruel as burning; and I am equally indignant that either course should have been taken.

I do not think I can say that I admire Queen

z

Elizabeth; because, not only was she cruel, but I think she was not quite as honest as she might have been. She was a Catholic out and out at heart, and only for political motives enforced Protestantism on our Church.

She was determined to sweep away the Catholic ritual from the parish churches, *but she used to have it in her own chapels*; and when the bishops came to her and said, "how can you expect the people to give up their ritual if *you* retain yours?" Queen Elizabeth's answer to them was "to mind their own business; for she intended to do just as she pleased." And she retained her candlesticks, censers, and whatever ritual she chose. She had political motives for trying to extinguish all Catholic feeling in the hearts of her subjects.

But I am not here to give a lecture upon the reign of Queen Elizabeth, or I should be able to draw out facts to prove the truth of what I am saying.

It was simply for political reasons that Queen Elizabeth supported Protestantism, in the Church of England; and I should like to advise those, who may wish to study the question, to read Mr. Hubert Burke's work, "Portraits of the Tudor Dynasty."

Then, we have seen that ritual, in the reign of Queen Elizabeth, received a still further blow; and we know how the tremendous religious cataclysm of the sixteenth century culminated in the political and religious catastrophe of the seventeenth. We know how Henry VIII. ruled with despotism and tyranny; and how he handed on an inheritance to his successors, which culminated in the martyrdom of Charles I.; who seems to have been the one upon whose head alighted the last woe of the tyranny—the fearful tyranny—inaugurated by Henry Tudor.

And if we compare the private life and disposition of Charles Stuart with that of Henry Tudor, who inaugurated that strange novelty of autocracy in British Government, we shall see that the innocent suffered for the guilty. It has always been so; and so long as wrong reigns, in this world of woe, these things will be.

In the Stuarts' time not only was ritual swept away, but even the use of the Prayer Book was forbidden, and a heavy penalty was attached to the infringement of the law in this respect.

With the head of the Archbishop of Canterbury, the head of the King of England fell—*with the dethronement of the Church came the dethronement of the State;* and Crown, Church and State fell for a time together. Afterwards, when the new state of things was successful, for a few years, we know how the tyranny of the Puritans proved even more vexatious than that of the king.

The Puritans determined to force their peculiarities upon an unwilling nation; so that I say the tyranny of the Puritans became more overbearing still than the tyranny of the Tudors, because it was of a kind, very, very deep and far-reaching —reaching even to the private life of British citizens.

Just imagine the Puritan body becoming dominant, with their severe ideas upon religion; and determining to thrust, *nolens volens*, their views upon the whole nation!

So England suffered under another tyranny at the time of the Commonwealth, which prepared the English nation for another tremendous revolution of feeling; and we soon find the people of London with bonfires blazing, with fountains of wine flowing, and with bells ringing, welcoming Charles II. back to the throne of his fathers.

Then, after the Restoration, the ritual of the Church of England became very, very dilapidated indeed; until, in the Hanoverian era, we find the Lion and the Unicorn taking the place of the Cross in the churches—the Cross of Christ had quite disappeared, and the arms of England had taken its place; as if to represent that the Church was a Church formed by the State, and was under the State, which we showed, in the address* last night, was not the case.

We can well understand that the worship of the Lion and the Unicorn, surmounting the motto "Georgius Rex," was not very spiritual; taken together with the extraordinary dilapidations in ecclesiastical life—if I may use such an expression; for we find many a parish priest hurrying his surplice over his shooting-jacket to conduct the weekly service, and many of the churches, meanwhile, in which it was conducted, damp, mildewed, miserable, and wretched; while the service itself was gone through in the most slovenly manner.

There are, in fact, ample grounds to justify us in the conclusion that English Church ritual, at this time, reached its very, very lowest ebb; and that this utter extinction of religious decency, in outward formalities, had a corresponding effect upon the spirituality of the people. We know quite well what a fearful spiritual gloom lay over our dear old National Church during the Georgian era.

Last night I referred to the action of the Countess of Huntingdon in attempting to put a stop to the scandals in Lambeth Palace; and I think we, at the present day, owe a great debt of gratitude to the

* Oration on "Church of England and Disestablishment."

movement which the Countess of Huntingdon set on foot. They called her, in that day, a madwoman; but numbers flocked to aid her in bringing about a purer preaching of the simple message of Jesus Christ.

Therefore this Countess was one of the first to inaugurate the early reformation in the Church of England.

Wesley and Whitefield then sprang up, at God's command. "The Lord gave the word: great was the company of the preachers."* The realities and fundamental doctrines of the true old Christian faith began once more to shed their beneficent light abroad; and crowds flocked, with eager, willing ears to hear a Whitefield or a Wesley tell that Jesus Christ was God's Own Son, and their Saviour. These men the Church of England persecuted, in the persons of her bishops.

The Church made a great mistake then, but has learnt her error since; and has received with open arms, at last, what is called the Evangelical movement.

The Evangelical movement was the commencement of the real Reformation which we are now enjoying. Yes; it did not begin by inducing people to go to Sacraments, in giving more frequent administrations; but it *began by offering a personal Saviour to each indi-*

* Psalm lxviii. 11; Pr. Bk. v.

vidual sinner; and that is the right way in which a spiritual reformation should begin.

The child has to be born before it can take milk of its mother; and the restoration and revival in the Church began with a revival of Evangelical and spiritual life; and it was the correct beginning; and it is because the Ritualistic movement and, to a very great extent, the Tractarian before it, did not more thoroughly endorse the Evangelical movement that they were not more successful.

Wesley and Whitefield were the forerunners of Newman and Pusey; and they were the forerunners of those who promote modern Ritualism. When the Tractarian movement arose, between fifty and sixty years ago, the Evangelical movement was, by a very great many of the promoters of the Tractarian movement, ignored or regarded as an opposition; but if they had endorsed the Evangelical movement, and had brought the revival of the Sacraments *into* the Evangelical movement, the two would have made a beautiful, living, and satisfactory whole.

What is the use of the Sacraments to a people who have not received the Spiritual life that the Evangelical movement brought? To give the Evangelical movement a "slap in the face," as so many of the Tractarians did, seems as though they were cutting the throat of their own movement by doing it. It does seem to me—and I speak from practical, Christian experience—that, unless I have first obtained the blessings of the Evangelical movement, the Tractarian movement will be to me a curse instead of a blessing. I do not believe in Sacraments unless the person who participates in them has a personal belief in a personal Saviour.

A great many of the Evangelicals, seeing the attitude which the Tractarians assumed, rose up in opposition to their movement; and thus the two movements, instead of coalescing, and working together, as two parts of a great whole, became antagonistic.

Hence the strife and bitterness, and the needless expenditure of strength upon questions of party differences!

I do not suppose that anyone who knew Dr. Pusey could love him, or reverence his memory, more than I do myself. Of Dr. Pusey the world knew very little, because his life of holiness was such a hidden life. Very few knew him more privately or more intimately than I had the privilege of knowing him; and, before my own conversion to the Evangelical faith, I had many a warning and many a reproof from the reverend Doctor for the bitterness with which I spoke against Dissenters. Dr. Pusey was not a Ritualist.

What do I see in him? A venerable old gentleman, in a tailed-coat, dressed like an ordinary Englishman, only very untidy—in fact, so untidy that I used often to think I should like to brush him up a little. I say this with all reverential respect.

But to call Dr. Pusey a Ritualist is nearly enough to make anybody, who knew him, laugh. I am sure he never put on a cassock; and I remember so well, when I was staying with him at Christchurch, his going to officiate at morning prayer, in the Cathedral. He came in at the last minute, picked up a dirty old surplice and a bundle of old crape—brown from age—hurried on the surplice, put the crape round his neck, and walked off to the Cathedral. This may shock some people, who regard Dr. Pusey as very punctilious in the matter of vestments; but they must remember that the Tractarian was quite distinct from the Ritualistic movement; in fact it was a very unritualistic movement; the Ritualistic movement grew out of the Tractarian movement, which restored the Sacraments to their former position, by having constant celebrations, by exalting the dignity of Holy Baptism, restoring the churches, and giving greater beauty to the outward form of Christian worship.

When, then, I look at the revival of Ritualism, I

think it did this good: it restored our churches, throughout the length and breadth of the land—those old shrines and sanctuaries which our forefathers, in their piety, had caused to be built, in their massive grandeur, and which were going to decay, or had been partially restored and greatly disfigured. We know the history of the term "Churchwardens' restorations!"

The second good that it did was to restore the outward beauty of Christian worship—slovenliness and irreverence in conducting service in the churches were done away with by degrees.

The next good that the Ritualistic movement did was to make our English Church outwardly more like the rest of Christendom than it was before.

I do not think, myself, that an Englishman should think it right to regard Christianity as a religion simply for the English. I think our insularity causes us to be a little narrow upon these matters; but I do think that, within the last fifty years, the Church of England, which, previous to that time, was totally unlike the rest of Christendom, in its outward worship, has been made more and more like the rest of Christendom, by Ritualism; and that is a good thing.

Next, I think that Ritualism is to the *converted* Christian—mark the stress I lay on the word "*converted*"—an outward expression of Gospel truth.

I see in the Ritualism of the Christian Church "JESUS ONLY," in every part: "Jesus only," as "the author and finisher of our faith"* by which His Saints "are perfected";† and I feel that in the ritual of the Church I am giving a simple and outward expression of my Evangelical faith.

But, on the other hand, what is the use of an outward expression of a thing which you do not inwardly possess? If people practice ritual without possessing the inward life, without having the Evangelical faith, Ritualism is a dangerous unreality to their souls.

Lastly, Ritualism has done good by bringing whole multitudes into the Churches who, otherwise, would never have gone into them at all; and if the preaching of the Gospel, in its simplicity, had followed up the ritual, I feel that a vast amount of spiritual good would have resulted from it.

Then, what do we find were the several faults of the movement? The first fault seems to me to have been that the Ritualistic movement, to a very great extent, has been devoid of simple, Evangelical teaching; and not only has it been devoid of such teaching, but there has been a distinct and determined resolution, on the part of some of its promoters, to set their faces, at the beginning, against Gospel preaching. They left out the idea of a good sermon, and you would

---

* Heb. xii. 2.   † Heb. x. 14.

hear them mumble through a short sermon of ten minutes' duration, much in the same way as they also mumbled through the Lessons. That was a very sad mistake, and it has done a great deal of harm; and has prejudiced a great many Christians against Ritualism, who would not otherwise have been prejudiced against it.

The next harm that Ritualism has done, is that it has attracted to our churches whole crowds of worldlings, and unconverted men and women, without converting them; leaving them just as they were, while outwardly professing to belong to the Catholic Church. They do not wish their enjoyment, and fellowship with the world, to be interfered with by their being in the Church; but we know that Jesus Christ says : "Ye are not of the world—I have chosen you out."*

Therefore I say that Ritualism has given comfort to worldly men and women, but has not attempted to draw them from the world, its fashions, its follies, and its pleasures; but has attempted to make these things harmonise with the Christian religion. We might just as well try to make oil and water mix.

The Ritualistic movement, I consider, has been very much hindered by the worldly element that has

* St. John xv. 19

obtruded itself into it. I know numbers and numbers of devout Christian people who point to the results of Ritualism in the persons of worldly men and women, who make outward professions, but who are not believers in Christ. "Look," they will say, "at that ritualistic young man; he will tell you he is a Catholic; and yet while he is partaking of the Sacrament one day, he is frequenting the haunts of fashionable dissipation the next."

So, brethren, this worldly element has been a detracting element in the movement.

And then, I repeat, it does seem to me that the leaders of the Ritualistic movement did wrong in repudiating the work of the great Evangelical leaders, Whitefield and Wesley. If Ritualism had only been the outward manifestation of the truths which the first reformers—Wesley and Whitefield—taught, I believe the movement would have been productive of much greater results.

It does seem to me that instead of making the Gospel, in its simplicity and fulness, the basis of the movement, they led people to believe that salvation is a matter of sacramental and ritualistic machinery— that you are in fact to be saved by machinery; as if the Sacraments could be of use to a man who has not really a personal faith. Ritualism is driving people to the Holy Communion whom it ought to have driven away from it, beginning at the wrong end with the individual sinner's heart and soul and life.

Probably you will wonder why I, who speak in such strong language, am such a Ritualist myself—in fact the Ritualists say I have gone too far for them; but I say if it be right—if their practices be right—we had better do the whole thing at once, and have done with it, and not be for ever torturing congregations with little additions and introductions month after month. Those very things for which my ritualistic friends have persecuted and abused me they are now doing themselves: I have had the kicks and they have had the coppers!

The point I want to make next is this: that, while knowing and profiting by the mistakes that have been made by so many individual actors in the movement, we have yet repelled numbers of really Christian souls who need not have been repelled.

I can tell of cases of Dissenters, and Low Churchmen, who have travelled hundreds of miles on pilgrimage to our monastery, to join in our worship. I remember at the last pilgrimage but one, how someone came and told me that a Dissenting family had arrived from Manchester, and wished to see me. I am nearly always overcome with work; but this was such a pressing invitation that I felt compelled to see the father of this family; and I told him that I was astonished they should have come to join in our "popery." "Oh!" said the gentleman, "you put it in such a totally different light; and although we are a Dissenting family we can thank God for all we have seen and heard at your services."

Again I would ask: "do not you think that we have positively, in the Ritualistic movement, really encouraged worldliness in the Church of Christ?" I have heard men say, "I do not approve of the cant of the Methodists; I do not think it is necessary to separate from the pleasures of the world." Then I have asked: "what do you mean by the pomps and vanities you renounced at your baptism and confirmation?" There do not seem to be any pomps, as far as they are concerned; for they do not renounce any of them. I remember asking a lady, a little time ago, how she could reconcile going to balls and theatres with constant Sacrament receiving. I said: "did not you renounce the pomps and vanities of the world at your baptism; and do not you confirm that renunciation each time you partake of the Sacrament?" "Oh!" she replied, "I do not consider these things are pomps!" "Then," I said, "what are the pomps? For if they do not mean participating in every kind of worldly pleasure, I know of no other definition of the word."

If we are Christian Ritualists, and want to bring

God's blessing into the movement, let us cast out the world entirely from the midst of it; and let us realise the word of the Apostle that "our conversation is in Heaven."* Let us not be ashamed of the word "Jesus," the name of Jesus, the love of Jesus, and the salvation of Jesus! If we be Christians shall we be ashamed of confessing Christ at all times?

Let us get rid of worldliness from our movement then we shall be doing more good to advance the cause of Ritualism than we can have any idea of. In many cases Ritualism has reduced religion to nothing but a mere outward form.

I have heard a young Ritualist speak in this way: "I must go and see Father So-and-so. I have such a cartload of sins to get rid of before I shall be able to enjoy myself again with a comfortable conscience!" Imagine such a thing as that! They seem to me to put the priest and the Sacraments entirely in the *place* of Christ.

We shall not remedy the matter by hiding these facts, or by covering them up. Rather let us drag them to the light, and ask ourselves this question: "What is the good of an outward form of religion, and all the machinery of an outward ritual, unless we have the reality in our worship; by which we shall be able to *die* as well as *live*?"

* Philippians iii. 20.

One more harm the Ritualistic movement has done: it has conspired to desecrate the Lord's Day—yes, positively conspired to desecrate the Lord's Day. Many Catholics of the Church of England are quite ready to have the Lord's Day secularised.

As a Christian, I cannot understand how this can be. We certainly know that the Sunday is not a legal sabbath, but is a freewill offering, consecrated to our precious Lord Jesus. The afternoon of Sunday belongs to Him as much as the morning; and if I love to worship in the morning I should just as jealously desire to consecrate the afternoon to the service of God.

I have six days for the world, and one day for God—that is our free-will offering: and I would not take one single hour away. Sunday cannot be kept too jealously by Christians, especially considering the moral atmosphere of the nineteenth century.

I know that one of the excuses made by some of our Ritualistic brethren is, that they want to be a little more like the Roman Catholics in this matter.

Here I say they make a mistake, for the religious Roman Catholic does not approve of the desecration of Sunday; and there is, at this present day, a regular Roman Catholic Society formed in France for the hallowing of the Christian sabbath.

In conclusion, I would point you to the remedy for the faults of Ritualism.

AA

It does seem to me, that the remedy is just simply this, and nothing else but this—*the lifting up of Jesus Christ, in His fulness, in our churches;* because, "I, if I be lifted up, will draw all men unto Me,"* says Jesus; and when once a man is drawn to Christ—be he Methodist or Ritualist, High Church or Low Church—there comes into his life a light, into his heart a power, into his conscience a cleansing, which enables him to live close to God.

The one remedy is "Jesus only;" and if the present Ritualistic movement only will take up, and bring prominently forward, the love of Christ and the simple teaching of His word, we shall be able to view it under a wholly different aspect; for all the bitterness of party spirit will then pass away; and as we are inspired to lift Christ up we shall "love one another as Christ also has loved us."†

---

* St. John xii. 32. † St. John xv. 12; xiii. 34; Ephes. v. 2.

XIX.

Why were the Monasteries of England Destroyed?

Oration.

Tuesday Afternoon, May 25th, 1886.

Why were the Monasteries of England Destroyed?

Prayer before Oration.

Grant, dear Lord Jesus, that the words which we shall hear and speak may be for Thy glory. Bless us, O Lord, with the realisation of Thy Presence, and be with us, for Thy dear Name's sake. Amen.

WHY WERE THE MONASTERIES OF ENGLAND DESTROYED?

Oration.

"Jesus said: Every one that hath forsaken houses, or brethren, or sisters, or father, or mother, or wife, or children, or lands, for My Name's sake, shall receive an hundred fold, and shall inherit everlasting life."—St. Matt. xix. 29.

These words, whether rightly or wrongly understood, have been the means of the formation of countless Monastic communities in the Christian Church. The venerable Bede quotes these words in treating of this subject; and they are used as one of the Monastic lessons on the festival of St. Benedict.

I am very sorry to say that it pleases God that most of my strength has gone; I cannot give you half the lecture that I should have liked to have given, because I am sitting here thoroughly done up from overwork. But may I ask you, before I begin my address, to picture to yourselves the magnificence of the venerable ruins which stud our country? May I ask you to contemplate, just for a moment, the grandeur, the magnificence of design, the gigantic efforts of art, which have combined to make these stupendous abbeys and priories, throughout our land, the wonder of every succeeding generation ?

What could have been the splendid force that produced such unutterably magnificent designs for religion's sake ? You have an instance of what they were in their splendour in the church close by, St. Peter's of Westminster. Hundreds upon hundreds of buildings, equal to that in beauty, are now the utter desolation of ruin.

Instead of the magnificent buildings, resounding with the perpetual praise of God night and day, for which purpose they were built—instead of the magnificent chapter-houses, in which the interests of the poor, and often of the kingdom, were discussed, by hearts and voices consecrated to Jesus; instead of the magnificent crypts, the libraries, which countless ages of Christian intellect and Christian enthusiasm had collected; instead of the marvellous hospices and houses of learning and charity, which then existed in connection with the monasteries, for the alleviation of every kind of human suffering; instead of all this splendour of Christian charity, learning and intellect, what have we now ?

Why were these splendid monasteries, a Christian

nation's provision for the poor; the houses of the benevolent and the learned; why were they destroyed? This is the subject of our lecture this afternoon.

First of all, we should ascertain the meaning of the word monk. A monk means a man who has made himself "a solitary;" a man who has separated himself from his fellow-men.

Man is, we all know, a gregarious animal. Humanity, generally speaking, is necessarily so, because God provided that it should propagate itself, and that it should increase.

But there were always, in the midst of this gregarious humanity, a few human beings who lived a life of separation from the crowd. A monk, therefore, means a man who lives alone—a Christian monk is one who does this for Jesus' sake. The Christian monk is a man who has left the world, and all that the world holds dear, for the sake of Him Who said: "Every one that hath forsaken father or mother, for my sake, shall receive an hundred fold."*

We are often reminded that Monasticism is peculiar to the Roman Catholic Church; but this is a great piece of ignorance, for all the Churches of Christendom have possessed their monastic institutions. The Church of Britain had her Monasteries on a very large scale; and it was the Monks of the British Church

* St. Matt. xix. 29.

who, in the first instance, repudiated the attempt of the Roman Church to assert supremacy over the British Church. Therefore, the idea that Monasticism is peculiar to Romanism is utterly false and unhistorical.

People often say to me: "how can you be a monk in the Church of England?" "I do not think you know anything about it," is my reply; and, as a matter of fact, people do not think about these subjects, or give themselves the trouble to inquire into them.

I suppose you know that every Church, either in connection with Rome or not, had her Monasteries; therefore the Church of Britain was not peculiar from the rest of Christendom in her possession of monastic institutions.

Remember that Christian Monasticism arises from the invitation of our Lord Jesus Christ, and that the monks were those people who loved Him with sufficient love to be led by the spirit of God, to dedicate themselves to the Lord, by a vow to lead a solitary life in His service.

And now I come to our question: "Why were the Monasteries of the Church of England destroyed?"

Are we not taught that they were destroyed on account of the vices of the monks and nuns?

As a boy, I remember, when I passed a ruined church, I admired its magnificence and the wonderful power, the wonderful force of intellect, of art and devotion, which my common sense told me had produced such splendid proofs of ancient piety; but I then thought that they had become so bad—the homes of vice and of rioting, in fact, instead of the houses of piety; and that therefore the Church of England, to quote the words of good old Bishop Jackson of London, " closed her Monasteries on account of the vices that were prevalent in them."

I remember, so well, an interview that I had with Bishop Jackson once at his house in St. James's Square, after several persons had petitioned him to allow me to preach in his diocese; but he had not granted the request.

I asked his Lordship : " Why will you not allow me to accept the invitation to preach in the churches of your diocese ? " He answered : " I am not prepared to sanction an order of preaching friars." " But, my Lord," I said, " I have nothing to do with preaching friars. A friar is a totally different thing from a monk. I assert that I am a monk by the call of God."

The dear bishop knew no more the difference between a friar and a monk than this brass knob does.

I then said: " you will not allow me to preach, because you are not prepared to allow what does not exist. There are no preaching friars in the Church of England ; and I do not want to be a preaching friar."

Then he said to me: "remember, Mr. Lyne, the Church of England, at the Reformation, closed the Monasteries because she found it necessary to do so."

I replied: "My Lord, I never heard that before, and I think you are very much mistaken. The Church of England never closed a single monastery at the Reformation. Henry VIII. smashed them all to pieces, and robbed them of their properties. The Church of England never closed one monastery; and the clergy and the people rose up in support of the monasteries when Henry VIII., by his hired mercenaries, smashed them to atoms, and gave their magnificent properties to the rascals and disgraceful characters whom he, by his own vices, had collected around his throne." Words to this effect were my rejoinder.

The bishop then said: "I see it is of no use talking to you."

But now let us be calm, and it is very necessary that I should be calm over this subject; for I feel so very deeply upon it.

"Why were the Monasteries of the Church of England destroyed?" We are told that they were destroyed because Henry VIII., through his Vicar-General, Thomas Cromwell, authorised a general visitation to the Monasteries of the Church of England, to ascertain their moral and religious condition. He chose, through this Vicar-General, Thomas Cromwell, for the general visitors of the monasteries, such men as Rice, London, and Leyton. These men visited the monasteries and reported that they were in a most desperate, immoral condition, and also that the nunneries were in the same horrible state.

But, brethren, it is a most extraordinary fact that Henry VIII. had himself only just written to the Pope of Rome to say in what an excellent condition the Monasteries of the Church of England were, and especially the Friaries; at the same time praising the moral and religious condition of the monks and nuns.

And again, when Henry VIII. wanted to destroy the lesser Monasteries, he publicly stated, before the House of Commons, that as for the great Monasteries of the realm, " religion was right well kept up and observed in them." So, by his letter to the Pope—Leo X. I think it was—and by his own confession, before the Commons of the country, the greater Monasteries maintained the discipline and piety of their profession.

This was the general acknowledgment of the man who destroyed them. I should like you to examine into the characters of these men—London, Rice, Lee, and Leyton—who were the King's visitors to the monasteries. They were men of the most infamous character, who were chosen, for this reason, by Thomas Cromwell, who gave them their instructions: "The king needs the monies of the Monasteries."

The king had spent all the accumulated wealth of his father, Henry VII. He was in a great state for want of money; and also the monks were the men who were courageous enough to reproach the king for his vices; and to refuse to accept the king's supreme headship over the Church of England. They also determinately rejected the legality of the divorce of the king from his lawful wife Queen Catharine.

Therefore, on account of the monks not being willing to assist Henry VIII. in the indulgence of his vices, and also seeing that the monks possessed one-seventh of the soil of England, for the benefit of the poor of England, Henry VIII. desired the destruction of the monasteries; and in order to pave the way for this, and make it more easy, he resolved to manufacture lies, of the most horrible and monstrous description, against the characters of the monks and nuns.

When the reports about the condition of the Monasteries had been published, by means of these visitors, the king was in hopes that the people of England would become more agreeable to his desires of appropriating the monks' property.

But did the people of England of *that* day believe the stories of the king's visitors respecting the monasteries ? Not a bit of it. Do you not think that the people of England, of that day, were in a better position to judge the monks than people of succeeding ages ?

Remember, the people of England, of that day, were the fathers and the mothers, and the uncles and the cousins, and the sisters of the men that formed the Monastic communities of England. In those days the boys and girls of the rising generation were the pupils of the monks and nuns, and lived with the monks and nuns, and saw their daily life. Did the people of England accept the reports of Henry VIII.'s visitors to the monasteries ? You know, as well as I do, that it is a matter of history that they utterly repudiated them ; and not only repudiated them ; but rose in thousands, all over the country, to protect the monks and nuns against the forces of Henry VIII., when he was determined to destroy the monasteries and appropriate their possessions.

Brethren, it is a very extraordinary thing that Henry VIII. was obliged to use hired, foreign mercenaries to destroy the monasteries. They were not British soldiers who overthrew those sacred homes of religion and piety. They were hired mercenaries of the vilest description from Switzerland and Austria, and Italy ; men who sold themselves to the different monarchs of the day for the express purpose of carrying out their wills.

So Henry VIII., by foreign, brute force, and in spite of the will of the people, robbed the Church of England of her monasteries. He tried to get an Act of Parliament passed in order to permit the dissolution, as it was called—a very euphonistic term—of the monasteries.

When this Act of Parliament was put before the British Legislature, how was it received? Unanimously the House of Commons rejected it. What was the result? The King, when he heard of it, strutted up and down the gallery of the House, and said: "Gentlemen, I hear you refuse to pass my Bill. If you do not pass my Bill I'll have some of your heads." That was the way in which the King secured the passing of the Act of Parliament.

I do not flinch from the closest examination into the question.

I do not deny that there were scandals in the monasteries. Of course there were. But was that any excuse for dissolution? If it be an excuse for dissolution, there are scandals in houses here in London; but I think it would be an extraordinary piece of injustice that, because of these scandals, these houses should be "dissolved," and smashed to atoms, and their inmates robbed of their possessions.

Professor Maitland, in his preface to the " History of the Dark Ages," as they were called—the Middle Ages—asserts: "Whatever the monks and nuns were in themselves, they were at all times, and in all places, much better than the other people." That is the testimony of a Protestant historian, who has given his mind energetically, and honestly, to a strict investigation of the subject.

So you see then why the Monasteries of the Church of England were destroyed. It was to gratify the lusts and the greed of an autocratic tyrant, who tore the Magna Charta of British liberty to shreds, and trampled it under his feet. My brethren, I ask you, if you are sufficiently interested in the subject, to look at Mr. Hubert Burke's accumulated testimony respecting the destruction of the Monasteries?

Take, for instance, the history of the Charterhouse in London. Read his essay on that one subject, and you will see that no charge is brought against the monks whatever, except that they refused to accept Henry VIII. as the head in spiritual, as well as temporal, matters of the Church of England; and also because they refused to accept the legitimate queenship of Anne Boleyn, when the king's lawful queen was alive.

These monks were dragged from their Monastery, kept in a state of filth and misery and torture, in the chains of Newgate; they were then dragged through the streets of London, on hurdles, to Tyburn Gate, amidst the grief of the weeping multitude; and the most holy and saintly men that English citizenship has produced were, then and there, disembowelled alive, drawn, quartered and burnt before the agonised crowd who beheld the horrible butchery and martyrdom of these holy men.

That is only one instance of the way in which the monasteries were " dissolved."

I have not the least hesitation in saying that, although it must be granted there were scandals—and there always will be scandals in every institution which is made up of human beings—the Monasteries were the abodes of holy, learned, self-denying, useful men.

Look at our own English clergy. They are, as a rule, a highly educated, moral set of English gentlemen; but there are some of whom we are not proud; these, however, are exceptions to the rule. And supposing I were to take one of these exceptions and show it as a picture of the English clergy, and send it all over the world, what a monstrous injustice, what a piece of moral torture and persecution and dishonesty would not that be! So, to take a story or two of the monks and nuns, and to give them as pictures of what they were generally, would be a very extraordinary misrepresentation, which the people of England, at that time, rose to refute *in toto.*

All I desire to say to you, in conclusion, is this: Seeing that the monks and nuns of the Church of England were the friends of science, agriculture, art, charity, and of religion; seeing that under the *régime* of the monks and nuns of the Church of England no charity by Act of Parliament, no poor's rates, no workhouses, were needed; seeing that the monks and nuns of the Church of England were, in very deed and truth, a sufficient supply for the wants of the poor; do you not think it would be a very grand thing for our Church, and for our country, in the present day, if, with all our secular restorations, we could attempt the restoration of the Monasteries and Convents of the dear old Church of England?

If the Church of England will not produce a Monastic restoration the Church of Rome will.

I have tried, for twenty-five years, to give to the Church of England a Monastery, and as far as the attempt has gone, I do not hesitate to say, it has utterly failed. You may say it is my fault. I know that there are a great many faults inherent in my peculiar character which are against the success of the work. No one knows them so well as I know them; but Almighty God put it into my heart to be the first to come out and dedicate myself to this work.

If some of our persecutors and critics would come forward and take my place, I would very thankfully retire into my own cell, and become an ordinary monk. I know my utter incapability for the leadership of so great a work; but God has called me to begin this work, just the same as He called St. Benedict, and put it into his heart, to begin his work.

I think that in this nineteenth century, Monasticism is more needed than ever it was, as an antidote to the sham religion and the restless spirit of the age. It is more than ever needed as a practical proof of Christian religious reality.

I repeat, brethren, that I should be happy to lay down the position I have held, by force of circumstances, for the last twenty-five years, if any of those who can sympathize with my incompetency for the work, will come forward and take my place, after undergoing a year's training. And if there be any one here present who will undertake to do this, with my whole heart will I thank God for calling out one who is willing, in this age of rationalism and unbelief, to come forward and give up all for Christ; and give a practical proof that the love of God is strong enough to draw out, from the people, a few—a very few, who are willing, for His sake, to live a life for "Jesus only," and the benefit of their fellow men.

I think I have said quite enough in order to help you, by a few data, to approach the subject of "Why the Church of England's Monasteries were destroyed;" and may I, in conclusion, again recommend to you those works of Mr. Hubert Burke on this subject? His works are valuable because they give such very voluminous, contemporaneous evidences.

"*Burke's Historical Sketches of the Tudor Dynasty.*" Will you make a note of that, because, if you will read that book, you will there see that the whole subject is brought very plainly and very voluminously, before the reader.

Brethren, may I ask you just to petition our blessed Lord to give me strength of will and body for my lecture to-night? It was almost impossible that I should come this afternoon to this service, and yet He has brought me here. I shall not have strength to sit, as the begging Monk, for the support of our only Monastery at the door, and I shall have to ask a very dear friend to take my place; but when I am out of sight, will you remember that my work is very hard and very single-handed; and that I am entirely dependent, for the support of the work, on the offerings that those, to whom God allows me to be a blessing, may give to help me in my very uphill, difficult, isolated position?

I thank you so much for your most courteous

hearing, because I know I have said a great many things that must seem new to some of you; and I would not, for all the world, say a word to hurt the feelings of my dear, kind hearers; for I thank God for the intense sympathy that He has given me in the hearts of my London congregations during the last two years. If He give me health and strength I hope to make this hall a centre for mission work twice a year, whilst He shall spare me.

Dear Lord Jesus, grant, I pray Thee, that the words that have been spoken, at this time, may not dishonour Thy precious Name; for Thy Name is above every name in our hearts; and if any word I have spoken be not for Thy glory, oh! let it be forgotten. Do Thou, if our work be the work of self-will, root it out of my heart, I beseech Thee; but if it be for Thy glory, if it be for the honour of Thy Name, and the salvation of souls, oh, raise us up friends to help us in our single-handed battle!

HYMN OF THE BENEDICTINE MONKS OF
St. Mary and St. Dunstan's Abbey of Llanthony.

We come, we come, the children of Salvation,
   The mystic spouses of our wondrous King;
For all the nations of the earth we're pleading,
   For Holy Church our solemn praises bring.

Amid the silence of our lonely mountains,
   Living for "*Jesus only*" and alone;
We come, we come, in joyous adoration,
   And pour our homage at His Altar Throne.

Benedictine Hymn.

Oh! grand and princely is our glorious calling,
   The Gates of Glory open at our word,
And pour their treasures o'er the weeping nations,
   Refreshing showers from JESUS Christ, our Lord.

O thought, most high!—all dedicate to Heaven,
   Earth's loves and treasures trampled 'neath our feet
We spend our lives at Zion's Golden Portals,
   Within the shadows of the Mercy Seat.

We bear the stamp of God's Predestination,
   The coronal of His electing love;
For "Day and Night" we raise our cry before Him,
   He will "avenge" us—throned in might above.

And wherefore cry we thus in full assurance,
   Our lives all full of priceless golden days,
Of which but "one is better than a thousand,"
   Lit as they are by God's own peerless rays,

It is because we live for things we see not,
   Things all eternal—lasting as our Lord,
Which fade not—change not—cannot disappoint us,
   Secured and promised by His Royal Word.

Ah! children of a dying world! we see you
   Straying to darkness,—weeping as you go;
For you we pray—for you His merits plead we,
   Ye *must be* saved from the dread ageless woe.

Like Moses on the mountain top—we bless you,
   A Host we bring, O peoples, to your aid;
Our praise like Mary's ointment shall refresh you,
   By Christ we are your greatest helpmates made.

For this we raise our songs and intercessions,
   Our praises from our Rolling Planet fling;
They glad the ear of our Triune JEHOVAH,
   Are precious in the presence of the King.

Then praise we mightily the GOD of Glory,
   O raise to JESUS, sweetest, loftiest songs,
Also to Thee, O Loving Patient Spirit,
   To Thee a universe of Praise belongs. Amen.

                    (IGNATIUS, O.S.B.)
                              MONK.

XX.

The Apparitions at Llanthony.

Oration.

Tuesday Evening, May 5th, 1885.

The Apparitions at Llanthony.

Prayer before the Oration.

O Jesus Christ, we have only a very few hours to stay here in this little, short, changing life: and Thou hast left us here for this little while to prepare for the great eternal Home-land. Grant us to hear words, at this time, that shall glorify Thy Name and help men to realize something of the sublimity, of the reality of the supernatural; and of the eternal life behind the thin veil that now hides it from our human ken.

Thou art able to use the very poor instrument of human words by anointing them with Thy Holy Spirit's power, and so bringing them home with a mighty force, which is divine, to our hearts first, and then to the intellects of those who are willing to be enlightened and comforted and instructed.

Thou knowest the different classes, the different schools of thought, the different tempers, the peculiar characteristics of all those who make up this assembly. Thou knowest those who would believe if they could; Thou knowest those who have given up all hope of ever believing in Thyself, or in the supernatural of any kind. But, O Lord Jesus, Thou art drawing so many men, such as those, to Thyself; and Thou givest us, Thy people, to see the transformation, the wondrous change that comes to them.

Grant that the word spoken to-night may only be Thy truth, and may be words of soberness as well as faith; words of power that shall carry peace and rest and light into the hearts of peaceless, restless, darkened souls.

Lord Jesus, Thou canst, and Thou dost, satisfy those who receive Thee; and wilt Thou use the strange story of Thy mercy to us, in such a way to-night, that it may be a weapon in the hand of Thy love for assisting doubters into the fold of the faithful sons of God!

Lord Jesus, let this meeting glorify Thee, and let it be a blessing to us who are gathered here. We ask it for Thy Name's sake. Amen.

THE APPARITIONS AT LLANTHONY.

Oration.

"Wherefore seeing we also are compassed about with so great a cloud of witnesses, let us lay aside every weight, and the sin which doth so easily beset us, and let us run with patience the race that is set before us." Heb. xii. 1.

I wish to give the congregation a text of Scripture as a preface to the address to-night, because it may give a key-note, at all events, to the thoughts of those present who believe in Christianity and in the Bible.

The text which I ask you to accept, as the substratum for the address, is the first verse of the 12th chapter of the Epistle of S. Paul to the Hebrews.

You will recollect that in the chapter before, reference has been made to several departed saints, and chapter xii. begins with these words: "Wherefore seeing we also are compassed about with so great a cloud of witnesses, let us lay aside every weight."

This text applies to the departed saints. The Apostle speaks of them as a cloud of witnesses round about us. He is using the simile of a race.

We, here, are still in the race; and the saints departed—within the veil—are round about us as a cloud of witnesses; therefore let us lay aside the *weight* that besets us—*especially our besetting sins*—because the saints are looking on like witnesses on a race-course or in a theatre.

Now, first of all, I want to appeal to those in this room who are Christians.

To Christians, who believe in the Bible, there will be no difficulty whatever in accepting the narration I have to give respecting the Apparitions which God has granted to us at the Monastery, among the Black Mountains of Wales. Christians cannot, on any hypothesis whatever, reject the visions, unless they believe them to be deliberate inventions of a company of impostors. But I shall not dwell on this just now, as I shall have to bring this thought forward more prominently when I appeal to *rationalists.*

Christians, you believe, do you not, as much as I do, that the Bible is the infallible, inspired Word of God? And this Book is full of the supernatural from beginning to end. From the very first chapter of Genesis to the last chapter of the Revelation—which is a Book of visions—there is nothing but one continuity of narrative regarding visions, miracles and apparitions. Therefore to you, Christians, who accept the Scriptures, as the Church has handed them to us, faith in apparitions and miracles, and the supernatural in general, is a necessary part of your Christianity. *You* do not doubt the possibility of apparitions and miracles; and *you* cannot quote the Scriptures to prove that miracles and apparitions should cease at any time in the Christian Church.

I wish, in speaking on this subject, to be careful of, and kind to, the feelings of others; still I must speak plainly. At all events I wish to speak very solemnly; and not to create a smile on any one's face. I hope that our Lord will make me mindful of the solemn position in which I stand to-night.

Yes, I am standing here in a very solemn position indeed; and what I am saying is either a narrative for God's glory, or an imposture for God's dishonour; because I have been standing forth, for twenty years and more, before the world, as a preacher of the Gospel.

Now, Christian people, let me ask any one of you— I shall make a pause after this question to give any Christian an opportunity of answering—" *Can you give me one single text in Holy Scripture to prove that miracles and visions are to cease with the Apostles?* " It is a very hackneyed argument, against the testimony for miracles and visions in these days, that those things ceased with the Apostles! That is the common answer we receive from Christian people.

Now I should be very glad to have my ignorance on this point instructed; and I ask any one of you to give me a single passage from God's Word to prove that miracles and apparitions *were* to cease with the Apostles. I pause for an answer from any Protestant or any Catholic Christian. (A pause, and no answer.) Then I shall conclude that there is no Christian here present who has a text ready to disprove the statement which I am making, that *there is no period in the history of Christ's Church in which the supernatural is to cease.*

Jesus Christ has left a supernatural legacy to believers. He has said, "these signs shall follow" not Apostles, *but* "them that believe; in My name shall they cast out devils; they shall speak with new tongues; they shall take up serpents; and if they drink any deadly thing, it shall not hurt them; they shall lay hands on the sick, and they shall recover."[*] Jesus also said of believers: "Verily, verily, I say unto you, He that believeth on Me, the works that I do shall he do also; and greater works than these shall he do; because I go unto My Father."[†]

Therefore, brethren, I say Christ's promise is to *believers*, and is not limited to any particular time or circumstances; it is a general promise, made generally to *the people of God.*

Therefore, brethren, when there is no exercise of the supernatural in the visible Church of Christendom

[*] St. Mark xvi. 17—18.   [†] St. John xiv. 12.

it is owing to the lack of faith; when we hear of miracles among the Jesuits, or any other body of faithful Christians in the Church of Rome, or any other Church; when we hear of miracles amongst dissenting, Evangelical congregations (and I could refer you to a house now opened by a Protestant minister in London for healing by faith); when we hear, in all directions, of the supernatural being manifested, we need not wonder, for we are living in a day which demands supernatural manifestations more than any other epoch in the Christian Church.

There never was a day that seemed to demand a voice from Heaven like the day in which we live; in which every species of attack is being made upon Christianity as a Divine Revelation; when every imaginable taunt is being flung from the little, puny chamber of man's wisdom; which man, in his pride, wants to apotheosize; when every sneer is being flung at the thorn-crowned Head of Jesus Christ.

Brethren, if ever there were a day when you Christians have a right to look for the supernatural, it is to-day.

As a matter of fact, the Christian world is quivering with the supernatural in every direction; as a matter of fact the supernatural is cropping up on all sides; but people have not the courage to come forward and tell of the things that they see and hear. Only this week have I received a letter begging me to say something to-night about a supernatural event which has recently happened in London; and I would gladly do so, were it not that I am bound in honour to be silent on the subject. Since I have been in London I have also received letters testifying to the supernatural in the experience of sensible, sober-minded Christians; and I find the same wherever I go. I repeat then, brethren, that there is not a word in the Scriptures to give any authority for the statement that the miraculous was to cease with the Apostles.

You cannot read the lives of such men as John Wesley, Ignatius Loyola, and the like, without, from time to time, finding the supernatural cropping up. John Wesley testifies to it in his life; and so do the saints of the different parts of the Catholic Church in their lives; and so do many Protestant saints of various denominations.

Although I may *seem* by some to take a unique position I am not actually doing so; for I might have this platform crowded with Catholic and Protestant Christians, who could bear testimony, from their own experience, of the supernatural both auricular and oracular. So that I do not feel alone on this platform. I know I am not alone in reality, for there are spirits all around me now, and no Christian can deny that we are thus compassed about.

I had been a witness to the supernatural, on other occasions, before the Llanthony visions. They have only been a climax; and there has been a hush since they appeared. God has granted us nothing further. It may be His will that we shall have no further manifestations; and no more are needed; but this is in His own Divine knowledge, and at His Divine disposal.

Christian people, is not the supernatural far more precious to you than this earthly life below? Do you feel at home in the crowded streets of the City, or in the Exchange, or on the busy quays? Do you feel at home in the market places and the places of pleasure on earth? No, these are all passing dreams to you; the supernatural world is your home. Year by year your darlings pass from you—one by one—through the filmy veil that hides the tremendous realities of the eternal world from our gaze. First, the last kiss of a darling wife, and she passes within the veil; and when she has passed you hear the voice you loved often come to you, even to your bodily ears.

Only yesterday some one said to me of a darling friend, "Oh, she has often spoken to me since she has been gone." Then an almost idolized child is taken from you, and, with a sweet bright face, just before death, the child has said: "Mother, I see the beautiful angels. I see them plainly; don't you see that angel?" And after she has spoken the words of the vision, which her dying eyes beheld, she has fallen asleep in the arms of the Mystic Shepherd—the Incarnate Son of God Almighty.

Then come the Christmas times. Christmas, when we are lonely and old, has no *earthly* music for our hearts; all the music of Christmas for us now is within the veil, where our darlings are gathered by the Shepherd's tender care. We put the empty chairs around the Christmas board and around the Christmas fire; and we think of those who are gone before into the real world of the immortal—the changeless life of liberty. And thus we realize, the longer we live, the *unreality* of the shifting scenes of this life of dreams; and the mighty *reality*, the stupendous beauty, and the calm rest of that supernatural life beyond the little stream that we name—death.

Oh, Christian people, our text is a very precious one. Our dear ones, within the veil, are round about us like a "great cloud of witnesses;" oh, so near—much nearer than we often think. When we go to our places of worship, we declare it to be one of the articles of our Creed, that we "believe in the Communion of Saints." It is a peaceful faith, it is a joyful faith, it is a faith that seems like a delicate, tender hand to brush away our falling tears.

He keeps my dear ones for me against the coming of the dawn, when, in the Home-land, we shall be united to part no more.

Oh, the supernatural! Oh, the life beyond this short, fleeting, dream of time! *That* is the REALITY. *This* is the *shadow*; *that* is the *substance*.

And, brethren, sometimes we ache in heart, and mourn in spirit, because we are surrounded by a crowd of men, with hearts of stone. They say: "no, we are on a par with the brutes; our wives and children, our loved ones, are nothing; we shall never see them again; they have ceased to exist. This life—although we may be dead to-morrow—this life, although there is nothing certain in it but death—this life is the only reality"!

To me, it seems a puzzle, how such men can drag on their wretched existence; for they can have nothing for which to live. There would seem to be for them no object in life. Oh! if Jesus Christ were to be taken from me, it would take away the sun from the sky; it would take away from me the spring and the summer-time, and the fruits, and the flowers, and the songs of birds; every thing would fall flat and dead, if the source of all beauty and joy were gone.

When once you have tasted what Jesus is, you cannot do without Him.

But they cannot take Him away; they can never touch the *faith*, that the Holy Ghost has stamped upon my soul, that, in Jesus, I am an immortal son of God; that I live in the Resurrection life of Him who lived and died and rose again for me, and Who says to me: "Because I live, ye shall live also."*

Oh! blessed life of the eternal years, hidden behind the veil! I wonder, oh, I wonder, and I marvel exceeding sore, that I see no more visions of thy beauty; that the light within the veil flashes not oftener on my earthly sight; that faces look not through the cloud to cheer me, and voices speak not to call me on; for "they compass us about as a cloud of witnesses!"†

Christian people, listen to the story of the Llanthony Apparitions, for they are testified to by credible, truthful, honest witnesses!

I have now spoken to Christians. I have reminded them of the state of the present day in which our lot is cast; and I have said that if ever the supernatural might be looked for, by Christ's disciples, it is at the present time.

And now, rationalists, I want to say a word very

* St. John xiv. 19.   † Hebrews xii. 1.

respectfully to you; and, believe me, I do not say "respectfully" with cant or hypocrisy. We are living in a day, when it is the common sentiment of the human race, that men have a right to speak plainly what they believe, without fear of bodily violence. The days of bodily violence, even for myself, seem to have passed by. I have not been beaten for my opinions since 1879; and I may say this, that I have received the greatest courtesy, on all hands, from freethinkers and rationalists. Therefore, in speaking to them I feel that I am addressing men who are willing to exercise their common sense upon the subject on which I speak, just as they would investigate any natural story as to its truth or untruth. I only want rationalists to treat the story I am going to tell them to-night in the same way in which a case would be investigated in a Court of Justice.

I am very anxious that the story I have to tell should be ventilated and examined; and when I have told it, I should like to refer you to a friend who will receive the names of any gentlemen who may be desirous of seriously investigating the matter. I should prefer the investigators to be rationalists, and, if possible, also lawyers. I do not want Christians to have anything to do with it; because *they* must accept the testimony, unless they say that I am telling deliberate untruths. There is no occasion for Christians to investigate the reality of the supernatural; but there is great reason for rationalists to do so.

The several persons who saw the visions—although now scattered and not, in any way, under my influence, can be questioned as to what they saw.

I shall be glad, therefore, to hear from any *bonâ fide* rationalists, (indeed I would prefer atheists—those who do not believe in God or in a future) who will form a committee to investigate the story of these Apparitions at Llanthony. I should not, of course, think of exposing myself to an enormous amount of correspondence, which I should be utterly unable to carry on; therefore it would have to be done upon the lines I suggest. I should expect to receive the names and addresses, of those proposing to act on such a committee, as a proof of *bona fides*—a reasonable *sine quâ non*, I think, on my part.

At the close of the lecture, if any persons present would like to put questions to me I shall be happy to answer them.

The best thing for me to do now will be to relate the story of the Apparitions, and then conclude by saying what it seems to me to be worth. I say "seems," because it is impossible for me to tell you how much it is worth. It may be, in God's merciful Providence, that we shall know more about what we have seen than we know at present.

First of all, I would remind my hearers generally, that the two points for which I have been, to such an extent, ostracised by my fellow-churchmen, have been these: the worship that we give to our Lord in the Blessed Sacrament, and the amount of veneration that we give to our Lord in His Mother.

Certainly, for nearly twenty years, we have suffered, as far as worldly prospects are concerned, on account of those two particulars. Churchmen, who would have liked to have helped us, have said: "no, you go to such extremes with regard to the doctrine of the Holy Eucharist, and the honour you pay to the Blessed Virgin, that we cannot *conscientiously* help you." Others have said: "we cannot *judiciously* help you; it would injure our work"!

We, on the other hand, have never thought about judiciousness or expediency; and therefore it is that we have the reputation of being very injudicious and of doing things that are very inexpedient, and "foolish" and "wrong."

In the year 1880 we were going on in our own practical matter-of-fact way at the Monastery, with every hour of the day carved out—because there we have to be our own servants; to be occupied with the minute details of daily, domestic service; to attend to a vast correspondence—all in addition, of course, to the religious services held in our own church by night and by day.

Besides the services, we each have an hour's watch of intercession in the Monastery church, before the Altar, for the conversion of sinners and the praise of God. I mention this in passing, to show that we have, and had then, no time for morbid sentimentality, hazy imaginations, and unreal wanderings of mind. We are thoroughly employed, and, generally speaking, every one is in a good state of health in the Monastery except myself. I have always been delicate; and the work that I have undertaken has entailed upon me a fearful strain, God only knowing all that I have had to pass through.

On Monday, the 30th of August, 1880, which was a very fine late summer's morning, a brother (Brother Dunstan) went, as usual, at nine o'clock, into the church to take his watch before the Blessed Sacrament. It has been said, to account for what follows, that we were all in a state of "receptivity." That is a very fine word, but there is no sense in it with regard to us; for our receptivity, at the time, was a receptivity for an amount of extra work. Monday is always an extra busy day with us; and this brother, if he had allowed his thoughts to wander at his watch—instead of their wandering to visions and miracles—they would probably have wandered to the extra amount of house work which he would have to do.

Dear friends, I am anxious not to say anything to create a smile;* but I want to be plain, and to help you to see the faultiness of some of the arguments which have been used against what I am saying. We were not in any state of receptivity at all; we were in a state of great hurry and business.

Well, this brother went into his watch at nine o'clock, and he was kneeling about twenty feet from the Altar. At the south side of the Altar there is a large window, which was not then filled with stained glass, and consequently a bright light shone upon the Altar. The church is divided with a screen, and only into the outer part of the church, are secular people, from the outer world, allowed to come.

The brother, who left the watch, had no communication with the sister who next came in to take her watch. She (Sister Janet) had been a schoolmistress in the neighbourhood for many years, and was now an associate of our Order.

The brother had been half an hour at his watch, (I may mention that this gentleman's sister is now in the congregation; she will give his name, and I am sure he will be willing to answer any questions of

* Some persons present smiled at this point.

investigation that may be put to him) when he raised his eyes and saw, in front of the Tabernacle, a kind of blue mist playing. As he looked at the mist he thought that his eyes must be affected, and he rubbed them, thinking it was an illusion; but as he still looked, the mist thickened and densified, until he saw the monstrance, or silver vessel which contained the Host, within the Tabernacle, glimmering in the mist, outside the massive door of the Tabernacle, which was locked. This door is of iron, nearly an inch thick. The key was in my cell, which I had not left that morning, because I had been very unwell, and had had a good deal of writing to do.

The mist gradually cleared away; and then the sacred vessel, containing the Host, was plain before the brother's eyes; and the sunlight, from the window, flashed upon it. He saw this for half an hour, and on leaving his watch, still looked back upon the Vision, as he went out.

Sister Janet then came in to take her watch; and knelt down, as usual, at the screen in the outer church. When she looked at the Altar she saw the same appearance; but she did not dream of its being supernatural—she imagined only that the Blessed Sacrament was exposed for some reason or other; but she was much astonished to find that the Host was exposed without the usual signs of reverence and devotion, which we always render when we have our three expositions in the year.

We only have the Host exposed three times a year, and they are very solemn occasions; and we pay our Lord a great deal of honour during those days. On this occasion there was no light burning; there were no flowers; and the sister was consequently much astonished, knowing how particular we are in these matters of detail and reverence. Directly her watch was over at 11 o'clock, she went to the Monastery porch, rang the bell, and asked to see the brother who had taken the watch before her. When he came to the grating, she said: "why has the Reverend Father left the Blessed Sacrament out?"

I may tell you that Brother Dunstan was a very matter-of-fact gentleman; he was brought up a Presbyterian, and was not at all inclined to believe in miracles or in the supernatural; in fact, the very opposite; and having felt convinced we should say that what he had seen was imagination, and laugh at him, if he told us about it, he had determined not to mention the matter at all. But when the sister came to the porch and asked: "why has the Reverend Father left the Blessed Sacrament out?" and when she explained precisely what she had seen, and Brother Dunstan knew that the Tabernacle had not been opened, he at once came to my cell to tell me what had happened.

I suggested that we should go to the church, for it was time for the mid-day office. When we went in the Apparition had disappeared. I said the brother and the sister had better say nothing about it.

I lay *particular stress* upon this, because people have said that the Vision which the boys saw in the evening was in consequence of what they had heard of the miracle in the morning. The boys knew nothing about it whatever.

In the evening, after Vespers, the choir-boys were in the meadow playing, as they do at recreation time, and were having a very noisy game. The children were very strong and healthy from the mountain air, and from their good, plain food. They were not withered, shrunk, imaginative, namby-pamby boys, fancying all kinds of nonsense, as has been suggested. I will give any one who likes, the name and address of the chief boy, so that those who care to investigate the matter may be able to ascertain for themselves what he saw. He is now employed in business.

All at once the noise of the game was stopped; and, in a very short time, one of the boys came running up to my cell, soon followed by others, saying: "Father, we have seen such a beautiful spirit in the meadow." That was the first thing they said. I did not pay much attention to it. I was still busy writing. It was then a quarter past eight in the evening. When, however, all the other boys came and told me the same story I was very much astonished.

The eldest boy, who was fifteen years old, said he was certain that what they had seen was the blessed Virgin Mary—quite certain. He said that first of all, as he was waiting for his turn to run in the game, he was looking towards an old ruined hut, where there had been a farm-house; and he saw a bright light over the hedge, and the figure of a woman, with hands upraised, as if in blessing, and with a veil over her face, coming to him. He stood still and was much astonished and alarmed. The figure came almost at right angles to him, and then she passed close enough even for him to see the material of the garments that she wore. The figure passed off at right angles, and stood in a bright light in a bush about fifty feet from the boy. The bush was all illumined with phosphorescent light. The figure passed through the bush; and the light was there for some little time after the form had disappeared. The rest of the boys saw, and described, the same appearance.

They had run out through the gate, so that they might go down the road to see more of this wonderful figure; but had seen nothing more.

After this I was determined to find out what it was

if we could. There was a young clerk, from a railway station, staying at the Monastery, who witnessed the boys' excitement on the subject.

I had all the boys in the church, where I spoke solemnly to them, separately, and heard what they had to say. I told them what an unlikely story it was, and that no one would believe them; and I asked them what could have put it into their heads to think of such a thing.

But they still maintained that what they said was true.

We watched Tuesday, Wednesday, Thursday, and Friday evenings after that.

A friend of mine from London, a lawyer, was staying in the neighbourhood, and I told him exactly what the boys had said. I asked him to interrogate them. He did so, very kindly, and I saw him afterwards; when he said: "of course, I cannot say what they have seen; but I am certain that the boys quite believe that they are telling the truth; and I have no doubt of their truthfulness."

Unfortunately I had to leave Llanthony on the Saturday, being under a promise to take the duty for a clergyman in the diocese of Exeter, where we had a convent at that time. He was going for a holiday for two Sundays; and he had entrusted his parish to me. I was therefore obliged to go, much against my wish; but I left strict orders that the brothers and the boys should watch every night, at the same time, about eight o'clock; and then write to me, telling of any experience they might have.

On Saturday night, September 4th, the boys were out playing as usual when, all at once, the same bush became illuminated with a very bright light. One boy called out: "The bush is all on fire again!"

For some little time they watched the light; then they ran to the Monastery to call out an elder brother.

In the meantime a junior brother had come out, had knelt down in the meadow before the illuminated bush, and had begun to say prayers and hymns. The boys were indignant because he was saying collects and hymns that had no relation to what they considered the vision to be, and they said: "do not say those prayers, but say a 'Hail, Mary'; for we are certain it was the Blessed Virgin. If we do our Lord will perhaps let the vision appear again."

While they were thus discussing, the senior brother came up, and he agreed that they should begin to sing "Ave Maria." That instant the figure flashed again, in a cloud of light, in the same place, where the first boy had seen it on the Monday.

As they sang, the figure in the light sent out rays

of light, sometimes appearing behind and sometimes in front of the hedge, and sometimes coming straight towards the illuminated bush. When they said the words in the "Hail, Mary" "Blessed is the fruit of thy womb, Jesus," they saw a second figure as of a Man, with only a cloth round His loins, appearing in the light, with His hands stretched out.

The boy, who first saw the vision, declared that he saw a Cross behind the hands, and saw the face distinctly; whereas the brothers said there was a mist over the face, and they could not discern any features. The face of the female figure was veiled as the boys had seen it on the Monday.

After this they watched, and on several occasions saw this same figure. The senior boy saw the figure on eight separate occasions.

As soon as my duty in Devonshire was over I was only too glad to get home; and when I returned to the Monastery, on the 14th of September, which was Tuesday night, we watched, but saw nothing.

On the 15th of September, between eight and a quarter past eight, we watched again. It was a very close, muggy evening. There was a heavy Scotch mist descending, and the mountains were looking very dull, and the sky leaden. It was so damp that we did not go into the meadow; but Sister Janet, who was not allowed to come to the

Monastery door, where we were standing, went into the meadow.

We were in the Monastery porch. The boys were standing on the front step; I was standing on the top step; one brother was at my left; and another brother on my right. Two farmers were behind in the back of the porch; and a gentleman visitor—an undergraduate of Keble College, Oxford, now in Holy Orders—was a little behind me to the right.

I suggested that we should sing three "Hail, Marys" in honour of each person of the Blessed Trinity. We began a "Hail, Mary" in honour of God the Father. Between the "Hail Marys" we, all of us, expressed our amazement at some very curious flashings of light which we saw in all directions in the meadow, like the outlines of figures. That was the impression I had. These outlines of light flashed here and there in all directions.

I then said: "Let us sing a 'Hail Mary' in honour of the Blessed Virgin herself;" and we began to chant the fourth "Hail Mary."

Directly we began to do so I saw a great circle of light flash out over the whole heavens, taking in the mountains, the trees, the ruined house, the enclosure, the monastery, the gates, and everything; the light flashed upon our feet, upon the steps, and upon the buildings; and from that one great circle of light, small circles bulged out, and, in the centre of the circles, stood a gigantic figure of a human being, with hands uplifted, standing sideways.

In the distance this gigantic figure appeared to be about sixty feet in height; but as it descended it took the ordinary size of a human being. At the moment it struck me that a dark appearance over the head of the figure was hair, not a veil; but I am convinced, from comparing notes with the others, and also from other reasons, that it was a veil which I saw over the head.

I saw distinctly the outlines of the features against the bright light, and also the exact form of the drapery from the sleeves of the upraised arms, as clearly and as plainly as it is possible for me to express.

It was all stamped with a most marvellous kind of reality upon my mind. But marvellous and glorious as the vision had been, staggered and astonished as I (who am naturally so impulsive, excitable, and demonstrative,) was at the time, I happily determined to say nothing of what I had seen to those about me; but to ascertain what they had seen in order that I might receive confirmation from them!

So after the vision had passed, I turned to the brother on my left and said: "did you see anything?"

"Yes, indeed I did, Reverend Father," he replied.

"Now, tell me," I said, "exactly what you saw." He told me exactly what he had seen, and his testimony was precisely confirmatory of what I myself had witnessed. The brother in front of me also declared that he saw exactly what the other brother had described.

A few minutes afterwards Sister Janet came in from the meadow, and walking up towards the gate, lifted up her hands, as if she wished to attract our notice and to speak. I went to her and said : "what is the matter ?"

"Oh! Reverend Father,'" she replied, "I have seen the most glorious vision of any yet."

I told her to be quiet, and to tell me exactly what she had seen.

She described precisely, without a word being said by us, what she had witnessed; and it was exactly what had been seen by us.

From that time no further visions appeared.

After seeing the vision, this was the thought that came to me. If I had seen it myself only, I should have felt that God had granted this vision to *me* individually, for some merciful purpose of His own ; but that it would not have been of much use to others, because people would naturally have said : "Father

Ignatius is enthusiastic, is of a very imaginative turn of mind, and it was all just the force of imagination." But when three other people, *at the same time*, saw *precisely the same thing* that I had seen, it became clear that their imaginations could not have been affected in exactly the same manner, and at the same moment. Therefore I felt convinced that our Lord had given to us these Apparitions for several reasons; and amongst them I believed that He had given them for the good of the Church of England, and for the comfort of those in the outer world.

I knew what an enormous storm of abuse, ridicule, and persecution would thereby be brought upon us; nevertheless, I determined to give a public testimony to the Apparition of the Blessed Sacrament, and to the Apparitions of the Blessed Virgin Mary.

As I expected, directly we gave our testimony, a torrent of storm, abuse, and ridicule poured upon us. Many of our friends deserted us, and did not care to have anything more to do with us; and, as far as pecuniary help, for our services and charities, was concerned, (which totally depend upon voluntary offerings) we lost a great deal.

In the midst of all this storm we had a letter from a man, not many miles off, who was a cripple, and he said he believed he might be healed through this vision; and asked me if I would send him some leaves from the bush where the Apparition had so many times appeared. I wrote to him and said: "certainly not until God had given me a token that He meant miracles to be worked in that way."

A few days afterwards, on the Festival of St. Matthew, the 21st of September (the last of the visions having been on the 15th), I sent to each of our nuns at Slapton, in Devonshire—as memorials of God's wonders amongst us, pieces of a wild rhubarb leaf, which had stood up dark against the dazzling garments of the Apparition, as it appeared in the bush.

Now, among our nuns was one middle-aged lady, who had been a cripple thirty-eight years. She had suffered from abscesses in the hip-joint, and from a contracted knee; and she had never been able to raise her limb without lifting it, with her hand or other foot; indeed she had had intense suffering ever since she was a child. Her knee was so contracted that she had not been able to put her foot to the ground for thirty-eight years.

On the morning of the day when this leaf arrived the sisters' meditation, at the eight o'clock service in the chapel, had been, "According to your faith be it unto you."* Those words had a very curious effect upon the nun.

* St. Matt. ix. 29.

I should tell you that this lady had been born and bred a Dissenter among the Moravians; and her brother is now a Dissenting minister. She had always had a prejudice against our extreme devotion to the Mother of our Lord; and though she wore a rosary, out of obedience to my wishes, she never, with her whole heart, had practised devotion to the Mother of our Lord as we do. I say this to show that she was rather prejudiced against paying honour to the Mother of Jesus.

But all through the day these words seemed to haunt her, "according to your faith be it unto you;" until at last she said, "yes, Lord, I know that; but I have no faith." She meant that she had not faith in the leaf, because, in her own mind, she had been thinking of applying it to her wounds. When she went to her cell after Compline, she was suffering more than usual; for on the Feast of St. Ignatius, the 31st July, some fresh abscesses had appeared, and some pieces of bone had passed through them.

On Tuesday, September 21st, 1880, just seven days after the last Apparition had been seen, she was quivering from head to foot with pain. She was going to lie down—but she never could lie down without lifting her diseased limb with the other foot on to the bed—when something told her to use the leaf, which she had put, wrapped up in an envelope, in her pocket.

She took the leaf out. She took the rosary and said ten " Hail, Marys ; " and, at the end of the " Hail, Marys ! " she took the piece of leaf, and laid it upon these painful abscesses. *The very instant the piece of withered leaf was laid upon the abscesses they closed up and the discharge ceased; her knee was loosened at the joint, her foot was on the ground, and she was cured instantaneously.*

She said that, at the time, she was inclined to scream for joy and gratitude, and to rush to the other nuns; but she knew that disobedience to the Rule would not glorify Him Who had done this for her; therefore she said: " I quieted myself, for obedience sake, and made up my mind that I would lie down until the morning."

When she was going to raise her limb upon the bed, as usual, she found there was no need for it; because she could put that limb up as well as the other, which for thirty-eight years she had not been able to do.

The next morning she told, and showed, the Rev. Mother, and her sister nuns, the miraculous wonder of God's infinite goodness towards her; and the news quickly spread in the village.

The vicar of the parish came to the convent, and the village people rang the village bells, for they were very fond of the nuns; and, in a day or two, there was a service of thanksgiving in the Priory chapel, for the miracle that God had wrought. There was also an account, in the local paper, of what had taken place.

I knew then that God had given me a sign, and so when letters came to me, by every post, asking me for these leaves we never refused them. There have been plenty of other healings following this one; but people are so peculiar and sensitive, that, even when they receive a blessing, they do not like to let it be known, and have their names published.

I am sorry to say that several people have bound me down in honour to say nothing of their blessed experiences; but with some this has not been the case. Only in the spring of 1885, a young man travelled some miles to my missionary service at Torquay, to show me a miracle that had been wrought upon his limb, which had been pronounced incurable by the doctor. For fifteen months he had had a great running sore, which was really sapping away his strength. He had had three doctors; and one of them had said that it would be many years before he was well; while another predicted that he never would be well again.

"I have come," he said, "to show you what has taken place. I had sent for a leaf, and I tied it on the wound. I want you to see it; for now it is as dry as the palm of my hand, and I am quite well."

The young man asked me to come into the waiting room, by the Mission Hall, that I might see his healed limb, and return thanks to God publicly for it. He offered to give his name and address to anybody.

But this young man is one of very few who are glad to come forward, and give publicity to the fact that God's hand is not shortened, in supernatural work and acts of healing love.*

Now, brethren, I have told you the story; and it

---

* The same young man, a few days ago, wrote to Father Ignatius the following note:—

"NEWTON ABBOT, DEVON,

"Sept. 28th, 1886.

"REVEREND AND DEAR FATHER,

"It is now nearly two years since I wrote and begged for a Leaf from the Holy Bush, for my poor leg; and which, by God's mercy, was healed. I am most thankful to say it is still well and healed, but when I say 'thankful' I am afraid I am not half so thankful as I ought to be.

"Will you ask those of the Community to remember to thank Almighty God for His goodness towards me?

"Pardon the liberty I have taken in writing you. Hoping you are restored to health,

"I remain yours truly,

"R. F. H——.

"I write this simply to let you know that it was not simply healed for a few weeks or so."

(Name and address were given in full.)

seems to me that there are only two hypotheses respecting it. The one is that what I have said is absolutely true, and the more investigation there is about it the better, because it would substantiate the truth; the other is that we have all conspired deliberately to palm off a most blasphemous imposture, in the name of the God of Truth, upon the people whom we want to delude.

The hackneyed explanation that it is all imagination—that it is the result of excitability of temperament, is manifestly absurd; because there were four persons, of different temperaments, who were all witnesses of the last Vision. Eight altogether had seen the Blessed Virgin, three men, one woman, and four healthy boys.

And now let me tell you, in conclusion, what I feel to be very much the meaning, and the value, of the Apparitions. First of all they are invaluable to the intellect of Christian people as showing the truth and the reality of that faith which they profess in the supernatural. There is an enormous amount of value indeed to those who already believe in Christ, in having their faith confirmed. Then I think they are of great value to the Church of England, because there has been so much of the supernatural in other parts of the Church; and the

Church of England has been without the least sign of it for so long a period.

The fact of God's granting this to the Church of England proves to my conscience, and to my heart, and to my understanding, that our Sacraments are valid, and that the Blessed Mother of Jesus would visit us as much as she would visit those in other parts of the Christian Church.

But there is so much bigotry of party and sect, that when the Vision was first promulgated, we had an enthusiastic letter from a Protestant lady in Hastings, saying that she believed in apparitions in these days, and that she believed there would be signs in the heavens; adding: "I am so sympathetic with you; please send me full particulars." We sent particulars; and we gave reasons why we were convinced that it was the Blessed Virgin Mary who had appeared.

But when she heard that we were convinced of *that*, she wrote a "furious" letter and told us that "*as we said it was the Virgin Mary she was convinced it was the devil who had sent the vision and not God!*"

Brethren, this was very sad and sickening to our hearts.

At the same time I had a letter from a Roman Catholic in Ireland, who said she quite believed that we had seen the Apparition, "*but*," she added, "*as you are not Roman Catholics I believe, instead of its having been a heavenly vision, it was satanic!*"

There again was party spirit. At all events, the wonders of mercy that have resulted from the Visions prove that they were of God; and that God's favour in the supernatural, is being restored to the Church of England, *if only there be faith to receive it.*

Last of all, it has been a great comfort to us personally, because it seems to have confirmed us on the two points upon which we have had most to suffer.

When I gave this address at Brighton, where the crippled nun had once kept a lady's school, for many years, a gentleman rose up in the congregation, and said that he had been her man of business for a long time, and that he could testify that this lady had been a cripple for many years. Then there were pupils of hers, and tradespeople, and friends, all of whom knew that my statements about her were true. And this gentleman further said: "I have had a letter from the lady to say that she was suddenly and instantaneously healed, and I know she would not tell me a falsehood."

Now, if any rationalist would like to ask a question I shall be very glad to answer it. I am sure that, if he will put his question courteously, he will be treated with the greatest courtesy by myself and by the audience.*

To sum up then:

A solemn, public testimony has now been given, to most startling, supernatural phenomena in a Church of England Monastery, in the midst of this unbelieving, materialistic age.

By these phenomena the mysteries of Christianity have been solemnly confirmed; and the Word of God has received one more "*So be it.*"

The Church of England has been supernaturally recognised as a true portion of the Catholic Church; and her Sacraments acknowledged by a miracle.

The Monastic revival, long persecuted because of the two especial points above alluded to, viz.: the Restoration of the Reserved Sacrament, and the Cultus of the Mother of our Lord, have now received a sanction from on High, by these marvellous manifestations.

Christians, who receive our testimony, must rejoice —our common Faith has been confirmed by God's Infinite Mercy.

English Churchmen have received from God a special approval, for their ancient Church, in spite of her sadly isolated position.

* No question whatever was asked.

We, at Llanthony, ought faithfully to hold on to the end, firmly believing that God has mercifully vouchsafed to bless our work there, and to accept it as pleasing to Himself.

Oh, if we could echo forth a thousand Alleluias of thanksgiving, it would be little indeed for so mighty a boon—as a Vision from the everlasting Glory, in the midst of the daring unbelief, and the denial of the Immortality of Man—in this woe-full age in which our lot is cast!

> Lift we now with thankful voices
> Hearts all filled with love and praise,
> Light the tapers! wave the banners,
> Sweetest clouds of incense raise.
> Deck the Shrine of our Great Mother
> For this wondrous Day of Days.
>
> All around was soul-felt darkness,
> Satan ruled in earth and air,
> For the things of days eternal
> Men had almost ceased to care.
> To deny all Revelation,
> Multitudes begin to dare.
>
> In the darkness of the valley
> As the ancient prophet saith,
> See the nations round us lying
> 'Mid the very shades of death.
> From the peoples long resisting
> Vanishes the Spirit's Breath.

Now indeed a night of sadness
Mantles o'er the souls of men,
How they long for some sweet vision
To enlighten earth agen.
And that GOD His Word would strengthen,
With but one more loud Amen.

Shout aloud! raise songs of gladness,
For our GOD hath heard our prayer,
And upon the still "Black Mountains,"
God hath flashed His Glory there.
MARY comes from Heaven in Beauty,
Fills with light the evening air.

'Mid Llanthony's silent Valleys,
O'er the meadows cool and green,
MARY comes in robes of silver,
Haloed as the Angels' Queen.
Raising up Her hands in blessing,
Thus GOD willed Her to be seen.

So the Monks and Convent Children
Gazed upon the Queen of Light,
Mother of the Glorious Day-spring,
Mother of the Morning Bright,
There all unbelief dispelling,
Chasing far the shades of night.

Praise our GOD! the silent Heavens,
Pour forth Glory once again,
And before the eyes of mortals,
Show that Christ as GOD doth reign
On the Throne of endless ages,
Who by death our Life did gain.

Mother MARY o'er the shadows
Of our dark and stormy day,
While men's restless rebel Nature
Strews with wreck life's troubled way.
Thou hast come as Star of Ocean,
Lit the darkness with Thy Ray.

Ray of Peace! O Ray of Gladness,
Joyous praise we humbly pour,
For Thy Gladness 'mid our Sadness,
Shining now the Mountains o'er.
And for this Thy Apparition,
MARY! we Thy Son adore.

Glory give we to the Father,
Glory to the Virgin's SON,
Glory to Her Spouse the SPIRIT,
While eternal years shall run.
Equal love, and equal glory,
To the Glorious Three in One.
     AMEN.

And now Lord Jesus, Precious Saviour, bless the words, in this book, to all who read them, for Thine own Glory sake. Let every eye, that scans these poor pages—scan at last and for ever—some of the glory of the Beatific Vision of Thy Face, O King of Beauty and Lord of Might.—Amen.

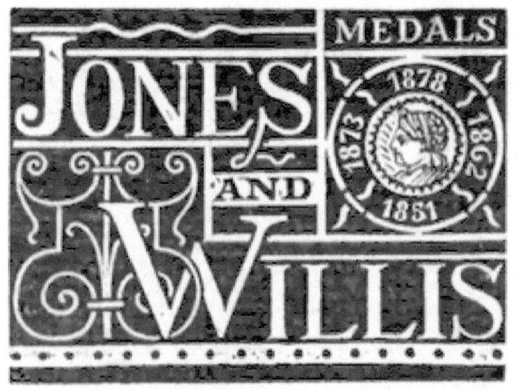

PARIS EXHIBITION PRIZE MEDALS AWARDED.

LONDON EXHIBITIONS, 1851 and 1862.

(WILLIS BROTHERS Co-PARTNERS).

BIRMINGHAM—EDMUND STREET;
LONDON—43, GREAT RUSSELL STREET, W.C.,
OPPOSITE BRITISH MUSEUM.
LONDON WORKS, 260, Euston Road, N.W.
BIRMINGHAM WORKS, Porchester Street.

MANUFACTURERS OF EVERY DESCRIPTION OF

CHURCH FURNITURE
AND MEDIÆVAL ART WORK.

TEXTILE FABRICS.

HANGINGS	ALTAR LINEN	VELVETS
CARPETS	FRINGES	CUSHIONS AND
CLOTHS	LACES	HASSOCKS.

ORIGINAL INVENTORS OF CELEBRATED RUG SEATING.

EMBROIDERIES.
In Ancient and Modern Designs.

| ALTAR COVERS | BOOK MARKERS | STOLES |
| BANNERS | HANGINGS | WOOL-WORK. |

Designs and Materials supplied to Ladies, and prepared for working if necessary.
ROBES, SURPLICES, AND CASSOCKS.

METAL WORK and LIGHTING APPLIANCES.
In Gold, Silver, Brass, and Iron.

COMMUNION VESSELS	CROSSES	LECTERNS
MEMORIAL BRASSES	STANDARDS	FINIALS
GATES	CORONA	CANDLESTICKS.

Special Estimates and Designs for Lighting Churches, Public Buildings, &c., on application.
Churches and Public Buildings lit by Electric Light, Gas, or the Patent Hesperus Lamp, light of which is equal to 45 candles.

WOOD WORK and CHURCH SEATING.

| ALTARS | STALLS | LECTERNS | PRIE-DIEU. |
| CHAIRS | PULPITS | REREDOS | |

SCHOOL FURNITURE AND FITTINGS.

Having erected special machinery for the execution of the above, J. and W. are able to supply them at very moderate prices, and tender for work to architects' designs.

STONE WORK.

| PULPITS | TOMBS | FONTS | REREDOS | CARVINGS, &c. |

MONUMENTAL STONES.

A CATALOGUE, containing 1,400 Woodcuts and Estimates, free on application.
Architects' own Designs estimated for and carefully carried out.

EDE & SON,
ROBE  MAKERS.

By Special Appointment to the Queen, the Lord Chancellor, and the Bishops.

PULPIT AND PREACHING GOWNS.
CLERICAL CLOTHING.
SURPLICES & CASSOCKS FOR CHOIR & CLERGY.
HOODS FOR ALL UNIVERSITIES & COLLEGES.
STOLES, BANDS, AND CLERICAL COLLARS.

ESTABLISHED 1689.
94, CHANCERY LANE, LONDON.
Price List by Post on Application.

"WAITING for the COMING
OF OUR
LORD JESUS CHRIST."

An Advent Sermon.

PREACHED AT ALL SAINTS', NOTTING HILL, ON THE EVENING OF DECEMBER 1ST, 1885.

By FATHER IGNATIUS,
(REV. JOSEPH LEYCESTER LYNE.)

Reprinted from the "Parish Magazine" of All Saints', Notting Hill.

LONDON:
WILLIAM RIDGWAY, 169, Piccadilly, W.,
AND OF ALL BOOKSELLERS.

PRICE 2d., BY POST, 2½d.

PRATT AND SONS,

CLERICAL OUTFITTERS, HATTERS, CASSOCK, SURPLICE, ROBE MAKERS,

AND

GENERAL CHURCH FURNISHERS.

Catalogues, Estimates, and Designs sent Free by Post.

23 & 24, TAVISTOCK ST.,
COVENT GARDEN, LONDON, W.C.

SHEPPARD and ST. JOHN,

Printers and Publishers,

6, ST. BRIDE STREET, LONDON, E.C.,

UNDERTAKE THE

PRINTING AND PUBLISHING

OF

BOOKS, NEWSPAPERS, MAGAZINES,

AND EVERY DESCRIPTION OF

COMMERCIAL AND LEGAL PRINTING

ON VERY MODERATE TERMS.

ESTIMATES FREE.

JOHN SEARY,

Clerical Tailor, Hatter, and Robemaker.

2 and 3, QUEEN STREET, OXFORD, and
13, NEW OXFORD STREET, LONDON, W.C.

(LATE 488, OXFORD STREET.)

CLERICAL DRESS.	JOHN SEARY'S "SPECIALITÉ" BLACK SERGE CLERICAL SUITS, price £2 17s. 6d., have been supplied to thousands of the Clergy during the last fourteen years, and the many expressions of satisfaction received prove this to be the most genuine and widely appreciated specialité ever introduced to the notice of the clerical world. Specialité Serge Suit ... ... £2 17s. 6d. Superior Black Cloth Suit, from ... ... 4 4s. 0d. The New Clerical Dress Coat, from ... ... 2 5s. 0d. Inverness Capes and Priest's Cloaks ... ... 2 2s. 0d. *Patterns and Prices on application.*
CLERICAL HATS.	Soft Felt Hats, all shapes, from... ... 5s. 6d. to 8s. 6d. Hard ,, ,, ,, ,, ... 8s. 6d. to 10s. 6d.
CLERICAL COLLARS & STOCKS.	The Linen-faced Clerical Collar (Registered) 1s. per dozen, 1s. 3d. post free, 10s. 6d. per gross; size required with order. Linen Collars, 10s. 6d. per dozen. Stuff Stocks, 2s. 6d. ; Silk do., 5s. ; Stock Bands, 5s. 6d. per doz.
SURPLICES & CASSOCKS.	Priests' Surplices, from ... ... 15s. 6d. to 42s. 0d. ,, Cassocks, from ... ... 21s. 0d. *For Choir Cassocks and Surplices see special reduced Price List.*
ALTAR FRONTALS.	THE RICH ITALIAN CLOTH, AND THE NEW FELT CLOTH, specially manufactured for us, have been found to be admirably adapted for cheap Frontals. An effective Frontal can be supplied, with silk Orphreys, etc., from 50s. *Designs and Estimates on application.*
VESTMENTS.	ITALIAN CLOTH Vestments (equal to silk in appearance) have received our special attention, and a complete set, comprising Chasuble, Stole, Maniple, Burse, and Chalice Veil, can be supplied for £2 5s., or with rich silk Orphreys, from £2 15s. Linen Chasuble, 21s. ALTAR LINEN from 9s. 6d. per set.
STOLES.	Coloured Stoles in ITALIAN CLOTH, with crosses and silk fringe, 21s. per set of four. Single Stole, 6s. 6d. Extra embroidered, per set, 30s. Single Stole, 8s. 6d. Rich Black Corded Silk Stoles from 8s. 6d.
PRICE LISTS	Will be forwarded post free on application.
TERMS OF BUSINESS.	Five per cent. discount on Cash payments within one month of delivery of goods. Accounts Quarterly.

COX, SONS, BUCKLEY & CO.,
Church Furnishers.

LONDON SHOW ROOMS.
SOUTHAMPTON STREET, STRAND, W.C.
STAINED GLASS STUDIOS.
MAIDEN LANE, W.C.
WORKS.
ESHER STREET, WESTMINSTER.
BRANCH OFFICES.
EDINBURGH: 118, GEORGE STREET.
NEW YORK: 343, FIFTH AVENUE.

METAL WORK.

WOOD WORK.

STONE WORK.

TEXTILE FABRICS.

Stained Glass
AND
Panel Paintings.

A Catalogue containing Woodcuts, also Designs and Estimates, free on application.

Architects' own Designs Estimated for and carefully carried out.

Should be read by every Englishman and Englishwoman, irrespective of Church, Sect, or Party.

"In all things let God be glorified."—   ✝   *Rule of S. Benedict, chap. 57.*

Jesus   **Only.**

Pax.

AN ORATION

Delivered at *Westminster Town Hall*, on *Tuesday Evening, October 27th, 1885*, on

THE CHURCH OF ENGLAND
AND
DISESTABLISHMENT.

BY

FATHER IGNATIUS, O.S.B.,
(REV. JOSEPH LEYCESTER LYNE).

Church of England Evangelist Monk, of Llanthony Abbey.

(From Shorthand Notes.)

With Preface, and Edited by **J. V. SMEDLEY, M.A. Camb.**

SECOND EDITION.

London: **WILLIAM RIDGWAY, 169, Piccadilly, W.,**
AND OF ALL BOOKSELLERS.

Price Sixpence, by post Sevenpence.

The *Church Review*, when referring to this Oration, in its issue of Nov. 27, 1885, said as follows:—

"We are glad to see that the oration which Father Ignatius delivered on Oct. 27, at the Town Hall, Westminster, on *The Church of England and Disestablishment*, and which he gave again in substance last Wednesday week at St. James's Hall, has been published in pamphlet form (W. Ridgway, 169, Piccadilly). Father Ignatius' oratorical power is a good wine that needs no bush; but if ever the property of the Church should be in danger again, the most effectual way of appealing to the popular mind to arouse feeling against such robbery would be to send him to stump the country. His oration of course loses much of its charm when reduced to the prose of print; but such a passage as the following, wherein he indignantly repudiates the doctrine that the Church receives her present pay from the State, when delivered with all the grace of rhetoric of which he is so consummate a master, must have carried away his hearers' hearts and heads:—" Supposing I were to go with a strong body of roughs to a gentleman's house, break open his door, push his children out of the window, break open his money-boxes, and take away say £30,000 from him—and supposing I were to say to that man, 'I will pay you back £2,000 of the £30,000 every year, and you must kindly consider I am supporting you'! I do not think that would be at all reasonable or fair. Do you?

"And now, dear people, supposing this robber comes back every year, and he pays £2,000 out of the £30,000 of which the ill-used man robbed him of years ago. Time goes on, somebody else comes and sets up a little house close by him, and as years go on another does so, until at last a dozen little houses are set up around him, and when the time comes for the gentleman to receive his £2,000, the other twelve little householders cry out for a part. I am perfectly confident that, if any of those twelve gentlemen were properly taught about the manner in which the other one had been treated, they would not only not ask for any of his money but would decline to take it if it were offered to them. Therefore I am quite sure that if our Nonconforming brethren were properly instructed as to the historical facts of the case, they would not condescend to touch any of the Church's money."—*Church Review*, November 27th.

www.ingramcontent.com/pod-product-compliance
Lightning Source LLC
Chambersburg PA
CBHW020835020526
44114CB00040B/790